Knowing
in Organizations

Knowing
in Organizations
A Practice-Based Approach

Edited by
Davide Nicolini, Silvia Gherardi, and Dvora Yanow

M.E.Sharpe
Armonk, New York
London, England

Library of Congress Cataloging-in-Publication Data

Knowing in organizations : a practice-based approach / edited by Davide Nicolini,
Silvia Gherardi, and Dvora Yanow.
    p. cm.
    ISBN 0-7656-0910-X (cloth: alk. paper) — ISBN 0-7656-0911-8 (pbk.: alk. paper)
    1. Knowledge management. 2. Organizational learning. I. Nicolini, Davide.
II. Gherardi, Silvia. III. Yanow, Dvora.

HD30.2.K6334 2003
658.4′038—dc21   2003000258

Printed in the United States of America

The paper used in this publication meets the minimum requirements of
American National Standard for Information Sciences
Permanence of Paper for Printed Library Materials,
ANSI Z 39.48-1984.

MV (c) 10   9   8   7   6   5   4   3   2   1
MV (p) 10   9   8   7   6   5   4   3   2   1

Contents

List of Tables and Figures

Tables

Figures

Knowing
in Organizations

1

Introduction: Toward a Practice-Based View of Knowing and Learning in Organizations

Davide Nicolini, Silvia Gherardi, and Dvora Yanow

Beginnings

In recent years the concepts of practice and activity have attracted the attention of academics and practitioners working on learning and knowledge in organizational and work settings. These scholars and practitioners have all begun to explore the implications for research and intervention of the notion that knowledge and learning are mainly social and cultural phenomena. The result is increasing interest in the thesis that organizational knowledge and learning cannot be conceived as mental processes residing in members' heads; rather, they must be viewed as forms of social expertise, that is, as knowledge in action situated in the historical, social, and cultural contexts in which it arises and embodied in a variety of forms and media.

Although they originate from different intellectual backgrounds, these views contribute to the emerging area of practice-based theorizing on knowing and learning in organizations. This approach assumes that knowing precedes knowledge, both logically and chronologically, for the latter is always an institutionalized version of the former. Scholars at work in this area investigate the theoretical implications and practical consequences of this depiction of organizational knowing as situated in the system of ongoing practices of action in ways that are relational, mediated by artifacts, and always rooted in a context of interaction. Such knowledge is thus acquired through some form of participation, and it is continually reproduced and negotiated; that is, it is always dynamic and provisional.

The aim of this book is to provide an overview of the work of authors who have taken up the challenge of addressing knowing, learning, and organizing processes from a practice-based perspective. The collection has grown from papers originally presented at a Symposium at the 1998 Academy of

Management Meeting in San Diego. The aim of this very well received symposium was to introduce this area of research to a broad academic public concerned with organization and management studies. Most of the presentations were then collected in a special issue of *Organization* (vol. 7, no. 2, 2000). Given the growing interest in these topics, we decided to supplement the material already available[1] with several other original studies in order to provide a broad overview of the variety of ways in which these new approaches can be put to work in organizational studies. Our aim was to assemble a volume representative of the major voices in the ongoing conversation. We were not trying to cover the current debate in its entirety; rather, we wanted to provide a representative and convincing snapshot of the state of the conversation on these topics and to set this kind of approach firmly on the map of organizational and work studies.

Accordingly, collected in this book are studies carried out within four distinct intellectual traditions that we believe currently represent the most promising ways to address the phenomena of knowing and organizing from a practice-based perspective: the interpretive-cultural approach, the "community of practice" approach, the cultural and historical activity theory approach, and the sociology of translation approach, also known as actor network theory. We would stress that the collection is not intended to be a thoroughgoing survey of these four approaches. Although several of the papers clarify their theoretical backgrounds and provide extensive references, the main purpose of the collection is to illustrate the contributions of each of the approaches when brought to bear on work and organizational studies.

Accordingly, this introduction highlights some of the common themes emerging from the book's chapters and reiterates the rationale and advantages of a practice-based approach to knowing and learning in organizations.

Why We Need a "Practice-Based" Vocabulary

For the last three decades a growing number of authors have emphasized the centrality and strategic importance of knowledge in postindustrial organizations. This emphasis has sprung from Galbraith's (1967) pioneering studies on "knowledge workers," Bell's (1973) thesis on the value of intangible and intellectual assets in the postindustrial economy, and Schon's (1971) essay on instability and change. This phenomenon is one aspect of the profound changes that affected societies worldwide in the last part of the twentieth century, and it goes hand in hand with the globalization of economic processes and markets, the declining importance of manual labor in the West, the diffusion of innovation, and the emergence of information and communication technologies. In describing these global phenomena, scholars have coined such expressions as "postindustrial era," "information age," and "knowledge society," which have become part of common parlance. By general agreement, the growing centrality of knowledge extends well beyond the limited domain of "knowledge intensive" organizations. All types of organization, the argument goes, increasingly depend on their capacity to effectively mobilize and manage knowledge in order to fulfill their missions and thrive (Nelson and Winter 1982; Drucker 1993).

One consequence of this emerging "knowledge-centered" discourse has been burgeoning interest, at all levels, in the issue of organizational learning and knowledge creation and management. For example, a bibliometric study conducted by two Canadian scholars in 1996 found that, between the end of the 1980s and the beginning of the 1990s, the number of articles on organizational learning in academic journals and business magazines grew exponentially, almost doubling in number year by year (Crossant and Guatto 1996). This striking trend slowed down at the end of the 1990s only to be replaced by expanding interest in the topic of "knowledge management" (Scarborough et al. 1999).

As appears from surveys of the literature on organizational learning and knowledge management over the years (Fiol and Lyles 1985; Nicolini and Meznar 1995; Easterby-Smith 1997; Dierkes et al. 2001), the majority of the scholarly and practitioner-oriented contributions on these topics use conceptual repertoires that take notions and constructs previously developed in the fields of biology, psychology, economics, cybernetics, or education and apply them in management and organizational studies.

A first group of authors uses approaches that conceive of knowledge as the codification of experience in some form of cognitive structure or behavioral pattern, and of learning as the process through which such structures and patterns change (Kim 1993; Fiol and Lyles 1985). Accordingly, organizations are equated with entities that process information, reflect on experience, and in this way acquire knowledge. To the extent that they modify their internal system of beliefs and their actual or potential behavioral repertoires, these organizations are said to have "learned." This understanding of knowing and learning constitutes the somewhat acritical transfer of a set of concepts from one field, individual psychology, where they have been linked to human development and cognitive capabilities, to organizational and management studies. In order to extend the same categories and concepts used to explain human cognition, learning, and behavior to social organizations and firms, however, these authors must perform one of two equally undesirable operations: either they must still conceive knowing as something that resides in the heads of individuals, and then use the artifice of "levels" in order to explain organizational phenomena (Kim 1993), or, alternatively, they must anthropomorphize organizations and conceive of them as superindividual entities in order to effectuate the transfer to them of individual human characteristics.

A second group of authors conceptualizes knowledge as an immaterial and atemporal substance: knowledge can thus be taken out of context, recorded, classified, and distributed. Davenport and colleagues, for example, define organizational knowledge as a form of "high value-added information" (Davenport et al. 1998: 43), while Nonaka et al. describe it as "a set of significant information which constitutes true and justified belief and/or implies a technical competence" (Nonaka et al. 1996: 295).

Finally, yet another group of scholars adopts an economic and finance-oriented approach. From this perspective, knowledge is an "invisible" asset and a form of "intellectual capital." It can be quantified, estimated, accumulated, and exchanged as a high-value commodity. For these authors, therefore, it is possible to establish measures of a firm's intellectual and knowledge capital, to ascertain its market value and its contribution to the profitability of the firm, and to put appropriate techniques in place to monitor and manage it (Stewart 1994; Bontis 1997; Nahapiet and Ghoshal 1998). As in the previous case, knowledge is reduced to something very akin to information that can consequently be stored, retrieved, and processed by modern communication technologies.

From our perspective, the main shortcoming of all three approaches is that they tend to translate uncritically into the organizational terrain conceptions of knowledge that have prevailed for centuries in Western cultures but which philosophers and social scientists of the last two generations have subjected to scrutiny and severe criticism. The conceptualization of knowledge as an object instead of a process—that is, as a mental substance mainly located in individual minds and manifested in written texts, representations, and routinized behaviors—is needlessly and, in our view, erroneously restrictive. Most of the debate in management and organizational studies ignores, for example, the growing attention to the social and processual aspects of knowing and learning that stems from traditions such as phenomenology, pragmatism, symbolic interactionism, Wittgenstein's thought, deconstructionism, and poststructuralism. As a consequence, much of the discussion on learning and knowing in organizations is carried out at an unacceptable level of simplification and superficiality, in a void exclusive of developments outside organizational studies, and appears at times intellectually unsophisticated and simplistic. Several of the topics and arguments are alarmingly antiquated. For example, Nightingale (2000) demonstrates that a significant part of the contemporary discussion of knowledge management is a revival or even merely a rehash of the debates conducted in the seventeenth century among such forerunners of modern Western thought as Hume, Locke, and Descartes. The difference, of course, is that the contemporary debate often lacks the innovativeness of those debates in their time, as well as their far-reaching political implications.

In order to update and give more depth to the discussion, we must therefore develop and employ "new vocabularies" of knowing and learning, to use an expression coined by Richard Rorty. New vocabularies, in fact, populate the world differently: they not only change existing ideas; they introduce new and alternative truth-values (Rorty 1989; Contu 2000). Put differently, we must develop new linguistic and conceptual repertoires about knowledge that free us from prevailing notions that depict it as the static result of the thinking of disinterested and autonomous individuals and that suggest that knowledge can be stored, transmitted, and circulated to other individuals able to assimilate it into some form of mental or material repository.

The main assertion of this book is that a practice-based vocabulary is a promising candidate for such rethinking. The notion of practice has, in fact, an ancient and solid lineage in cultural traditions that have offered views of knowing and learning that are alternative to the prevailing representational-ist and idealist tradition. The authors of the papers collected in this book all concern themselves with questions of practice in the context of organizational life, ranging from cooking to roof-laying, from flute-making to bridge-building. As we will discuss below, these several approaches have as many points of difference as they have commonalties. Neither they nor we have made any effort to force-fit this variety into a single practice-in-knowing conceptual box. But as they all take up questions of practice, it is worth beginning, briefly, with an historical review of the intellectual heritage that undergirds this concept.

At the Root of Polisemy: A Brief Reminder of the Historical Legacy of the Notion of Practice

Although a thorough reconstruction of the history of the notion of practice goes well beyond the scope of this introduction, we would point out three of the major cultural roots—or tributaries, had they been watercourses—that support the work of the authors in the present collection: Marx's work, phenomenology and symbolic interactionism, and Wittgenstein's legacy

A first tradition is the Marxist notion of practice. Marx was, in fact, one of the first authors seriously to challenge the entrenched and institutionalized neglect of practice in the political philosophy of his day. One enduring legacy of his work is its successful attempt to challenge centuries of

Western rationalist and mentalist traditions and to legitimate "real" activity—what people actually do in their everyday lives—as an object of research and as an explanatory category in social sciences. As Marx stated in *The German Ideology*:

> Men, developing their material production and their material intercourse, alter, along with this, their real existence, their thinking and the products of their thinking. Life is not determined by consciousness, but consciousness by life. . . . Where speculation ends—in real life—there real, positive science begins: the representation of the practical activity, of the practical process of development of men. (Marx 1846: 123)

Practice plays a central notion in Marxist epistemology. It is an epistemological principle in the sense that we know only that which becomes the subject of our practice: thought and world are always connected through human activity; they are inseparable. On the one hand, people are always actors and producers; on the other, thinking is only one of the things people do. Even social scientists and philosophers do not spend all their time thinking; they also eat, play music, jog, fight, make love. In Marx's view, the object of inquiry for philosophers (and what we would today call social scientists) should therefore be *praxis*, understood as what persons say, imagine, conceive, and produce, *and* think while attempting to carry out these activities.

Practice is both our production of the world and the result of this process. It is always the product of specific historical conditions resulting from previous practice and transformed into present practice. The material process of production involves both the production of goods and the reproduction of society. The important contribution of this tradition is its epistemological and methodological insight that practice is a system of activities in which knowing is not separable from doing, and learning is a social and not merely a cognitive activity. As many of the authors in this book argue in their chapters, and as Blackler once wrote (1993: 870): "Social learning is a creative achievement, therefore, which involves a degree of personal investment; it can only be achieved by active participation."

Marx also introduced the idea that understanding human action requires one to focus on the entire social and historical context of that action—a tenet central to the work of several of the authors working with a practice-based approach, and especially those with a background in cultural and historical activity theory. Only by considering the concrete totality of interconnected activities that engender socially productive activities can one grasp the meaning of human action. Because productive actions are inherently social, moreover, in order to grasp meaning and intelligibility, one must understand the social and historical context in which they take place. As Marx wrote: "Activity and mind are social in their content as well as in their origins; they are social activity and social mind" (Marx 1975: 157).

A second notable tradition of thought that provides practice with a solid lineage is phenomenology. According to the phenomenological tradition, in everyday organizational life, such activities as work, learning, innovation, communication, negotiation, conflict over goals and their interpretation, and history are copresent in practice. They are part of human existence, of the "human life-world." At the same time, within this flow of existence, within any practical endeavor, there is no distinction between subject and object; there is no dualism. Heidegger (1962) and the phenomenological school, drawing on Hegel (see Bernstein 1971), used the term *Dasein* to denote this "being there" or "being-in-the-world" in which subject and object are indistinguishable. Both are concurrently part of a situation, and both exist within a social and historical setting.

Winograd and Flores (1986) elaborate on Heidegger's argument to provide an illuminating example of the relationship among subject, object, context, and knowledge. Consider a carpenter hammering a nail into a piece of wood. In the carpenter's practical activity, the hammer does not exist as an object with given properties. It is as much a part of his world as the arm with which he wields it. The hammer belongs to the environment and can be unthinkingly used by the carpenter. The carpenter does not need to "think a hammer" in order to drive in a nail. His or her capacity to act depends upon the familiarity with the act of hammering. His/her use of the practical item "hammer" is its significance to him/her in the setting "hammering" and "carpentry." When the carpenter is hammering unimpededly, the hammer with its properties does not exist as an entity: in the usable environment, the understanding of situations is prereflexive activity, and the world of objects thus becomes "simply present" (*Vorhanden*). The hammer as such acquires a separate "existence" only when it breaks or is lost: that is, when its unreflective use becomes problematic. For reflexive, investigative, theoretical knowledge to come into play, something previously usable must become unusable. This breakdown only occurs when the carpenter has already understood the hammer in practice. Only when a nonusability situation occurs will the carpenter's activity of "hammering" take on a problematic form. The traditional Western hierarchical privileging of theoretical, discursive knowledge over practical understanding is hence reversed: knowing in practice predates reflexive theoretical knowledge and makes it possible.

Hammering is a paradigmatic example of prereflexive learning, of comprehension that takes place in situations of involvement in a practice. This theme has been extensively developed by Polanyi (1962) under the rubric of "tacit" and "personal" knowledge—two concepts that appear in many of the essays in the present collection (e.g., Strati, and Gomez et al.). Polanyi's position is in fact quite akin to the phenomenological tradition that he only in part embraced. He asks: Does an analytic description of how to keep one's balance on a bicycle suffice as instruction to someone wanting to learn how to ride a bicycle? And he answers: "[R]ules of art can be useful, but they do not determine the practice of an art; they are maxims, which can serve as a guide to an art only if they can be integrated into the practical knowledge of the art. They cannot replace this knowledge" (Polanyi 1962: 50). In this, says Polanyi, we "know more than we can tell" (Polanyi 1962: 4).

The example of hammering is also paradigmatic of the knowledge that arises when breakdown occurs and reflexive activity intervenes. Accidents, for example, are cases of breakdown in everyday life that bring what previously was unproblematic to the surface, as is clearly seen in Gherardi and Nicolini's essay. In the phenomenological tradition, the concept of practice shows how comprehension in situations where one is "thrown headlong into use" is prereflexive and does not draw distinctions among subject, object, thought, or context; it also shows how reflexive understanding arises at moments of breakdown. Ethnomethodology has used the breaching of rules to show the operation of those rules in producing a "normal" situation. The approach exploits the social, cognitive, and emotional breakdown brought about by rule-breaking events.

Organizations as systems of practices therefore exist in the dimension of "simply usable" tacit knowledge, which becomes the object of reflection when a breakdown occurs. Symbolic interactionism adds a strong social and interactional dimension to this view. Herbert Blumer (1969) posited three core ideas as the basis of this approach: (1) the notion that human beings act toward things on the basis of the meanings that those things have for them; (2) the notion that such meanings arise out of the interaction of the individual with others through language practices, so that language gives people a means by which to negotiate meaning through symbols; (3) the notion that an interpretive process is used by the individual in each instance in which s/he must deal with things in his/her environment. For symbolic interactionists, therefore, every kind of knowledge both represents and embodies (interactional) work and can only be accessed through interaction. Tacit knowledge is not only prereflexive; it is also and above all social, and hence open-ended, provisional, and subject to local negotiations. Accordingly, as suggested by some well-known studies carried out within this tradition (e.g., see Becker 1953), and as reiterated here in the papers by Wenger and Gomez et al., for example, becoming knowledgeable in any field, from computer science to smoking marijuana, requires participation in the interaction and engagement with the local web of meaning-making processes: that is, becoming a member of the group, community, or local culture that collectively sustains these interpretive processes.

A third tradition contributing to the richness and polysemy of the notion of practice is Wittgenstein's legacy and its insistence on the relation among practice, language, and meaning through the notion of linguistic game (Wittgenstein 1953). For Wittgenstein, in fact, language is mainly a practical and social endeavor. Linguistic terms arise within a social practice that encompasses meaning construction. Participation in a practice entails taking part in a professional language game, mastering the rules, and being able to use them. "Having" a concept means that one has learned to obey the rules within a given practice. Speech acts are units of language and action; they are part of a practice. They are not merely descriptions, but types of action like any other in a given practice.

Language is not only the expression of social relations; it is also the medium for their creation (Czarniawska-Joerges 1991). Those who participate in the practice of a linguistic game must share in the "life form" in which that practice is possible: intersubjective consensus is more a matter of shared environment and language than of abstract opinions (Wittgenstein 1953).

Sharing a "life form" (a praxis) is the prerequisite for the understanding and transmission of so-called propositional knowledge. The latter is the type of knowledge acquired through the practical understanding of an operation. For example, carpenters participate in a professional language game, and they are able to "tell" the procedures that they follow in making a chair. But the (propositional) knowledge that one can acquire in this way is different from the practical understanding of the real operation of "making a chair." The propositional knowledge of how to make a chair, and how to describe the process, is qualitatively different from the procedural knowledge of how to use a saw or a plane, or of when their blades need changing.

As amply illustrated by many of the papers in the present collection, there is knowledge that is transmitted through the senses by virtue of familiarity with previous situations and of refinement of that sensibility. As pointed out by Yanow, knowing how to imagine the sound of a flute is part of the practice of knowing how make a good instrument. Practical understanding is often tacit: not because flutemakers do not wish to talk about explicit measures of the feel of the instrument, but because they can talk about the feeling in other ways as they participate in that language game.

In sum, a practice-based vocabulary possesses such potency because it has a long intellectual pedigree. Although not all the scholars who use it today may be wholly aware of this derivation, the notion of practice is imbued with diverse traditions of thought, including those discussed here. These traditions simultaneously constitute the basis of the richness and the reason for the multiplicity and irreducible variety of the voices that make use of the approach. Together, these voices articulate knowledge in and about organizing as practical accomplishment, rather than as a metaphysical transcendental account of decontextualized reality.

Four Practice-Based Ways to Talk About Knowing and Learning

We have argued at the outset that a practice-based theoretical approach allows us to address the topics of organizational and workplace knowing and learning from a perspective that is different from, and yet complementary to, the still prevailing engineering and economic models utilized in management and organizational studies. As the previous section indicates and the papers collected in the present volume demonstrate, there is no such thing as a unified practice theory or practice-based approach, only a number of research traditions and scholars connected by a common historical legacy and several theoretical family resemblances. Four of these traditions are represented in this book.

Dvora Yanow and Antonio Strati develop their contributions from within a *cultural interpretive framework;* Wenger and Gomez, Bouty, and Drucker-Godard concentrate on *social learning,* although the former focuses on "community of practice" and adopts a symbolic interactionist perspective, while the latter operate within a "habitus" framework derived from the work of Pierre Bourdieu; Engeström, Puonti, and Seppänen and Blackler, Crump, and McDonald utilize *cultural and historical activity theory,* an account of practice and change that has emerged in the West at the point where Vygotsky's cultural psychology, the Marxist notion of praxis, and elements of symbolic interactionism intersect. Finally, Law and Singleton, Suchman, and Gherardi and Nicolini work within the *sociology of translation,* a theoretical sensitivity that in many ways combines the processual, materialist, and antideterminist elements of all the traditions mentioned above with Foucault's reflections on the pervasiveness of power and Wittgenstein's notion of meaning making. In the following sections we shall seek to summarize how each of these have contributed to the emergence of a new vocabulary centered on the notion of practice and practice-based knowing and learning.

Understanding Knowing as Culture and Aesthetic Understanding

Dvora Yanow and Antonio Strati present a first way to talk about practice using terms and notions derived from cultural and, in Strati's case, aesthetic perspectives.

Describing flute-making and agency identity-creation, Yanow argues in Chapter 2 for the benefits of an interpretive perspective, both substantively and methodologically used to understand knowing as practice. When an interpretive cultural perspective is employed, in fact, some of the conceptual tools used to understand the notion of culture are translated into the realm of practice-thinking; this makes it possible to focus on practices as collective endeavors and it directs attention to actions and interactions, the objects and language used in these social transactions, including the site-specific meanings of various artifacts to the actors in the situation, as well as to the site-based set of interpretive methods designed to access and analyze these data. The interpretive cultural perspective emphasizes the context-specific, collectively held meanings embedded in practices sustained by and reproduced in all organized human activity. It highlights how mastery depends on social processes both for its existence and for its communication: the practice of flute-making is at the same time the medium through which mastery is expressed and communicated, and the outcome of that mastery. The interpretive cultural perspective also shows how artifacts and interactions sustain both meaning- and knowing-in-practice without an intervening process of representation being necessary: flutemakers use vague and very abstract expressions such as "the flute doesn't feel right"; yet these comments are readily understood and they prompt very specific acts to correct that "feel" (cf. Cook and Yanow 1993).

The reference to the kinesthetic, tacit, and aesthetic dimensions of knowing as practice is developed by Antonio Strati, who in Chapter 3, discusses the aspects of the practice of roof-making and unmaking. Strati notes how perceptive-sensorial capacities and aesthetic judgments prove particularly important not only for working on a roof but also for deciding to take up that kind of work, for teaching others how to do it, and for selecting the personnel able to do it. Strati thereby stresses the aesthetic dimension of knowing-as-practice. In so doing, he gives voice to a growing number of practice-oriented authors for whom sentience is an integral part of their discourse—a feature that sets them apart from the cognitivists, who tend to underplay or ignore this dimension of human intelligence and action, as well as from most organizational scholars, who have extended the "logos over pathos" hierarchical discourse to the realm of social and business organizations (Gagliardi 1990).

Conceptualizing aesthetic knowledge as the form of competence that persons acquire by activating specific capacities of their perceptive-sensorial faculties and aesthetic judgment brings to the fore the central importance of personal knowledge in the processes of organizational knowing, as well as its corporeality. The socialized, inscribed, trained, habituated, and conditioned sentient human body described in Strati's chapter (and in others in this volume) becomes a critical locus of connection and of the reproduction of social order, such that the sensuous and the cultural take central place in the processes that enable social and organizational order to be reproduced and/or disrupted and/or reconstituted. These disciplined bodies are in fact carriers of social order; as Strati notes, they are aesthetically and emotionally doing and redoing organization.

An aesthetic take on practice thus emphasizes knowing as a form of aesthetic experience at once personal and social. By highlighting the importance of the tacit dimension of knowing, Strati's approach allows us to think of practical knowledge not as what has not yet been rendered explicit, like a continent ripe for scientific exploration, but as what cannot be spoken because it is not verbal in itself.

Understanding Knowing as Community and Habitus

In Chapter 4, Etienne Wenger develops a now well-established way to talk about practice-based learning and knowing in organizations that uses the notion of "community of practice." Wenger claims that associating the terms "practice" and "community" yields a more tractable characterization of the concept of practice and defines a special type of community characterized by joint enterprise, mutual engagement, and a shared repertoire of actions, styles, artifacts, concepts, discourses, stories, and histories (cf. Wenger 1998, ch. 2).

For Wenger, communities of practice are the basic building blocks of social learning systems in that they function as the social containers of the competencies that make up such systems. Communities grow from the intersection between competence and personal experience within a context of mutual engagement in a common practice. Competence is historically and socially defined in communities, and knowing is a matter of displaying the socially defined competence sustained by the community. At the same time, however, because we experience knowing on the basis of our own personal stories, the enactment of such knowing is always a matter of negotiation. The interplay between knowing and competence gives all constituents opportunities for learning and innovation.

The community of practice perspective thus emphasizes knowing in practice as joint enterprise and belonging. Although communities of practice should not be romanticized too much, as Wenger stresses, the approach focuses on shared repertoires, communal resources, common language and routines, and shared artifacts and stories. These dimensions support the mutuality among members of the community which constitutes the social fabric of knowing and learning. At the same time, the approach focuses on the developmental process of becoming part of a community of practice. This

perspective, in fact, conceives of knowing not so much as a way of understanding the world but as a way of being in the world: competence and identity are inseparably intertwined and depend on recognized participation in a
community of practice. Wenger explores forms of belonging to communities
of practice that go beyond physical copresence, thereby extending the notion
of mutuality to include imagination and alignment as ways to participate in a
social learning system.

The approach also emphasizes that the process of becoming a member of
a community of practice is a crucial source of learning for both novices and
the community. "Legitimate peripheral participation" is a term that refers to
the progressive involvement of newcomers in a practice as they acquire growing competence (Lave and Wenger 1991; Gherardi et al. 1998). The adjective "peripheral" denotes the existence of a route that the new member must
follow in order to gain the esteem of the community's established members.
At the same time, the idea of "legitimate participation" emphasizes that as
the newcomer passes through the various stages of learning, he/she must
necessarily connect with others performing actual practices. Since knowledge
is integrated and distributed in the life of the community and learning is an act
of belonging, learning necessarily requires involvement. Learning cannot take
place if participation is not possible: the professional development of members and the development of the practice sustained by the community go hand
in hand; their identity and that of the community evolve in parallel.

The focus on social processes as the fabric of knowing and learning is
also a central theme in Gomez, Bouty, and Drucker-Godard's essay (Chapter
5). Studying the practice of French haute cuisine and the chef's work, the
three authors examine this highly valued and highly volatile form of practical knowledge from the notion of "habitus." The latter was introduced by the
French sociologist Pierre Bourdieu as a way of providing an account of practices and practical knowledge that explains both our experience of a world
prestructured with respect to our possibilities of thinking and acting, and the
active apprehension and engagement with the world of persons and objects
that takes place within this prestructured field of practical possibilities. Habitus
is defined as "a system of durable, transposable dispositions, structured structures predisposed to function as structuring structures" (Bourdieu 1990: 53).
It is conceived as a set of "principles that generate and organize practice and
representations that can be objectively adapted to their outcomes without
presupposing a conscious aiming at ends or any express mastery of the operations necessary in order to attain them" (ibid.). Social and historical in
nature, habitus is deeply inscribed in the body. Moreover, habitus always
operates in conjunction with a practical endeavor that it helps define and
structure: habitus is only actualized in the context of real and significant

practical circumstances; only then does it sustain the mutual adjustment among practices and coordination among actors, while at the same time allowing personal trajectories to take shape.

The language of habitus addresses practical knowing in terms of bodily predispositions that generate and reproduce specific courses of action associated with specific social positions and structures. Here, too, socialization and habituation assume central importance as ways to become part of a practice. One cannot enter the "magic circle" of haute cuisine by instantaneous decision of the will, but only by a slow learning and initiation process that requires a good amount of "obstinacy," as one of the informants quoted in the chapter by Gomez et al. put it. Unlike others, this approach to practice is highly sensitive to disparities in the distribution of knowledge brought to bear by habitus, which is in fact a principle that incorporates, enacts, and reproduces hierarchical social positions and unequal power relations, together with the practices that go along with them.

The habitus approach therefore characterizes knowing in practice as an embodied practical sensitivity—a *sens pratique*—learned and remembered by the body as practical dispositions that present us with a world in which it make sense to do some things and not others. This way of knowing is different from a traditional form of computational logic in that it is based not so much on the application of explicit or tacit rules as on responding to a feel: a feel for the game, for example, the game of cooking, a feel for what is appropriate within the existing conditions (will a new dish still be recognized as "haute cuisine"?), and a feel for the social positioning that goes with it.

Understanding Knowing as a Feature of Cultural and Historical Activity Systems

Chapter 6 by Blackler, Crump, and McDonald and Chapter 7 by Engeström, Puonti, and Seppänen introduce a further way to talk about practice-based forms of learning and knowing, both centered on the conceptual apparatus of cultural and historical activity theory.

Activity theory originates from the work of Vygotsky and emphasizes the historical, mediated, and transformational nature of collaborative endeavors (a brief account of the origins of the approach is outlined in an appendix to Chapter 6). According to this approach, activities are culturally situated and mediated by linguistic and technological artifacts. Activities are always enacted in communities and imply a division of labor among participants; activities provide motives and are oriented toward objects of work that are partly given and partly generated within the activity itself. Because the accomplishment of the object of an activity requires the assemblage of several simpler actions, the units of analysis of the practice-as-activity approach are complex activity systems. Activity systems comprise a variety of actions with different histories and logics of action associated with them. For this reason, activity systems always entail conflicting aspects and inherent contradictions that make them by definition disturbance-producing systems. As Blackler et al. note, the existence of paradoxes, tensions, and incoherences is inherent in the nature of activity systems and fuels their ongoing transformational drift: within activity systems, both the understanding of the nature of the object of work as well as the activities that go along with it are in constant "expansion." Such an expansion requires the activity system to learn new ways of accommodating all different composing elements, an effort that is bound to affect the very nature of the object of work and spur new inconsistencies and contradictions, thus triggering a new cycle of transformation. Change, expansion of objects, and learning are fundamental and integral aspects of this approach to practices.

Blackler and his coauthors examine the practices of strategic renewal and technological innovation in a high-tech firm to illustrate how activity theory can be used to interpret knowing simply as an aspect of collaborative endeavors that are social and transformational in character. Thus, the cultural and historical activity theory approach emphasizes in particular that social and historical conditions are both the outcome of and the precondition for social activity. These conditions, however, are in continuous flux, so that practice carries within itself the germ and principles of both its perpetuation and its transformation. The approach also highlights the mediated nature of activity and the central role played by artifacts both material and symbolic in actualizing these conditions and structuring current and future endeavors. Finally, this approach emphasizes more than any other the opportunities for innovation and development of collective competencies inherent in any practice and the fundamental fluidity of activity systems.

This latter aspect is extensively developed by Engeström, Puonti, and Seppänen, whose chapter illustrates the object-oriented and expansive nature of knowing from this same perspective. The account of three emerging practices—white-collar crime investigation, crop rotation in organic farming, and caring for patients with multiple illnesses—shows how a practice-as-activity approach can articulate the recursive relation between practice and its object. This relation becomes especially visible when there is an expansion of either one, as in the cases discussed in the chapter. The expansion of the object of the activity triggers the creation and emergence of a new mediating instrumentality that recursively reconstitutes the activity and its object. This cycle of mutual interaction is an endless process that creates new practices as well as new ways to address them.

The two chapters, informed by a cultural and historical activity theory sensitivity, show how this particular approach enables interpretation of expertise as a collective, heterogeneous, and evolving phenomena, and organizations as distributed, decentered, and emergent systems of practical knowledge. Also stressed is the centrality of mediating artifacts and objects as organizing centers for regimes of practical expertise (see also Knorr-Cetina 1999). Finally, cultural and historical activity theory stresses the relation between knowing and change, depicting practical knowing as a historically situated accomplishment subject to an irrevocable process of expansive change. The modification or emergence of new objects of work has, in fact, the effect of bringing out the contradictions inherent in any activity system, and therefore requires the development of new rules, mediating artifacts, and ways of working that will inevitably modify the object of work in an endless process.

Understanding Knowing as Heterogeneous Engineering and "Action Net"

The final three chapters in the collection—those by Suchman, by Gherardi and Nicolini, and by Law and Singleton—all work within the framework of sociology of translation, also known as actor-network theory.[2] The sociology of translation began as a development of the social studies of science and technology. It can be described as an interpretive sensitivity and a literary genre based on the notion that "the social" is nothing other than a patterned network of heterogeneous materials—not only people but also machines, animals, texts, money, architectures—kept together by active processes of ordering (Law 1992). Although it has never been codified into a full-fledged theory, the approach unites scholars who find it useful to conceive of the world in terms of effects, relationships, and performativity.

Thinking of the world as a performative effect entails acknowledgement that all entities are performed in, by, and through the relationships in which they are involved: organization, stability, and persistence are, hence, the result of an effort, not an intrinsic quality of things (Law 1999). The order and "nature" of things is therefore always a reversible and uncertain outcome, an effect of operations, maneuvers, and processes that keep things in place. The main challenge for social science is to do empirical research that can explain how the durability of orderings is achieved in practice, how facts become such, how order is performed, how things are put in place and stay that way, and how change comes about—what authors operating within this framework call the tactics of translation of ordering in time and space. Knowing a practice is equated with being able skillfully to participate in and influence the ordering of the world while pursuing one's own interests; that is to say, knowing is a different way to describe the capacity to proceed unhampered in whatever we do. One of the characteristics of this approach is that it does not limit its focus to language, discourse, or human interactions, granting instead equal citizenship to a range of disparate and heterogeneous elements (technologies, artifacts, symbols, places) as active players in the processes of ordering—although not necessarily as volitional and intentional "actors" (Brown and Capdevila 1999). Knowing is therefore another way to describe the successful alignment of human and nonhuman elements ("heterogeneous engineering") and the human capacity to produce an effect on the world.

This latter aspect is evidenced by Suchman in Chapter 8, which is centered on understanding the engineering practice of bridge building. Suchman gives a detailed description of how the endeavor of building such a large and significant artifact as a bridge implies the complex work of alignment involving not only different professional knowledges, centers of expertise, and technological artifacts but also social and political relations, interests, and conflicting demands by human and nonhuman elements. She emphasizes that bridge building is a process of sociotechnical ordering and heterogeneous engineering that is historically, socially, and geographically (as well as geologically) situated. In this sense, the collective knowing involved in building a bridge cannot be understood as a self-standing body of knowledge; it is instead an irremediably contingent process of performing competence and making oneself accountable, artfully balancing compliance and the endless need for practical subversions in order to get the work done.

Though using the same overall framework, Gherardi and Nicolini (Chapter 9) are instead more interested in the processes through which knowledge is constituted as such; that is, the way in which legitimate knowledgeable practices emerge, are sustained, become durable, and eventually disappear. As they analyze how safety is attained on construction sites, Gherardi and Nicolini describe how the creation, shaping, stabilization, and circulation of safety knowledge—or better, "safety-knowing"—is coterminous with the emergence of an ecology of actions and interests that sustains a particular practical regime of what constitutes a safe site and of how to go about making work on construction sites safe. They describe safety-knowing as distributed among several intermediaries (artifacts, discursive practices, and norms) and as sustained by the process of their circulation, exchange, negotiation, distortion, use, and non-use. In this sense, safety-knowing does not reside in any of the nodes of this seamless web; instead, it is the emergent effect of the entire heterogeneous "whole." This network of actions and intermediaries can be considered in many senses to be the "author" of the accomplishment of safety, and its contingent character and composition determine what safety means in practice in that particular part of the world and at that particular time.

The Suchman and Gherardi and Nicolini chapters, then, put forward yet another way to understand knowing-in-practice, namely as arising from the alignment of a number of heterogeneous materials and interests. From the vantage point of the sociology of translation, knowing-in-practice is the creation of a complex web of elements in mutual interrelationship and continuous struggle. Knowing is, in this sense, the result of a system of ongoing practices and political processes that are, in effect, two sides of the same coin. One could say that the subject of the knowing is the "action net" identified by these processes. It does not reside in any of its parts, and even less, in any of the representations produced by its different constituencies.

The relation between representation and knowing is the central concern of Law and Singleton in Chapter 10, which concludes the book. Unlike the other authors in this collection, Law and Singleton focus less on the description of a practice than on the practice of description. They examine the trajectories of alcoholic patients with liver disease in the UK health sector and reflect on their finding that different constituencies use different, inconsistent, and mutually interfering ways to map them—with major repercussions for the care given to the patients and its outcomes. Law and Singleton ask themselves, and the readers, what is to be done with this irreducible multiplicity, and they reflect on the relationship between representing and doing and on the possibilities and limits of the practice of inscribing and representing.

In certain respects, this essay is a most fitting conclusion to the book because it draws attention to the limitation inherent in a practice-based vocabulary *qua* vocabulary. As de Certeau has aptly put it, describing practices is necessarily a form of colonization through description (de Certeau 1984). If a practice is to be captured in discourse, it must first be severed from the lived world: science only knows dead objects. Applying the practice-based approach reflexively to itself, Law and Singleton bring us to the limit of a practice-based vocabulary, showing its shortcomings and giving us a sense not only of what it can do for us, but also of what it cannot do. Their chapter leads to what Wittgenstein once described as the point at which "language goes on holiday," the point at which we must let practice speak for itself (Wittgenstein 1953; Johannessen 1996).

Elements of a Practice-Based Vocabulary for Knowing and Learning in Organizations

The above brief overview of the approaches used in this book is an illustration of the abundant insights yielded by the perspectives described into a practice-based understanding of knowing and learning in organizations. It also outlines the similarities and differences among the approaches. On the one hand, the contributors to the book do not speak with a uniform and homogeneous voice, and it is evident that in organizational studies, as elsewhere, there is no such a thing as a unified practice approach (Schatzki 2001). On the other hand, this multiplicity is a source of richness and redundancy that defines a complex terrain of partly overlapping, partly diverging discourses marked not only by differences but also by family resemblances and similitude. For example, all the approaches reviewed above believe that such phenomena as knowledge, meaning, human activity, power, language, organizations, and historical and technological transformations take place and are components of the field of practices. At the same time, they make recurrent use of a common set of terms and notions, which together delineate a recognizable practice-based linguistic and theoretical repertoire—the sort of new vocabulary mentioned by Richard Rorty (1989). Without any attempt to silence the extant multivocality or reduce the existing multiplicity of views by crafting a single unified theory of practice, in the next section we shall seek to describe the overall features of such a vocabulary or repertoire, attempting to capture, within the space available, what distinguishes a practice-based approach to knowing and learning in organizations from other approaches.

Some Characteristics of a Practice-Based Vocabulary for Knowing in Organizations

In the first place, one may argue that a distinctive characteristic of a practice-based vocabulary is the presence of verbs, often declined in the gerund. This lexical characteristic, which derives from the inherent process-oriented stance of a practice-based approach, conjures up a world that is always in the making, one in which "doing," more than "being," is at the center of attention; they signal the constructive nature of the social and material world and convey an image of knowing as materiality, fabrication, handiwork, the craftsman's skill, conflict, and power struggle; they denote a world in which "reality" is experienced as solid, stable, and certain matter, but in which this condition is an effect, a result, a machination—in short, something that perhaps is but that could have been different. A practice-based vocabulary is, then, a vocabulary made of verbs: *learning, organizing, belonging, understanding, translating,* and *knowing* are among the terms most recurrent in the essays collected in this book. Several of the most frequently used nouns indicate performativity as well: *activity, alignment, construction,* and *enactment* are all key terms in practice-based approaches. This is because all practice-oriented approaches focus on what people actually do. Attention is directed toward understanding how and under what conditions action is actually carried out. The object of inquiry becomes the capacity of humans to perform actions competently, the temporal organization of such actions, and the resources that make them possible.

A second distinctive feature of a practice-based theoretical repertoire is the predominance of socially related terms. For all the authors in this collection, knowing and mastery are by definition social accomplishments, even when they are attributed to individuals; the adjective "social" points to the localization of learning and knowing not in the mind of the individual but in a social subject, a subject that simultaneously thinks, learns, works, and innovates. Within a practice-based perspective, knowing is always conceived of as a social ecology sustained by processes of participation in, enculturation into, and belonging to social patterns like communities, activity systems, and local cultures—all of which are terms that differentiate the approaches represented here from more traditional individual-centered social cognition perspectives. Significantly, however, the social dimension of knowing, which springs from the inherently social nature of practices, goes hand in hand with the use of a range of terms (habitus, sense, feeling, touch) that refer to knowledgeable people whose mastery is sensorial and emotional in character. Among the protagonists of this book are Strati's bricklayers, who feel and fear the roof; Yanow's flutemakers, who share knowledge and build mutual intelligibility by passing to and fro the artifact they are creating; as well as Gomez's chefs, whose competent activity requires learned and sophisticated senses of smell and touch. The sociality evoked by a practice-based linguistic repertoire is therefore very different from the refined, clean, aseptic abstractions predicated by functionalist social scientists. In the world depicted by practice-based terms, people act and interact, but they also look at, listen to, and ignore each other. They have bodies; they touch, smell, taste; they have sentiments and senses; they argue, yell, fear, get nervous, and even die. They are not solely ephemeral social entities (agents); they are living beings who inhabit a world of life that, far from constituting a "problem," is the object itself of study and representation by this approach.

A third salient aspect of a practice-based vocabulary is the presence of a host of object terms referring to material artifacts as well as to specific historical conditions. The sociality referred to by practice-based approaches is a sociality not only with other human beings but also with artifacts, both material and symbolic. Most of the essays in the book talk about mediated action, but they also recount stories that are social and material in character. Flutes, roofs, pots and pans, crops, diseases, bridges, cement mixers, and buildings—as well as rules, norms, and mapping conventions—all figure prominently as active "characters" in the stories of organizing that constitute the chapters of this book. Unlike in other approaches, here these artifacts do not play a merely background role. On the contrary, they participate actively in the stories, carry history, embody social relationships, distribute power, and provide points of resistance. Historicity and heterogeneity—two key terms in a practice-based vocabulary—combine to articulate a world where not everything and everyone is the same, where inequalities and power are continuously produced and reproduced as the pattern of what is doable and sayable, of what is possible, of who can or cannot do or say.

Fourth, just as practice-based approaches articulate knowing as social, they also insist on its spatio-temporal localized nature. In articulating the "where" of knowledge, most practice-based approaches refer to its situated nature, the latter being another recurrent term in a practice-based vocabulary. The term "situated" indicates that knowledge and its subjects and objects must be understood as produced together within a temporally, geographically, or relationally situated practice. All practice-based approaches therefore employ a variety of terms that signal not only the locality in time and space of ordering efforts but also their ephemeral, provisional and emergent nature. "Knowing as performance," as "an occurrence," as "an event," are all expressions that belong to a practice-based repertoire.

Finally, practice-based approaches and vocabularies grant citizenship to a host of terms—for instance, *uncertainty, conflict, incoherence*—that run contrary to the deeply rooted antitheses between order and disorder in Western discourse. As we have seen, for many practice-oriented social scientists, incoherences, inconsistencies, paradoxes, and tensions are all fundamental and ineliminable elements of practices. Breakdowns and "disturbances" are not only observational occasions for the researcher but also reflexive learning and fundamental innovation opportunities for the activity system. The learning trigger is the misalignment produced by the expansion of the object; the innovation arises from the attempt to constitute new actionable trails or extend existing ones into the newly constituted "territory," to populate the emergent practical space with new forms of symbolic and material instrumentality. Disorder, not order, generates meaning (Atlan 1979). In practice-based approaches there is no respite to this rhythm. As Suchman says in her chapter, quoting a previous piece by John Law, perhaps there is ordering (or knowing, or acting), but there is certainly no order (or knowledge, or unequivocal action). This is because orders and ordering efforts, knowledges and actions are never complete—they are verbs, not nouns, as we noted above. But there is another more disquieting reason. As Law and Singleton point out in Chapter 10, even when considered as processes and not substances, ordering and knowing efforts do not coexist in an orderly fashion. Instead, they permanently interfere with each other, resist each other, annul each other in a game of partial connections, of order *and* disorder that escapes representation and only offers itself through the art of evoking.

This is also evident in the context of the present collection, which illustrates not only the connections, resemblances, and commonalties among different practice-based approaches but also the significant differences and discrepancies in style and content among them. A divergence of focus is, for example, visible between authors like Strati, Wenger, Yanow, Gomez, and Gherardi and Nicolini, who concentrate on identity, community, and established actionable and structuring principles that are somehow passed down from generation to generation, and others, for instance the authors working within the cultural and historical activity theory tradition, who by contrast emphasize the outward-looking transformational nature of collaboration. While for the former change is a "variation" stemming from unexpected events in the reproduction process, for the latter change is constitutive of practice itself. While the former authors focus on learning as enculturation and as the transmission of a legacy and a shared repertoire that is somehow given, the latter emphasize that learning always results from the mutual expansion of the object of work and the array of mastery, tools, and relations that goes with it. The former emphasize the power of tradition; the latter stress expansion, creativity, tension and unease.

A different fracture line between practice-based approaches is generated by their differing emphases on mutuality, collaboration, and sharedeness, on the one hand, and power inequalities, silencing, and hegemony on the other. Power- and hegemony-related terms—such as conflict, resistance, voice—are not equally distributed among the chapters. They figure most prominently in the essays rooted in a poststructuralist sensibility, namely those based on the notion of "habitus" (Gomez et al.) and the sociology of translation (Suchman, Gherardi and Nicolini, Law and Singleton). They are less prominent in the work of more phenomenologically oriented authors like Strati, Wenger, and Yanow. For the former authors, practices organize and reproduce the distribution of power, knowledge, and the inequalities that go with them. Distributing knowing is not a voluntaristic act but rather the result of the open or tacit collision and maneuvering of divergent interests. As a result, while some of the terms used in the practice-based vocabularies are clearly oriented toward emancipation and critique, others are more attuned to a terminology of management and control.

A final difference that divides the approaches used in the book along yet another dimension is their differing focus on bounded social units (community, system) versus less defined, more contingent sociotechnical arrangements (action net, culture, alignment). While some of the essays use terms that suggest partial closure (e.g., Wenger's discussion of boundaries, Blackler et al.'s discussion of networks of activity systems and communication among them), others use terms that evoke a more diffuse bonded-ness among the elements included in a practice, so that it can be said that the former conceive the community or the system as performing a practice, while for latter the opposite is the case: practice performs the community or system-ness.

In sum, a practice-based vocabulary opens up a space of discursivity that enables us to think and talk about knowing, learning, and organizing in novel, broader, and thicker terms. This practice-based theoretical vocabulary is bound to remain a multi-voiced, partially aligned and partially connected repertoire, more than being a coherent unified theory. Nevertheless, it offers a palette that colors knowing in organizations as a phenomenon that is social, processual, and materially and historically situated.

Concluding Remarks

As the above sections illustrate, practice thinking is by no means new, and in many ways it stands in the background of a number of the major developments in contemporary social theory. The issue is therefore this: Why a renewed interest in these themes now? Why bring practice back into the center of debate?

As we noted at the outset, the answer lies in the growing centrality of knowledge-related issues in contemporary organizations and society, and in the related inadequacy of many of the existing ways to understand these phenomena. On the one hand, this renewed attention is an effect of the emergence and hegemony of the discourse according to which modern society is becoming a "knowledge society." One of the corollaries of this discourse is that to the extent that society increasingly relies on expert knowledge, there is a pressing need to deepen understanding of the organizational conditions and processes that can sustain and foster its creation, circulation, (unequal) distribution, and reproduction. On the other hand, the disappointing results of most knowledge management tools and technologies expose the shortcomings of the traditional cognitive and economic assumptions upon which those tools are built. As Richard McDermott aptly put it, traditional approaches and their IT instantiations can "inspire but not deliver knowledge management" (McDermott 1999) because they fail to recognize the inherent social, processual, and historical nature of knowledge processes. Because of these failings, the limitation of the traditional approaches and their technological and managerial embodiment cannot be resolved by devising more sophisticated IT systems or new management intervention techniques. On the contrary, what is required is recognition that both knowing and knowledge are first and foremost effects of social practices, and that it is toward practices and a practice-based approach that we need to turn to advance our understanding of these processes.

Accordingly, the main aim of this introduction has been to make a case for the adoption of a practice-based approach as articulated by the different contributions to this book. We started by discussing the need to find a way to gain understanding of knowing in organizations that can stand as an alternative to the intellectualist tradition that views knowledge as a mental content, a quasi-substance, or an asset, and learning as a form of accumulation by individual or superindividual entities. After a brief historical excursus on the legacy of the notion of practice, we then articulated four of these ways as set out by the chapters in this collection, showing that the authors in this book conceive knowing-in-practice as culture and aesthetic sense, as community and habitus, as activity, and as heterogeneous engineering. Although they describe activities as diverse as flute-making, roofing, cooking, bridge-building, crime investigation, technological innovation, crop rotation, caring for the ill, creating a safe work site, and mapping disease trajectories, the authors use an overlapping repertoire of terms and figures of speech that broadly outline a practice-based vocabulary of knowing in practice. This vocabulary depicts knowing in organizations as social, processual, materially and historically mediated, emergent, situated, and always open-ended and temporary in character.

Our main claim is that a practice-based approach is a promising way to address the issues of knowing and learning in organizations in such a way that the richness and depth of the phenomenon is given full consideration. As demonstrated by the contributions to this book, far from being the locus of mechanical repetition and mindlessness, practice is instead a key to the comprehension of knowledge-related phenomena. It is in practice, in fact, that knowledge comes to life, stays alive, and fades away. It is in practice that institutionalized, historically determined, and codified expertise acquires sense and becomes both a resource and a constraint for action. At the same time, it is in practice that such knowledge is enacted and reproduced (together with the power relations that it carries) or is transgressed, translated, and betrayed, generating in the process new institutions and patterns of order.

Because it takes us close to the point at which action is generated, a practice-based sensibility makes it possible to observe knowing as an intimate feature of daily organizational life, the locale in which traditional dualisms lose their meaning and dissolve. In the "here and now" of real time practices, knowing and doing are difficult to conceive of as separate: the knowing subject and the known objects cannot be treated in isolation and opposition; repetition and innovation, the given and the emergent coexist and presuppose each other; the body and the material dimension of our existence cannot be excluded from the processes of mind, because the inscribed, trained, and institutionalized body (along with its artifacts) carries knowledge, just as does the inscribed, trained, and institutionalized mind. Finally, in real time practices, knowing and knowledge, process and institution are not opposed: competent performance always presupposes an institutionalized and constraining context of action. But what this context is and to what extent it is perceived as an "external" persuasive force depends on how it is represented, how it is translated in time and space, what patterns of interest it can mobilize in its support, and above all how it is appropriated and put to work in practice.

A practice-based approach offers, in this way, a radical alternative for the study of knowing and learning in organizations because it offers both a new ontology and a new epistemology. The ontology envisaged by a practice-based approach and vocabulary is relational, constructive, heterogeneous, and situated. From a practice perspective, the world appears to be relationally constituted, a seamless web of heterogeneous elements kept together and perpetuated by active processes of ordering and sense making. Practices—including discursive practices—are a *bricolage* of material, mental, social, and cultural resources. Not only are people active *bricoleurs,* but the world is not docile or passive. To know is to keep all these elements in alignment, given that order is not given but is always an emergent process.

Practice-thinking also connotes a world in which activities and knowing always have a specific "where" and "when": they are always "situated." The latter adjective communicates the idea that competent action always happens within a materially, historically, and socioeconomically defined horizon, a "context" that, far from being pre-given, emerges as the result of the conditions put in place by the practices themselves. The adjective "situated" also denotes that, from a practice-based perspective, knowing as well as knowledges and the world are accomplishments, transient effects, temporary alignments that bear within themselves the seeds of their demise. The world of practices is a world in constant flux in which persistence and change coexist because they are not opposed to each other (Bauman 1999). Stability is not, in fact, a static ontological attribute but an outcome of work. Obtaining the same result in our shifting world, achieving stability, creating and sustaining an institution, keeping an organization going require effort. The world is as it is, but it could have been different and can be different: change is an option.

A practice-based approach and vocabulary thus resonates with a sensitivity to what is local, what is temporary, what is partially connected, what is changing. As we have said, practice-talking reiterates that beyond grand constructions like discourses, paradigms, or logics there is a daily reality of local tactics, pockets of resistance, dialects, collusions, contradictions. A practice-based approach emphasizes that tradition, institution, and culture—like knowledge and organizations—are verbs, not nouns. Perpetuating them requires work, tricks and skills, suffering—all of which are phenomena that should become the object of social science.

This processual, relational, constructive, and situated ontology involves a specific epistemic sensitivity and a set of related methodological preferences that allows the researcher to remain consistent with a practice-based approach. A practice-based approach directs the researcher's attention to what people do and say, to the world of life made of the details and events that constitute the texture of everyday living and organizing. Here, the legacies that converge in practice-thinking speak with one voice: everyday life is not something that we need to transcend in order to produce good science. On the contrary, the study of everyday practices should constitute a major concern for social scientists: "The basic domain of study of the social sciences [is] social practices ordered across space and time" (Giddens 1984: 2).

In order to follow the rugged contours of practices and knowing-in-practice, their study should adopt some version of the methodological principle stated by Hughes (1971) as "follow the actors." At the same time, given the "institutionalized" and often embodied and encultured form in which we encounter and experience practices, comprehending them requires us to focus on instances of practice-making or practice-changing. In other words, practice is better observed when some "breakdown" occurs in an entrenched practice or when some substantial change requires major realignments of the extant configuration of practice.

In sum, we believe that the ontology and epistemology, as well as the practice-based vocabulary, provided by the contributions to this book constitute a promising way to understand knowing, one that comes closer to our everyday experience and that helps us enrich our comprehension of the organizing process. Not only does "practice" assist us in thematizing the richness and importance of what is tacit, what is taken for granted, what is familiar, but it is also a more agile tool with which to understand complexity in general and the complexities of the modern organizational world in particular (Law and Mol 2002). Although practice requires attention to less grand things, its modesty becomes a potentially winning factor in approaching big and often seemingly intractable issues. Because practices do not respect boundaries, because they connect things, people, and events that are distant and only partially congruent, because they allow the coexistence of old and new, because they are able to deal with change and disorder while explaining persistence and order, they constitute a highly promising candidate for deepening our understanding of the organizational world in postindustrial society.

Notes

1. Of the authors who contributed to the special issue of *Organization*, only Alessia Contu and Hugh Wilmott are not represented in this volume. An expanded version of their original piece will in fact appear elsewhere (cf. Contu and Willmott, in press).

2. A good introduction to the original version of the sociology of translation can be found in Law (1992). That paper includes an extensive reference list of most prior actor-network theory (ANT). John Law also maintains a very complete and updated online bibliography of ANT works. The reference list can be found at: www. comp.lancs.ac.uk/sociology/antres.html.

References

Atlan, H. (1979). *Entre le Cristal et la fumée.* Paris: Seuil, 1978.

Bauman, Z. (1999). *Culture as Praxis.* 2d ed. London: Sage.

Becker, H.S. (1953). "Becoming a Marijuana User." *American Journal of Sociology* 59: 235–242.

3ell, D. (1973). *The Coming of Post-industrial Society: A Venture in Social Forecasting.* New York: Basic Books.

Bernstein, R.J. (1971). *Praxis and Action.* Philadelphia: University of Pennsylvania Press.

Blackler, F. (1993). "Knowledge and the Theory of Organizations: Organizations as Activity Systems and the Reframing of Management." *Journal of Management Studies* 30(6): 864–884.

Blumer, H. (1969). *Symbolic Interactionism: Perspective and Method.* Berkeley: University of California Press.

Bontis, N. (1997). "Intellectual Capital: An Exploratory Study that Develops Measures and Models." *Management Decision* 36(2): 34–47.

Bourdieu, P. (1990). *The Logic of Practice.* Cambridge: Polity Press.

Brown, S., and Capdevila, R. (1999). "Perpetuum Mobile: Substance, Force and the Sociology of Translation." In J. Law and J. Hassard, eds., *Actor Network Theory and After* (Sociological Review Monograph), 26–50. Oxford: Blackwell.

Certeau, M. de. (1984). *The Practice of Everyday Life.* Berkeley: University of California Press.

Contu, A. (2000). "Learning and Semiotics of Practice: 'New Vocabularies' for Learning and Organising." In C. Grey and S. Fox, eds., *Proceedings of the 2nd International Conference "Connecting Learning and Critique,"* 71–86.

Contu, A., and Willmott, H. (in press). "Re-embedding Situatedness: The Importance of Power Relations in Learning Theory." *Organization Science* 14(3): 283–284.

Cook, S., and Yanow, D. (1993). "Culture and Organizational Learning." *Journal of Management Inquiry* 2(4) (December). Reprinted in Michael D. Cohen and Lee Sproull, eds., *Organizational Learning.* Newbury Park, CA: Sage, 1995.

Crossant, M., and Guatto, T. (1996). "Organizational Learning Research Profile." *Journal of Organizational Change Management* 1: 107–112.

Czarniawska-Joerges, B. (1991). "Culture Is the Medium of Life." In P.J. Frost, L.F. Moore, M. Louis, C. Lundberg, and J. Martin, eds., *Reframing Organizational Culture,* 285–287. Newbury Park, CA: Sage.

Davenport, T.H.; De Long, D.; and Beers, M. (1998). "Successful Knowledge Management Project." *Sloan Management Review* (winter): 43–57.

Dierkes, M.; Berthoin Antal, A.; Child, J.; and Nonaka, I. (2001). *Handbook of Organizational Learning and Knowledge.* Oxford: University Press.

Drucker, P. (1993). *Post-capitalist Society.* Oxford: Butterworth Heinemann.

Easterby-Smith, M. (1997). "Disciplines of Organizational Learning: Contributions and Critiques." *Human Relations* 50(9): 1085–1111.

Fiol, C.M., and Lyles, M. (1985). "Organizational Learning." *Academy of Management Review* 10(4): 803–813.

Gagliardi, P. (1990). "Artifacts as a Pathway and Remainings of Organizational Life." In P. Gagliardi, ed., *Symbols and Artifacts: Views of the Corporate Landscape*, 3–38. Berlin: De Gruyter.

Galbraith, J. (1967). *The New Industrial State.* Boston: Houghton Mifflin.

Gherardi, S. (2000). "From Organizational Learning to Practice-Based Knowing." *Human Relations* 53(8): 1057–1080.

Gherardi, S.; Nicolini D.; and Odella F. (1998). "Toward a Social Understanding of How People Learn in Organizations: The Notion of Situated Curriculum." *Management Learning* 29(3): 273–298.

Giddens, A. (1984). *The Constitution of Society.* Cambridge: Polity Press.

Heidegger, M. (1962). *Being and Time.* New York: Harper and Row.

Hughes, E. (1971). *The Sociological Eye.* Chicago: Aldine.

Johannesen, K. (1996). "Action Research and Epistemology. Some Remarks Concerning the Activity-relatedness and Contextuality of Human Language." *Concepts and Transformation* 1(2/3): 281–297.

Kim, D.H. (1993). "The Link Between Individual and Organizational Learning." *Sloan Management Review* 35(1): 37–50.

Knorr-Cetina, K. (1999). *Epistemic Cultures: How Science Makes Knowledge.* Cambridge: Harvard University Press.

Lave, J., and Wenger, E. (1991). *Situated Learning: Legitimate Peripheral Participation.* Cambridge: University Press.

Law, J. (1992). "Notes on the Theory of the Actor-Network: Ordering, Strategy, and Heterogeneity." *System Practice* 5(4): 379–393.

———. (1999). "After ANT: Topology, Naming and Complexity." In John Law and John Hassard, eds., *Actor Network Theory and After*, 1–14. Oxford and Keele: Blackwell and the Sociological Review.

Law, J., and Mol, A., eds. (2002). *Complexities: Social Studies of Knowledge Practices.* Durham, NC: Duke University Press.

McDermott, R. (1999). "How Information Technology Inspired, But Cannot Deliver, Knowledge Management." *California Management Review* 41(4): 103–117.

Marx, K. (1975). *Early Writings.* L. Coletti, ed. Harmondsworth: Penguin.

Marx, K., and Engels, F. (1846). "The German Ideology." In K. Marx and F. Engels, *Collected Works, Vol. 5*,106–143. New York: International Publishers .

Nahapiet, J., and Ghoshal, S. (1998). "Social Capital, Intellectual Capital, and the Organizational Advantage." *Academy of Management Review* 23(2): 242–267.

Nelson, R., and Winter, S. (1982). *An Evolutionary Theory of Economic Change.* Cambridge: Harvard University Press.

Nicolini, D., and Meznar, M.B. (1995). "The Social Construction of Organizational Learning: Conceptual and Practical Issues in the Field." *Human Relations* 48(7): 727–746.

Nightingale, P. (2000). "Knowledge Management Fads in Seventeenth Century Science Policy: Tacit Knowledge, 'Codification' and the Bishop of Chester." Paper presented at the Knowledge Management: Concepts and Controversies Conference, Warwick, UK, 10–11 February.

Nonaka, I.; Umemoto, K.; and Senoo, D. (1996). "From Information Processing to Knowledge Creation: A Paradigm Shift in Business Management." *Technology in Society* 18(2): 203–218.

Polanyi, M. (1962). *Personal Knowledge: Towards a Post-Critical Philosophy.* 2d ed. Chicago: University of Chicago Press.

Rorty, R. (1989). *Contingency, Irony and Solidarity.* New York: Cambridge University Press.

Scarborough, H.; Swan, J.; and Preston, J. (1999). *Knowledge Management: A Literature Review.* London: IPD.

Schatzki, T. (2001). "Practice Mind-ed Orders." In T. Schatzki, K. Knorr-Cetina, and E. Von Savigny, eds., *The Practice Turn in Contemporary Theory.* London: Routledge.

Schatzki, T.; Knorr-Cetina, K.; and Von Savigny, E. (2001). *The Practice Turn in Contemporary Theory.* London: Routledge.

Schon, D. (1971). *Beyond the Stable State.* New York: Norton.

Stewart, T. (1994). "Your Company's Most Valuable Asset: Intellectual Capital." *Fortune*, October 3, 68–74.

Wenger, E. (1998). *Communities of Practice: Learning, Meaning and Identity.* New York: Cambridge University Press.

Winograd T., and Flores, F. (1986). *Understanding Computers and Cognition: A New Foundation for Design.* Norwood, NJ: Ablex.

Wittgenstein, L. (1953). *Philosophical Investigations.* Oxford: Blackwell.

2

Seeing Organizational Learning: A "Cultural" View

Dvora Yanow

> *Keep your hands dirty with the data.*
> —Don Schon (personal communication, 1976–1982)

> *The years teach much which the days never know.*
> —Ralph Waldo Emerson[1]

What is learning such that an organization, as distinct from its individual members, may be said to do it? That "the experiential referent for the term 'organizational learning' is elusive" (Weick and Westley 1996: 441) makes a difficult claim for such collective learning. Yet another source of difficulty emerges from the ontological, epistemological, and methodological problems of *seeing* organizations—and, hence, of seeing organizations learn. If "organizations cannot be perceived," as Sandelands and Srivatsan (1993) argue, then it will of necessity be difficult to research and to theorize about them, let alone about their properties and processes.

A colleague and I sketched a path out of this ontological, epistemological, and methodological impasse when we proposed a cultural perspective on organizational learning (Cook and Yanow 1993; I will refer to this work as COL henceforth). At the time of its writing I had the sense that we were, implicitly, invoking "culture" in two ways: substantively, in its anthropological sense, to denote a collective and its acts and artifacts; and methodologically, in the sense in which today I would talk about an interpretive mode of analysis (Yanow 2000)—one that is grounded in an interpretive (phenomenological-hermeneutic) philosophical position and that focuses on situated meaning (in this case, what is meaningful to those actors engaged in organizational learning activities). As this essay has since been taken up by others as exemplifying a cultural approach to learning (e.g., Easterby-Smith,

Snell, and Gherardi 1998: 265; Henriksson 1999; Weick and Westley 1996),
I would like here to reflect on and clarify the argument, in light of subse-
quent work in organizational culture, the philosophy of (organizational) science, and organizational learning.[2]

In contrast to the view that scientific theories are a mirrored reflection of
their research subjects, an interpretive epistemological perspective posits that
scientific perception is mediated by the theoretical constructs that researchers bring to their observations. In Kuhn's (1970) words, research "force[s]
nature into the conceptual boxes supplied by professional education" (5).
Embedded in these conceptual boxes are metaphors that assist in mediating
both perception and theoretical formulation.[3] One such conceptual box/meta-
phor approaches organizational learning drawing on the elements that characterize cultures; it is this approach that Scott Cook and I took in arguing in
COL that the construct of "culture" was useful in theorizing about the collective aspects of organizational learning, as observed in a company making
flutes. Invoking culture allows the researcher to "see" and conceptually even
to experience a social or collective aspect of learning because of the conceptual entailments it carries, in a metaphoric process, from its theoretical source
in anthropology (as distinct, for example, from its sources in art, music, or
literary criticism, expressed in the phrases "high culture" and "low culture").
I will begin by exploring these entailments with an eye to addressing two
questions: what vision of organizations does the language of "culture" allow,
and what might it then mean to take a "cultural" approach to the study of
organizational learning? I will extend the arguments made in COL to another
field-based study, to address the issues of organizational size and geographic
dispersal. The essay concludes with a brief comparison with the entailments
of a second metaphor, "communities of practice," which also enables a collective approach, and with some observations on the implications of a cultural-interpretive approach for research methods. Such metaphor analysis
follows the Greek etymology of the word "metaphor": to transfer or bear, in
this case meaning, from one context to another. It asks, What meanings are
being moved from metaphorical sources to organizational settings, and what
do these meanings enable the researcher/theorist to see?

Seeing Organizations "Culturally":
COL as Interpretive Analysis

Scenario: Imagine that you are watching people seated side by side, working
at a table, making flutes. One person is holding the long tube into which tone
holes have been drilled, forming the body of the flute. She is affixing to it the
structure that holds the key mechanism. When she finishes her work, she

passes it to the next flutemaker, who assembles the key mechanism and fits it quite precisely to the body. He hands this keyed tube to the next flutemaker, who puts pads into the keys and adjusts the mechanism by hand to very fine tolerances. Another maker assembles the head joint and embouchure hole, each of which is hand finished with great care.

At every point along this "line," as a piece is passed, each maker assesses the work of the previous flutemaker. If the flute "does not feel right"—and that is the language they use, rather than the more numerically precise language of calibration or specs (specifications)—the worker will say so while handing the piece back to the previous flutemaker for further work.

What the observer-researcher sees on site—"in the field"—(and later reports on) is a number of people engaged in acts involving artifacts produced by the company, interacting between and among themselves concerning these acts and these artifacts (and any other social interaction or banter that might transpire). The researcher does not see any single individual making an entire flute. If we were being precise, we would also say that the researcher does not *see* people "making flutes." The researcher sees people working on parts of the instruments; a finished flute appears after several actions and interactions take place. The statement "people are making flutes" is an ex post attribution made after watching these acts and interactions over time.

A researcher "sees" a culture in the same way: seeing a practice—a set of acts and interactions involving language and objects repeated over time, with patterns and variations—and inferring back that a culture exists. Using "culture" in its substantive, anthropological sense allows us to address the ontological problem of "organization": "What is an organization . . . ?" (Argyris and Schon 1978: 8). Taking the ontological position that an organization needs to be real in the way that tables and chairs, or even humans, are real brings us to the impasse noted earlier. Approaching an organization as a culture in an "as if" analogic-metaphoric way bypasses this problem by drawing on the reality status that "culture" carries.[4]

A major piece of the COL argument was made in this way, riding implicitly on the unspoken, and in a sense intertextual, entailments of "culture." The concept has an established standing in social science, particularly in anthropology. The term itself asserts an ontological status and ascribes that status to its research subject. It is accepted in its own scientific circles (as well as in daily parlance) as a condensed referent to and connoter of a broad range of observed human actions—"the totality of socially transmitted behavior patterns, arts, beliefs, institutions, and all other products of human work and thought characteristic of a community or population" (Morris 1975: 321).[5] This collective reality status is confirmed in the English language (at least) by the use of singular verbs to denote what the collective does.

Researchers in anthropology do not begin their reports by arguing for the ontological standing of the group they have been studying as a collective entity, collectively acting; they do not need to. Naming it a "culture" does that work for them.

In conferring ontological status on the collectivity that produces these acts, language, arts, and so forth, the term "culture" applied to organizations enables us to sidestep two difficulties. For one, it makes "organization" as a collective "seeable" as an entity. This is how it addresses the ontological problem: the organization is real not in the sense that tables are real, but in the sense that cultures are real (which is to say, through the same process of ex post inference that sees "flute-making" in observed patterns of "parts-making"). Second, the metaphor allows us to escape the problem of seeming to anthropomorphize an inanimate object: in the same way in which "cultures" (in the sense of "societies" or "tribes") could be said to exist and to hunt and so on, organizations can be said to act.

Using "culture" in its substantive, anthropological sense also allows us to address the epistemological-methodological problem of whether organizations can be known, and if so, how to generate such knowing. This is intertwined with the ontological problem. If we claim that organizations exist in the way that chairs do, then it makes sense to claim to know them by direct, objective (or external) apperception through one or more of our five senses. But if we comprehend that knowing whether something is an organization or not requires interpretation by members and researchers of their sense data, then we are in a different epistemological realm. Indeed, this is the realm out of which I am writing here: the claim that theoretical metaphors (those embedded in theories) shape perception and understanding reflects an interpretivist epistemological presupposition. Using the metaphor of culture to understand the flutemakers positioned analysis in the realm of knowledge claims based on interpretation (theirs, of their experiences; ours, of observational and interview data).

It is in this mode that "culture" is also used in COL, even more implicitly, in a methodological sense, implying that "cultures" were best studied "culturally." The methods used for knowing the flutemakers organizationally are present by implication (and named there in note 11): the narrative includes details, quotes, and paraphrases that suggest that observations and interviews were conducted; its tone and word choice imply an intimate understanding of flutes-as-musical-instruments (rather than just as a company product, for instance) of a level gained by participant-observation to some degree. Knowability of this sort requires such site-specific methods as observation with varying degrees of participation (see Gans 1976), including conversational interviews and supplemented, where appropriate, by document analysis.

These interpretive methods are designed to produce a record of "local" knowledge (Yanow 2000): detailed descriptions of the activities that groups actually engage in, and members' sensemaking of those actions from their own points of view. In accessing the local knowledge that is the possession of the actors in the situation, interpretive studies seek to understand lived experiences of the realities of the workaday world. As Blumer put it, the "social world is constituted by the local production of meaningful action" (quoted in Suchman 1987: 56). It is this recognition of the importance of local knowledge that seems to be driving the engagement of "chief learning officers" in various companies "to gather the best knowledge from a company's far-flung divisions and apply it where it will do the most good" (Ward 1996). Local knowledge entails and informs "practical judgment," the situationally contingent reasoning and deliberation that underlie acting and taking action. Such practical reasoning seems to rest on the kind of listening, attending, and appreciating that characterize interpretive methods—"some sort of complex responsiveness to the salient features of one's concrete situation."[6] These methods also allow for retrospective sensemaking, the kind of reflexivity identified by phenomenologists (and akin to the baseball umpire's humorous observation about pitched balls, "They ain't nuttin' till I calls 'em"). This points to the ex post dimension of "sight": learning may be less evident in the moment than it is in the longer run, as Emerson so poetically observed.

So, taking an interpretive cultural perspective means a focus on:

- collectives
- and their acts (including interactions)
- and the objects that are the focus of these acts
- and the language used in these acts,
- together with the site-specific meanings of these various artifacts to the actors in the situation
- as well as the site- (or "field"-) based set of interpretive methods designed to access and analyze these data.

A cultural perspective, both substantively and methodologically, makes strong claims for situation-specific knowledge and much weaker ones for universal generalizability. This is seen clearly in anthropological studies, which claim to generate knowledge about the language or rituals or kinship practices, for example, of one group of people or even of only one individual (e.g., Behar 1993). These are the methods used by cultural anthropologists (and community and occupational sociologists and other social scientists interested in accessing local knowledge); they are carried into the COL analysis with and by the culture metaphor.[7]

Substance, methodology, and method intertwine. Substantively speaking, the concept of culture refers not only to a group of people, but also to the artifacts they create (including the values, beliefs, feelings, and other forms of meaning embedded in those artifacts). In this vein, we would say both "The French are a culture" (meaning they constitute or produce or create it) and "The French have a culture" (meaning a set of artifacts embodying culture-specific meanings).[8] These artifacts range from the group's acts (sitting at the table, talking to each other, working on what will become flutes) to the language they use (and that others use about them) to the objects that are the focus of these acts and talk. These observable elements—acts, language, and objects—are the data that are accessed and analyzed using interpretive methods. Such a cultural methodological approach gives as much emphasis to physical artifacts as to acts and language (see, e.g., Gagliardi 1990b; Yanow 1996, esp. ch. 6). Hence, the flutes themselves—the objects—were a focus of analysis, including their appearance in company stories and in myths of the flute world more broadly.

An interpretive methodological approach focuses on two relationships: the constructive character of the relationship between artifacts and their creators, in which the former are seen as embodying the intentions (or "mind" or "consciousness") of the latter;[9] and the symbolic (representational) character of the relationship between artifacts and their embodied meanings. This entails an analytic focus on meaning: what values, beliefs, and/or feelings an artifact represents beyond any "literal," nonsymbolic referent. This focus on meaning, together with the epistemological point about site-specific knowledge, mandates understanding the meanings of artifacts from the point of view of organizational members who created and/or engage them. It also underscores the process through which ongoing engagement with artifacts sustains those meanings.[10] This is what we implicitly brought to the organizational learning analysis of the Powell flute company. These are the hallmarks of phenomenological-hermeneutic approaches to human and social action, which is why, writing today, I would call this an interpretive approach.[11]

Seeing Organizational Learning
Culturally-Collectively-Interpretively

Once we can "see" organizations, we should be able to extend that vision to organizational learning. For if a culture can be said to produce institutions, beliefs, and other human artifacts, then it can also be said to learn. The problem for a cultural approach is not, then, to argue for the collective reality of "organization," but to enable the sighting of learning done collectively, organizationally.

The culture metaphor frees researchers from looking in collective actions for what is accepted as learning in individuals. Instead, it enables exploring what learning by a collective—*organizational* learning—might look like, grounded in empirical observations, which the lens of a collectivity-enabling metaphor makes visible. The culture metaphor provides both terminology and a conceptual vocabulary for talking about field-based observations: the language of culture implicitly makes group action that could, COL argued, reasonably and usefully be called "learning." The difficulty in doing so arises from the conceptual limitations placed on the term "learning" by its sources in individual learning, and especially by approaches to individual learning that limit it to cognition.

Because culture entails a broader range of human action than just cognition, because an interpretive-cultural approach looks, among other things, at the creative relationship between meaning and artifact, a cultural perspective on learning focuses on what we can see when we look at what people do, rather than searching for what might be going on only in their heads. This approach to organizational learning requires researchers to expand the realm of what has traditionally, especially under the influence of organizational behavior with its individualistic psychological roots, been recognized as learning.

One field observation was that *one flutemaker alone did not make an entire flute; making a flute required the group as a whole.* This led to the inference that *the flutemakers held knowledge together, as a group, collectively.* What could be seen and heard were the acts and interactions that yielded complete flutes and the language use (or "speech acts") that that entailed, as well as the handling of the objects that were the focus of these acts and language. Because the makers *were* as a group turning out completed flutes that worked, and because of the international acclaim in which these instruments were held, we could infer that collectively they had mastered the practice of flute-making—that is, the knowing how. And because this knowledge was not inborn, and indeed because new organizational members (including veterans of other flute companies) could be trained to produce flutes in this particular company's way of producing its own recognizable flute styles, we inferred that learning took place. That knowing and learning were displayed and were visible only in the group: members had learned how to make their work practices (what they knew) visible to each other—by way of talk in the context of embodied acts (e.g., pointing) and objects (the flute sections)—in order to carry out relevant action. This view of organizational learning emphasizes learning to become a practitioner—in a specific workgroup, in a specific organization—over learning about practice, and that is a collective undertaking (both in learning and in knowing).[12] It entails individual mastery, certainly, but there is a crucial collective, interactive dimension.

Seeing the process of acts and interactions by which a group of people together made a single flute as collective, "organizational" knowing and learning follows the same ex post reasoning that occurs when a researcher claims to see people making flutes: the observable outcome serves as a basis for inferring and attributing characterizations to prior acts. Inferring back from observed practices and the evaluation of these practices (the flute company produces "the best flutes in the world") yields the interpretation that they therefore know how to do what they do and that, therefore, they learned it.

Another field-based observation was that *the knowledge regarding flute-making was expressed and communicated in reference to aspects of the flutes as the makers handled them, worked on them, and handed them on to the next maker or back to the preceding one and commented on them.* That is, *the knowledge was expressed and communicated through the vehicle of the flute* in acting on it, in interaction with and concerning it. The knowledge was learned in the acts and interactions, the speaking and handling and working, of making flutes—that is, in the common practice of becoming and being Powell flutemakers. What we see when we look culturally-interpretively at flutemakers or other organizational members is their collective and several acts and language with respect to object use—the act(s) (I am including speech as an act) of creating and engaging artifacts and endowing or embodying them with meaning. Artifactual interactions—handing the flute sections back and forth, talking about the feel, and so forth—recreate and reinforce (and potentially change) the meanings they embody.

This entails a kinesthetic dimension (quite aside from cognitive understandings). The flutemakers made judgments of hand and eye (that were both individual and conjoint). Today I would also emphasize the aesthetic dimension (Gagliardi 1996; Strati 1992) of knowing and learning: a flutemaker trained at another company had to learn how to make a flute whose feel, as well as tone, marked it clearly as a "Powell" flute.

It is precisely in this handing back and forth of the flute sections, in evaluating their feel and accepting or rejecting them, and in the latter case in evaluating the rejection, that organizational learning is taking place. The flutemakers hold a multifaceted sensory image of how a Powell flute feels. The aesthetic and kinesthetic judgments assess the flutes-in-process against this image. What is accepted is what fits the image (see Kuhn 1977).[13] Organizational learning entails developing and acting out a collective, shared sense of this image. When Powell flutemakers adopted the Cooper scale, they struggled with the question of how that difference would or would not fit the image of the Powell flute. The company "learned" how to produce a Powell-flute-with-a-Cooper-scale without it ceasing to be "the

Powell flute." For company members, the central question was how to learn to do something different without changing their identity—without ceasing to be "the Powell company," producer of the best flute in the world (by general acclaim in the flute world, even before Albert Cooper introduced his new scale). That they learned both these things can be seen from the fact that after adding a second line of flutes, members felt they were still "the Powell company" still producing "Powell flutes."

Yet another field observation was that *the language used by flutemakers in communicating to one another about the flutes was often of a seemingly general and abstract, noncalibrated or -quantified nature (makers spoke to one another of the "feel" of the flute); but even so they understood one another, and these "abstract" communications from one prompted explicit, concrete actions from another with respect to the communication (i.e., a comment that some part of the flute "did not feel right" prompted very specific acts to correct that feel).* This led to the inference that these kinesthetic (and aesthetic) judgments of feel drew on and reflected *knowledge shared by the makers that was known tacitly,* in Polanyi's sense (1966), *within the collective* and not just the cognitive knowledge of individuals that could (or should) be made explicit (whether in the form of measurements or instrumentation).[14] The fact that the flutemakers could successfully bring in new members while keeping language use "abstract" in this way meant that *tacit knowledge could be communicated*—and was done so in interaction with and through the artifacts, leaving their embodied meanings unspoken.[15] It is in this sense that makers might be said to have learned to make their tacit knowledge "visible" to one another.

Such observations and inferences led to the definition in COL of organizational learning as "the acquiring, sustaining or changing of intersubjective meanings through the artifactual vehicles of their expression and transmission and the collective actions of the group." Organizational learning, in this view, is a collective ability expressed in and through product- or service-oriented acts related to the organization's enterprise. It is these acts or practices that can be seen; the learning (and knowing) is (are) seen only obliquely, by inference after the fact. What can be measured is the mastery of these acts or practices; the learning itself cannot be measured directly.[16] At times what is learned can be made explicit; at other times, it is tacitly known, although organizational actors who are practitioners of it are more likely to be able to make parts of it explicit when they are required to interact with practitioners of different knowledges (including, at times, a researcher asking questions). It is best seen obliquely, while engaged in looking at or doing something else (which is Polanyi's formulation for tacit knowledge: something learned while focusing on something else; see Polanyi and Prosch 1975).[17] Hence, COL argued that organizations learn tacitly, while focusing on the activities of daily work.

Such an approach to organizational learning, then, focuses on:

- the collective
- and its situated acts (including language use)
- engaging the artifacts that are the focus of daily work-related practices
- including the nonexclusively cognitive (such as tacit, kinesthetic, and aesthetic knowledge) and the nonexclusively change-oriented.

"Culture," in enabling a discourse about collective action, bearing both conceptualizing possibilities and descriptive terminology, makes these actions seeable as collective, organizational learning. It shifts the research question from "Who is learning?" to "What is being done, and what needs to be learned in order to do it?" or "What is being learned, and to what effect?" It enlarges the scope of questioning to include, "What is made visible, to whom, for what purpose(s)?" As Weick and Westley (1996: 442) noted: "[W]hen researchers focus on organizations as cultures, they focus less on cognition and what goes on in individual heads, and more on what goes on in the practices of groups" (see also Normann 1985). In looking at what people *do*, a cultural-interpretive perspective focuses on organizational learning not just as organizational change but as organizational maintenance or sustenance as well.[18] It decouples learning from change and from progress: it is possible to engage in organizational learning to stay the same (to maintain an identity or image, for example), and it is also possible to learn things that are not true or that are speculative (either because their disproof has not yet been widely accepted, or because a group wants intentionally to know things that have been proven false). This perspective also decouples learning from error-correction, adaptation to environmental changes, and other systems-theory-infused metaphors of learning. This is not to say that organizational learning cannot be change-related, but that it need not be that exclusively.

The social, interactive dimensions of learning have captured the attention of other organizational researchers (see, e.g., Barley and Orr 1997; Blackler 1995; Blackler, Crump, and McDonald 1998; Brown and Duguid 1991, Gherardi, Nicolini, and Odella 1998; Lave and Wenger 1991; Orr 1996). It is no accident, I think, that much of this work is being done by scientists borrowing from or with training in anthropology, with its presupposition that human acts, including knowing and learning, can usefully be studied and understood as activities of collectives.[19]

Collective Organizational Learning in a Larger-Sized Organization

One of the questions raised for discussion in the COL essay was the extent to which one might see such tacit, artifactual learning in an organization larger and more highly differentiated than the Powell flute company. Longitudinal field-based research in a national, geographically dispersed, government Corporation of Community Centers in Israel (ICCC) suggests that the approach is, indeed, applicable.[20]

At the time of the agency's creation, the idea of a "community center" was new, an import both in name and in concept from the United States (and later known as a *matnas*). There was much discussion at various levels and at various times concerning what community centers should look like and do. The Minister of Education and Culture whose idea it was to create them had already sent out two deputies to research the matter. One of them he asked if she knew what a "community center" was before charging her with forming a study commission; it later became the Board of Directors, and she later became its Chair. The other deputy became the new agency's first executive director.

At one of the early planning meetings, a member of the Board said, "The community center will be a functional supermarket." This metaphor entered into the conceptualization of agency functions across the board, guiding members in decision-making about the design of community center buildings, norms for staff roles, program types, program evaluation criteria, and so on. The agency developed an unknown concept into a clear organizational identity and image.

Ten years after its founding, the agency had over 100 town- and neighborhood-based community centers dispersed throughout the country. In an interview conducted one year later (i.e., after the tenth anniversary of the agency's founding), the director of a community center in a small city remote from agency headquarters, who had been hired some years after that early planning meeting, said, "There's no subject that we can 'push' only as supermarket 'owners' or 'clerks.' We must also be outside [the building]."

The entailments of the supermarket metaphor had never been spelled out, not in that initial planning meeting in which it was spoken nor at any other time. Neither in-service training sessions and annual agency meetings nor annual reports and other agency documents and correspondence instructed members in thinking about or acting with respect to their local community centers as if they were supermarkets. And yet, this center director not only knew to use the metaphor; she understood some of its entailed meaning. So much else of agency action also reflected that knowledge. The agency "learned" how to do its work—what it "meant" to be a *matnas,* a community center in its own particular style—from the entailments of the metaphor, from what it meant in Israel in the late 1960s–early 1970s to be a supermarket (as contrasted with an open-air market or corner grocery store, or with a department store or library or city hall), without making any of this explicit. How to be a community-center-as-supermarket was learned across levels of the organization, by street-level bureaucrats (Lipsky 1980) providing direct service at the front lines as well as by staff and directors at agency headquarters. This was learned, indirectly, through ongoing interactions among center directors and other staff at annual and monthly meetings focused on normal work-related activities to plan programs and discuss strategy, such that newcomers came to use the metaphor (although not *as* a metaphor) as common knowledge in relation to practice. They learned how to make this knowledge-in-practice "visible" to one another so that they could do *matnas* work. This is organizational learning through tacit, artifactual interaction over size, geographic distance, and time.

Culture and Organizational Learning, Interpretively

To treat organizational learning culturally-interpretively does not require an analysis of organizational cultures or the equation of organizations with cultures. The difference is perhaps subtle. Analyzing organizational culture, whether from a functionalist, symbolic, or other perspective (see Smircich 1983), requires at a minimum an identification of the presence of one or more artifacts in the organization (see, e.g., Deal and Kennedy 1982), and more broadly, an attention to the meanings embedded in those artifacts by organizational actors, whether leaders (see, e.g., Sergiovanni and Corbally 1984; Schein 1985) or others (e.g., Kunda 1992; Louis 1985; Yanow 1996). To analyze organizational learning "culturally," one does not need to identify rituals, myths, trophies, and so forth. What is required (or enabled) by such an approach is a meaning-centered focus on whatever work people in the organization do together. Analysis may focus on what they know and/or on the processes by which they learn it, collectively and interactively, on acts and interactions, and on the physical artifacts that are the focus or subject of these acts and interactions and the language used in and with them. Interesting parallels to this approach are emerging from research that derives from studies of human-computer interaction and computer-supported collaborative work, which also focus on situated, action-oriented, collective learning and knowing through the media of "tools" and language (see, e.g., Engeström and Middleton 1996; Goodwin and Goodwin 1996; Shaiken 1996; Star 1996; Suchman 1996).

What is required is an insistence on the centrality of meaning, both as a substantive focus and as a methodological device.

Learning in this view looks nothing like what has commonly been recognized as learning when individuals do it. Researchers looking for that kind of experience or evidence of learning will not see it in cultural-interpretive learning studies; their expectations will be disappointed, and they may claim that this is not learning.[21] Yet this is what collective learning is; it is not individual learning.

Gagliardi (personal communication 1998) argues that knowing and learning are, indeed, attributes of individuals and that we see the collective dimension in the practices that display and represent their individual mastery of the subject. While this makes intuitive sense, there is also a very real sense in which sports teams or groups of musicians (from trios and quartets to choruses and orchestras) or theater troupes learn and know their "plays" not as individuals—who learn their parts—but only together, as collectives.[22] Flutes were made by more than a single individual; community center buildings and programs were designed and implemented by the whole organization. In this sense, to say that a tribe has "learned," "knows," and acts out its traditions, or that a chorus has "learned," "knows," and performs a particular song, is to point to the collective, interactive, social dimensions of learning linked to practice-relevant artifacts, and this cannot be reduced to whatever individual members learn and know. As Tsoukas (1996: 14) notes, "Individual knowledge is possible precisely because of the social practices within which individuals engage. . . ." The argument hinges on whether a theorist sees it as a meaningful statement to say that Pele, alone on the field, is (was) able to play a soccer match. Certainly, we say that he knows how to play soccer; but that statement is only meaningful, it seems to me, as an empirical observation of his play in the ball- and teammate-focused practices that constitute "playing soccer." Observing him alone on the field, dribbling the ball, we could not make the same statement about him with the same meaning (except if we knew about his play from having seen him beforehand with the team). As Connie Mack, the manager of the Philadelphia Athletics baseball team, once said about the late Joe DiMaggio, "As one of nine men, DiMaggio is the best player that ever lived" ("Joe DiMaggio" 1999). Situating DiMaggio among his teammates, this captures something important that researchers are trying to say about what we see that we call organizational learning: that it resides in what people do interactively with practice-relevant artifacts.

There is another metaphor of organizational learning that focuses on the collective aspects of organizational actions.[23] Drawing on the work of Lave and Wenger (1991; see also Wenger 1998), it invokes the concept of communities, seeing learning as an attribute of a "community of practice" (Brown and Duguid 1991; Raelin 1997; see also Barley and Orr 1997; and Orr 1996). Seeing the work group or the entire organization as a "culture" or as a "community" provides two different, yet ontologically and methodologically compatible, lenses for addressing the collective quality of organizational learning; both are "generative metaphors" (Schon 1979) for the study of the social dimensions of learning. It has seemed to me that the phrase "community of practice" captures much of what COL described; the defining criteria of a community of practice (nicely summarized in Raelin 1997: 7–9) are not materially different from what we observed and analyzed among the flutemakers.

What the two phrases share is an emphasis on groups of people acting together: both "culture" and "community" imply a group bonded together in some fashion. However, although we were careful to say in COL that we did not intend to imply by the use of culture a monolithic organization, that connotation is apparently hard to avoid (Henriksson 1999). "Community" suggests a smaller unit; it is seemingly easier to conceptualize several communities within a single organization than it is to conceptualize several cultures. Part of this is due to the entailments of language: while we did not claim that the flute company constituted "a culture," neither did we name the collective unit we were analyzing, other than to use the language of "group" or "collective." The "community of practice" language fills that need. "Community" bounds the action-engaged collective more visibly; culture is a more diffuse and global term.

Culture is more useful than community for focusing on the tacit elements of organizational learning and for conceptualizing cross-group communication and the friction that at times ensues from tacitly known habits colliding. The language of community invokes a tighter, less diffuse bondedness within a group, which highlights potential boundary crossings more strongly than the language of culture: clashes of practice are more easily conceivable in work-focused analysis and conceptually more amenable to intervention than culture clashes and bi- or multiculturalism.

Both cultural and community-of-practice perspectives take a pragmatist orientation, focusing on learning/knowing in and through action. The community-of-practice phrase brings action-as-practice front and center, which is its conceptual strength and advantage over the more diffuse cultural approach. Culture has too often been treated in the organizational studies literature as a set of values and beliefs alone (see Gagliardi 1990a on this point); even when feelings have been included, the treatment has usually lacked a sense of pragmatic action. While interpretive cultural analysis has moved from "reading symbols" to "analyzing practices" (Assad 1993)—from seeking understanding of organizational culture in isolation from context, much like the anthropologist's trait lists or the corporate tourist collecting souvenirs, to seeing situated meanings embedded in artifacts, including what people do— it seems to fall victim to the more widespread, if erroneous, noninterpretive perception of culture as artifacts alone. By making the language of action explicit, "community of practice" highlights what has been missing from many treatments of "culture."

What it risks, however, is precisely the opposite of these advantages. For one, it risks being taken as privileging acts over or to the exclusion of linguistic and physical artifacts. Moreover, the language of community has a long intellectual history with several connotations that culture avoids. It implies affinity and closeness (both affective and geographic proximity, although the emphasis on practice seeks to replace the geographic connotations). There is a conforming or controlling or constricting, at times punishingly so, aspect of living in community, as those from small towns and many non-U.S. national cultures know, which is not as strongly present in the culture metaphor, perhaps because of its diffuseness. Whether this will shape views of organizational learning seen from a community of practice perspective should become clear with further empirical research. Second, its "local" aspect may be less useful in certain organizational contexts. As I think back to the ICCC case, community of practice could have been a very useful way of conceptualizing the community organizers within the agency, whose professional practice brought them into conflict with the dominant, agencywide understanding of the supermarket metaphor (Yanow 1996: ch. 5). But the metaphor did become an organizational metaphor, and the organization as a whole learned how to "do" community-center-as-supermarket across what might otherwise be considered several communities of practice. In this broader context, it is not clear to me that the more bounded and local community of practice metaphor would have an advantage over the more global notion of culture. Perhaps this suggests the need for a level-wise nesting of concepts of collective learning, from the more local to the more global.

Third, unlike the claims processors examined by Wenger (1998) or the copy machine technicians observed by Orr (1996), the ICCC community organizers did not engage one another daily. They met, at most, and for a limited period, once a month for two days for in-service training sessions. Despite this, in many respects they did constitute a community of practice, much like a high-tech firm's design engineers who initially form a face-to-face community of practice in a single location only to become dispersed around the world as a consequence of mergers and acquisitions and other "globalization" activities. At the same time, the community organizers' professional practice entailed daily interactions with community residents, center staff, professional counterparts in schools and other agencies. It is possible that the very diffuseness of the culture metaphor is more suitable for such an arrangement—cultures surviving in a diaspora—although the affective ties (a virtual "proximity") borne by the community metaphor is also relevant.

Both collective metaphors enable researchers to "see" and study organizational learning when to other researchers, organization and collective learning remain invisible. In both cases, however, observation and insight are theoretically informed: the researcher does not *see* a culture or a community; she/he sees the members of the organization act and interact as if they were cultural or community groups.[24] Using the five senses alone, one cannot see an individual, let alone an organization, learn. What we see are acts, practices, degrees of competence and of mastery. The ability to "perceive" organizations, in a cultural-interpretive perspective, requires more than sense-based perception; it relies on theoretically and experientially informed interpretation as well. That experience, in turn, is lived experience, which leads methodologically to situated participant-observation.

To study organizational learning culturally-interpretively, then, requires *in situ*—which is to say, field—observational work, not least because the tacit knowledge entailed is embedded in situation-specific practices, requiring the "active participation of the knower"—in this case, the researcher—"in the situation at hand" (Raelin 1997: 2). As we move from mind to act, we move from armchair theorizing to dirty hands (in Schon's sense). Along the way, thinking, knowing, interpreting, and acting become less "pure" (or isolated) as activities (in the pre-Heisenbergian understanding that researchers were to be careful about "contaminating" their data). The activity of researchers, like that of the "practicers" they are studying, becomes a situated bricolage, working together bits and pieces of local knowledge (which in the researchers' case means also their own practical judgments based on their own context-specific "local" knowledge). The researcher's intimate familiarity with and insight into these actions are what is required for theorizing, because organizational learning is as much about act and artifact and their meanings as it is about cognition. It is this methodological imperative, together with the ontological and epistemological presuppositions on which it rests, that makes this cultural approach an interpretive one.

Notes

This essay was sparked during the third plenary discussion at the 1998 George Washington University–sponsored organizational learning conference when I was asked to describe what organizational learning in the flute company looked like. An earlier version was presented at the Academy of Management Annual Conference, San Diego, CA, August 9–12, 1998, and appears in *Comportamento Organizacional e Gestão* 5: 2 (1999): 55–67. My thanks to Silvia Gherardi for challenging me to articulate what it means to take a cultural approach to organizational learning and to Pasquale Gagliardi and Davide Nicolini for their careful readings of the first version and for generative conversations on the theme.

1. My thanks to Frank Blackler (personal communication July 7, 1998) for the epigraph from Ralph Waldo Emerson and for pointing me to the link between time and "sight."

2. I feel I must add a writer's note. The 1993 essay was coauthored in the best sense of that practice: the fieldwork among the flutemakers was Scott Cook's and appears at length in his doctoral dissertation; I brought the concept of "culture" and a theoretical approach from my own dissertation to the reinterpretation of his observational and interview data as a possible solution to problems he and I had identified in organizational learning theory, particularly as articulated by Don Schon; the analysis and conceptual development were worked out jointly over a period of ten years. I am not comfortable attributing intent in an editorial "we" ex post facto to my coauthor; when I cannot clearly do so, I will claim an authorial "I" as regards the intentions underlying the arguments presented there.

3. This line of reasoning has been articulated by, among others, Richard Harvey Brown (esp. 1976 and 1977; see also 1987 and 1992). I am drawing here on Yanow (1992a and 1996, ch. 5).

4. This line of reasoning parallels that articulated by Smircich (1983). I am using "metaphor" more broadly, however, following Miller (1982), who treats it as a general category with seven variants, among them metaphor proper and analogy.

5. Indeed, it reifies this status, unless we constantly remind ourselves that cultures (and organizations) are human creations—an argument that phenomenologists would make to critical theorists, who might themselves argue back that just because it's a social construction doesn't mean it doesn't "really" exist and have power to control behavior.

6. The quote is from Martha Nussbaum, "The Discernment of Perception: An Aristotelian Conception of Private and Public Rationality," in her *Love's Knowledge: Essays on Philosophy and Literature* (New York: Oxford University Press, 1990); cited by Annette Sassi (personal communication October 7, 1997). I owe this formulation of what Aristotle called *phronesis* (practical reasoning) to Ms. Sassi; see Hawkesworth (1988: 54–57) and Ruderman (1997) for discussions of this concept and some of its contemporary exponents.

7. In the COL case, the concept of culture actually entered long after the initial fieldwork had been done. Because the flute company analysis had been based on field observation and interviews, it fit conceptually to bring in the culture theory that I had been developing in analyzing the Israeli community centers.

8. This parallels Kuhn's (1970) dual sense of "paradigm" as both the worldview shared by a community of scientists and the community sharing that worldview.

9. This is, in general, the argument made by phenomenologists such as Schutz, and Berger and Luckmann or hermeneuticists such as Husserl and Gadamer. For introductions to their ideas, see, for example, Bernstein (1976) or Polkinghorne (1983). For extended discussions, see Berger and Luckmann (1966), Rabinow and Sullivan (1979), Schutz (1967; 1973).

10. This is the hallmark of cultural or symbolic anthropology, ethnomethodology, symbolic interaction, ethnography, participant-observation, and other modes of analysis informed by and/or consistent with interpretive philosophical positions.

11. This position is a philosophical cousin to the argument made by Marta Calás and Linda Smircich (1987) that "culture is dead."

12. I owe the formulation of this idea in part to Henriksson (1999: 53); see also Brown and Duguid (1991).

13. I am indebted to Pasquale Gagliardi for helping me to make this part of the argument explicit.

14. This was the heart of our disagreement with Don Schon (see Argyris and Schon, 1978), who required that cognitive maps be made explicit in order for learning to take place. For different reasons, and informed by different field research, Cook and I argued that this was not necessary. In my view, in fact, it could at times be harmful (Yanow 1992b).

15. When Polanyi says that "we know much more than we can tell" (1966: 4), he does not rule out the possibility that tacit knowledge might be communicated through other than verbal means. Research on nonverbal behavior argues that a high percentage of what is communicated interpersonally is achieved through nonverbal modes (as much as 93 percent, according to some studies). Elsewhere I have argued that tacit knowledge may be, and is, communicated through artifacts other than language (Yanow 1996).

16. I thank Pasquale Gagliardi for helping me articulate this point.

17. But focusing on what is known tacitly, if that is possible, may enable making at least some of it explicit. Tsoukas (1996: 14) has the best discussion that I have found of Polanyi's concept, including ways in which it has been misunderstood. But on this point even Tsoukas misses the extent to which Polanyi's example contradicts his definition: even if one were to focus on all that one knows in order to ride a bicycle, one is unlikely to be able to make all of that knowledge explicit in a communicable fashion such that someone else hearing or reading it could get on a bicycle and ride away. We lack the verbal language and the cognitive ability to make kinesthetic—and perhaps aesthetic—knowledge explicit, except in approximations to what we know in these ways.

18. Henriksson (1999) notes the paradox that this poses, as stability is seen as antithetical to learning in other, noncultural approaches.

19. I may be shortchanging my own "home" fields of political science and public policy analysis, which also begin, at least in some approaches that are not limited by behaviorism, with a consideration of the collective. For one example that seeks to cross this border, see Bennett and Howlett (1992).

20. The following is drawn from Yanow (1996); the specific example is taken from ch. 5.

21. Goodwin and Goodwin (1996) describe through field observations how airport personnel come to "see"—perceive and comprehend—things as they do. Although I am using sight in relation to researchers and theorists, the arguments are quite parallel.

22. This is one of the points that was demonstrated in the All Academy theme session, "From Theatre to Management: Reflections on Second City Improvisation Company" (Academy of Management, Chicago, August 9, 1999).

23. The following section is based on Yanow (1999).

24. Kuhn (1970; 1977) and others remark on this "seeing as" quality of interpretation and the extent to which it constitutes a pattern-matching activity.

References

Argyris, Chris and Schon, Donald A. (1978). *Organizational Learning*. Menlo Park, CA: Addison-Wesley.

Assad, Talal. (1993). *Genealogies of Religion*. Baltimore, MD: Johns Hopkins. Cited in Catherine Bell (1997), *Ritual*.

Barley, Stephen, and Orr, Julian, eds. (1997). *Between Craft and Science: Technical Work in the United States*. Ithaca, NY: Cornell University Press. [See esp. chs. 1, 2, 7.]

Behar, Ruth (1993). *Translated Woman: Crossing the Border with Esperanza's Story*. Boston: Beacon Press.

Bennett, Colin J., and Howlett, Michael. (1992). "The Lessons of Learning: Reconciling Theories of Policy Learning and Policy Change." *Policy Sciences* 25: 275–294.

Berger, Peter L., and Luckmann, Thomas. (1966). *The Social Construction of Reality*. New York: Anchor Books.

Bernstein, Richard J. (1976). *The Restructuring of Social and Political Theory*. Philadelphia: University of Pennsylvania Press.

Black, Max. (1962). *Models and Metaphors*. Ithaca, NY: Cornell University Press.

Blackler, Frank. (1995). "Knowledge, Knowledge Work, and Organizations." *Organization Studies* 16(6): 1021–1046.

Blackler, Frank; Crump, Norman; and McDonald, Seonaidh. (1998). "Managing Innovation in Complex Activity Networks." Presented at the Academy of Management Symposium, "Situated Learning, Local Knowledge, and Action," San Diego, CA, August 9–12.

Brown, Richard H. (1976). "Social Theory as Metaphor." *Theory and Society* 3: 169–197.

———. (1977). *A Poetic for Sociology*. Cambridge: Cambridge University Press.

———. (1987). *Society as Text*. Chicago: University of Chicago.

———, ed. (1992). *Writing the Social Text: Poetics and Politics in Social Science Discourse*. New York: Aldine de Gruyter.

Brown, John Seeley, and Duguid, Paul. (1991). "Organizational Learning and Communities of Practice." *Organization Science* 2(1): 40–57. Reprinted in *Organizational Learning*, ed. Michael D. Cohen and Lee Sproull. Newbury Park, CA: Sage, 1995.

Calas, Marta B., and Smircich, Linda. (1987). "Post-culture: Is the Organizational Culture Literature Dominant but Dead?" Presented at the Standing Conference on Organizational Symbolism, Milan, Italy.

Cook, Scott, and Yanow, Dvora. (1993). "Culture and Organizational Learning." *Journal of Management Inquiry* 2(4) (December). Reprinted in *Organizational Learning*, ed. Michael D. Cohen and Lee Sproull, 430–459. Newbury Park, CA: Sage, 1995.

Deal, Terrence E., and Kennedy, Allen A. (1982). *Corporate Cultures*. Reading, MA: Addison-Wesley.

Easterby-Smith, Mark; Snell, Robin; and Gherardi, Silvia. (1998). "Organizational Learning: Diverging Communities of Practice?" *Management Learning* 29(3): 259–272.

Engeström, Yrjö, and Middleton, David. (1996). "Introduction: Studying Work as Mindful Practice." In Yrjö Engeström and David Middleton, eds., *Cognition and Communication at Work*, 1–14. New York: Cambridge University Press.

Gagliardi, Pasquale. (1990a). "Artifacts as Pathways and Remains of Organizational Life." In P. Gagliardi, ed., *Symbols and Artifacts*, 3–38. New York: Aldine de Gruyter.

———, ed. (1990b). *Symbols and Artifacts*. New York: Aldine de Gruyter.

———. (1996). "Exploring the Aesthetic Side of Organizational Life." In S.R. Clegg, C. Hardy, and W. Nord, eds., *Handbook of Organization Studies*, 565–580. London: Sage.

Gans, Herbert. (1976). "Personal Journal: B. On the Methods Used in This Study." In M. Patricia Golden, ed., *The Research Experience*, 49–59. Itasca, IL: F.E. Peacock.

Gherardi, Silvia; Nicolini, Davide; and Odella, Francesca. (1998). "Toward a Social Understanding of How People Learn in Organizations." *Management Learning* 29(3): 273–298.

Goodwin, Charles, and Goodwin, Marjorie Harness. (1996). "Seeing as Situated Activity." In Yrjö Engeström and David Middleton, eds., *Cognition and Communication at Work*, 61–95. Cambridge: Cambridge University Press.

Hawkesworth, M.E. (1988). *Theoretical Issues in Policy Analysis*. Albany, NY: State University of New York Press.

Henriksson, Kristina. (1999). *The Collective Dynamics of Organizational Learning*. Lund Studies in Economics and Management 49. Lund, Sweden: Institute of Economic Research, Lund University.

"Joe DiMaggio, 1914–1999." *San Jose Mercury News*, March 9, 1999, 14A.

Kuhn, Thomas S. (1970). *The Structure of Scientific Revolutions*. 2d ed., expanded. Chicago: University of Chicago Press.

———. (1977). *The Essential Tension*. Chicago: University of Chicago Press.

Kunda, Gideon. (1992). *Engineering Culture*. Philadelphia: Temple University Press.

Lave, Jean, and Wenger, Etienne. (1991). *Situated Learning*. New York: Cambridge University Press.

Lipsky, Michael. (1980). *Street-level Bureaucracy*. New York: Russell Sage.

Louis, Meryl Reis. (1985). "Sourcing Workplace Cultures." In Ralph H. Kilmann, Mary J. Saxton, Roy Serpa, and associates, eds., *Gaining Control of the Corporate Culture*. San Francisco: Jossey-Bass.

Miller, Donald F. (1982). "Metaphor, Thinking, and Thought." *Et cetera* 39(2) (Summer): 134–150.

Morris, William, ed. (1975). *The American Heritage Dictionary of the English Language*. Boston: American Heritage and Houghton Mifflin.

Normann, R. (1985). "Developing Capabilities for Organizational Learning." In J.M. Pennings, ed., *Organizational Strategy and Change*, 217–248. San Francisco: Jossey-Bass.

Orr, Julian. (1996). *Talking About Machines: An Ethnography of a Modern Job*. Ithaca, NY: Cornell University Press.

Polanyi, Michael. (1966). *The Tacit Dimension*. New York: Doubleday.

Polanyi, Michael, and Prosch, Harry. (1975). *Meaning*. Chicago: University of Chicago.

Polkinghorne, Donald. (1983). *Methodology for the Human Sciences*. Albany: State University of New York Press.

Rabinow, Paul, and Sullivan, William M., eds. (1979). *Interpretive Social Science*. Berkeley: University of California Press.

Raelin, Joseph A. (1997). "A Model of Work-based Learning." *Organization Science* 8(5): 1–16.

Ruderman, Richard S. (1997). "Aristotle and the Recovery of Political Judgment." *American Political Science Review* 91(2) (June): 409–420.

Sandelands, Lloyd, and Srivatsan, V. (1993). "The Problem of Experience in the Study of Organizations." *Organization Studies*.

Schein, Edgar. (1985). *Organizational Culture and Leadership*. San Francisco: Jossey-Bass.

Schon, Donald A. (1979). "Generative Metaphor." In A. Ortony, ed., *Metaphor and Thought*, 254–283. Cambridge: Cambridge University Press.

Schutz, Alfred. (1967). *The Phenomenology of the Social World.* Chicago: Northwestern University Press.

———. (1973). "Concept and Theory Formation in the Social Sciences." In Maurice Natanson, ed., *Collected Papers*, vol. 1, 48–66. The Hague: Martinus Nijhoff.

Sergiovanni, Thomas J., and Corbally, John E. (1984). *Leadership and Organization Culture.* Urbana: University of Illinois Press.

Shaiken, Harley. (1996). "Experience and the Collective Nature of Skill." In Yrjö Engeström and David Middleton, eds., *Cognition and Communication at Work,* 279–295. Cambridge: Cambridge University Press.

Smircich, Linda. (1983). "Concepts of Culture and Organizational Analysis." *Administrative Science Quarterly* 28(3): 339–358.

Star, Susan Leigh. (1996). "Working Together: Symbolic Interactionism, Activity Theory, and Information Systems." In Yrjö Engeström and David Middleton, eds., *Cognition and Communication at Work,* 296–318. Cambridge: Cambridge University Press.

Strati, Antonio. (1992). "Aesthetic Understanding of Organizational Life." *Academy of Management Review* 17(3): 568–581.

Suchman, Lucy A. (1987). *Plans and Situated Actions.* New York: Cambridge University Press.

———. (1996). "Constituting Shared Workspaces." In Yrjö Engeström and David Middleton, eds., *Cognition and Communication at Work,* 35–60. Cambridge: Cambridge University Press.

Tsoukas, Haridimos. (1996). "The Firm as a Distributed Knowledge System." *Strategic Management Journal* 17: 11–25.

Ward, Leah Beth. (1996). "In the Executive Alphabet, You Call Them C.L.O.'s." *New York Times*, February 4.

Wenger, Etienne. (1998). *Communities of Practice.* Cambridge: Cambridge University Press.

Weick, Karl E., and Westley, Frances. (1996). "Organizational Learning: Affirming an Oxymoron." In Stewart R. Clegg, Cynthia Hardy, and Walter R. Nord, eds., *Handbook of Organization Studies.* London: Sage.

Yanow, Dvora. (1992a). "Supermarkets and Culture Clash: The Epistemological Role of Metaphors in Administrative Practice." *American Review of Public Administration* 22(2) (June): 89–110.

———. (1992b). "Silences in Public Policy Discourse: Policy and Organizational Myths." *Journal of Public Administration Research and Theory* 2(4) (October): 399–423.

———. (1996). *How Does a Policy Mean? Interpreting Policy and Organizational Actions.* Washington, DC: Georgetown University Press.

———. (1999). "The Language of 'Organisational Learning': A Palimpsest of Terms." In M. Easterby-Smith, L. Araujo, and J. Burgoyne, eds., *Organizational Learning* (Proceedings of the 3d International Conference, Lancaster University, June 6–8) 2: 1075–1086.

———. (2000). *Conducting Interpretive Policy Analysis.* Newbury Park, CA: Sage.

3

Knowing in Practice: Aesthetic Understanding and Tacit Knowledge

Antonio Strati

Introduction

My main argument in this chapter is that an aesthetic approach to understanding the tacitness of organizational knowledge can provide the researcher with crucial insights into the interpersonal nature of knowing in practice in organizational life. Study of the dynamics of organizational learning focuses on people's work and organizational skills and the social construction of the latter by processes of organizational interaction that are not always explicit, formalizable, or even apparent. In these cases, one talks of tacit knowledge, of practical expertise, and of learning situated in the social practices that people implement within organizations or on their behalf. But one should also talk of aesthetic knowledge, for this would induce scholars to break with the dominant tradition of cognitive theory on organizational learning and managerial training. Aesthetic understanding, in fact, prompts considerations that question and undermine the exclusive reliance on cognition—on the rational and mental—by studies of social phenomena in organizational settings that take due account of our knowing in practice, as experienced and supported by the senses rather than just the way that we think.

This is the thesis argued in this chapter, which is organized as follows. I first outline what is meant by aesthetics in organizational theories and management studies and then show the close interweaving between aesthetics and tacit knowledge. I conclude with discussion of the meaning of an approach to the study of organizations that concentrates on the aesthetic dimension, and the value that derives from it for the traditional analysis of organizational learning.

Aesthetic Understanding and Organizational Studies

Aesthetic knowledge is the form of knowledge that persons acquire by activating the specific capacities of their perceptive-sensorial faculties and aesthetic judgment (Baumgarten 1750–58; Kant 1790; Vico 1725) in the day-to-day lives of organizations. Aesthetics highlights and legitimates the personal sentiment as an intersubjective form of knowing (Carchia and D'Angelo 1999: 257), that is, a sentiment which is both individual and collectively constructed in the interactive acts by individuals of experiencing, understanding and judging through senses and taste. Aesthetics has been the matter of much controversy during the last three centuries, and radical transformations occurred in the last century especially because of the interplay between the conceptualizations of artists and the studies of social scientists. Yet a common ground emerged from these debates, and it regarded the central topic of this chapter, namely the close relationship between aesthetics and knowledge.

Contemporary discussion of aesthetics draws a distinction between "continental philosophy"—which focuses on the culturally constructed subjects of study and their historical roots—and "analytical philosophy," which stresses structured and rigorous analysis and is grounded in logical positivism and empiricism. Both styles of philosophical research emphasize the contribution of aesthetics to knowledge. According to continental philosophy—which is the intellectual background to this chapter—in recent decades the aesthetic experience has been redefined as "vital to an understanding of the relationship between mind and world. The aesthetic, formerly exiled from mainstream attention, assumes centre-stage as the region to which we can turn for new cognitive possibilities and a sensibility that is critical of the divisions exercised by modern thought" (Cazeaux 2000: xiii).

Analytic philosophers place different emphases on the contribution of aesthetics to knowledge. As regards art, for example, Eileen John comments that it is a source of cognive stimulation—thoughts, feelings, desires—which prompts conscious activity, creates or shapes categories of knowledge, and is an important resource "for studying the role of such factors as creativity, surprise, interest, and choice in the emergence of new ideas" (2001: 340).

Some three centuries ago, philosophical aesthetics was formed and debated in terms of:

(a) the antithesis to Cartesian rational explanation constituted by emphasis on mythical poetry, the *mythos*, the mythological imagination, reasoning by metaphors, or mythical thought, and the close and constant connection between what is thought and what is felt by the body's sensory and perceptive faculties (Vico 1725);

(b) the sensitive judgment that enables assessment of feelings, phantasms, fictions, and other things that the intellectual judgment is unable to understand (Baumgarten 1735, 1750–58). Involved here is whatever impinges on our senses and is part of our sensory experience, or in other words, the complex of representations that subsist beneath the analytical distinctions drawn by the science of sensible knowledge and the art of fine thought, the goal of which is the perfection of sensible knowledge in itself;

(c) the aesthetic judgment applied to the perfection or imperfection of a particular thing. This is a sensible judgment that does not yield judgments, but rather evaluations of perceived perfection or imperfection that have the nature of sentiment and taste (Addison 1712; Baumgarten 1735; Kant 1790) or a judgment in harmony with feelings instead of concepts.

The aesthetics addressed and discussed in organizational theories is therefore *aisthánomai, aisthetes, aisthetikós, aisthánesthai,* that is, expressions that all highlighted—in ancient Greek—the act of perceiving, and to which Baumgarten referred when coining the modern term "aesthetics." It concerns feeling the pathos of an organization's material and nonmaterial artifacts, perceiving an organization's beauty, appreciating the grandiosity of certain organizational practices, feeling disgust at certain courses of organizational action. As the act of perceiving and judging sensorially, *aesthetics is that form of organizational knowledge which is personal and collectively socially constructed at once.* To have a good eye or a refined taste is a personal sensorial faculty acting in—and shaped by—interpersonal relationships in organizational settings and in society. This is a source of differentiation among organization participants, given that not everyone sees the same things, reacts to the same odors, or has the same taste: there are those who "have an eye" for things while others do not; those who have an "ear" or a "nose," those who are "good with their hands," or "have taste." This socially constructed personal knowledge is ineradicable and irreducible: indeed, a remark on an organizational event to the effect that "I don't like this" may be unarguable, given that further reason-based negotiation on the matter is impossible. This is an aesthetic judgment and it brings to the fore the close connection between aesthetics and art in organizational understanding (Dégot 1987; Jones, Moore, and Snyder 1988; Strati and Guillet de Montoux 2002).

Art has a cognitive value and can be a source of both knowledge and pleasure, since it provides insights about ourselves and our styles of living social matters (Young 2001). Moreover, art is pure formativeness, writes Luigi Pareyson (1954), and the artistic action is a process of inventing and making that is not intended to produce speculative or practical works, but is instead addressed to the production of the form itself. Formativeness, however, refers to every human action, since all human actions are directed to forming something—the art of managing beautifully, for example—even though only in art *per se* is shape given to the form itself.

To resume, debate on art and aesthetics in organization theories has led to valorization of:

1. the *central importance of the human person* in the process of organizational knowledge;
2. the *corporeality of personal knowledge* in organizational life;
3. the *socially constructed character of aesthetic knowing* in organizational settings;
4. the *relationship between persons and forms*, since everyday life is characterized by an inexhaustible process of interpreting, inventing, and reshaping forms by its participants.

What bearing, therefore, does the study of aesthetics and organization (Dean, Ottensmeyer, and Ramirez 1997; Gagliardi 1996; Hatch 1997; Linstead and Höpfl 2000; Strati 1999) have on organizational learning? It shows that the latter cannot be confined to the sphere of cognition and of the translation of all forms of knowledge into cognitive knowledge. Rather, due account should be taken of the personal knowledge based on the faculty of aesthetic judgment and the perceptive-sensorial capacities. On this rests the radical break with the dominant tradition of cognitive theory on organizational learning that aesthetic understanding entails. On this is grounded the interweaving between aesthetic knowing and tacit knowledge.

The practical knowledge acquired through the five senses of sight, hearing, smell, taste, and touch, and the faculty of aesthetic judgment connected to them, was also considered by Michael Polanyi (1962) when he drew the distinction between explicit knowledge and tacit knowledge: the former type of knowledge is formalized in scientific terms; the latter is constituted by the *awareness of knowing* how to do something without being able to provide an adequate analytical description of it and, therefore, without being able to translate it into formal, universalistic, and generalizable knowledge. It is for this latter form of knowledge that the aesthetic understanding is fundamental.

Aesthetics and Observations in the Field

In research and study on learning in organizations as social contexts (Strati 2000), when attention has focused on organizational practices, the use of tacit knowledge described by Polanyi (1962) has sometimes emerged

(Baumard 1996; Brown and Duguid 1991; Cook and Yanow 1993; Fox 1997; Gherardi 2000; Nonaka and Takeuchi 1995). This form of knowledge constitutes the common ground between the debate on organizational aesthetics and that on organizational learning. This is one of the main themes of this chapter, and it will be examined on the basis of empirical observations of the work of stripping and re-laying a roof. These observations will be set out using an evocative rather than analytical style, given that this is the distinguishing feature of the aesthetic approach (Strati 1992), and that style is like theory in the study of organizations since "staking out a theoretical position is unavoidably a rhetorical act" (Van Maanen 1995: 134).

I was observing a meeting for the purposes of my research. When I looked out of the window I saw three workmen dismantling the roof of a nearby two-storey building. My attention had been drawn by the racket made by the workmen as, with an almost rhythmic cadence, they threw the tiles and other material stripped from the roof down into the yard below. Distracted but also intrigued, I watched what was happening on the roof and in the yard, and I was struck by the workmen's apparent disregard for safety systems, although these had apparently been adequately installed. For example, none of the workmen was attached to the ropes, and they ignored the hand-grips provided to move around the roof. The latter, in fact, sloped steeply, and as the building was two stories high, there was a considerable risk of injury if a workman slipped or lost his balance. But I was most struck, as I have described elsewhere (1999: 89),

> by the movements of one of the workmen. Although plump to the point of obesity, he moved up and down the roof with surprising agility. He was obviously in charge because he was gesticulating orders to the others. If he saw that one of his workmates was doing something wrong or had not understood, he went to help him, hanging onto the rope with one hand to descend the roof, hauling himself up with the rope to ascend, on some occasions even grabbing the chimney stack. Once he had reached the other workman, he took over, almost pushing him out of the way. I also gained the impression that his was the most satisfying, most difficult and most demanding job. All three workers, however, were intent on removing the old tiles from the roofing timbers. They then took the stripped materials and threw them down to the yard below. As the debris hit the ground, it made a variety of thumps and crashes, all equally annoying, and all of which disturbed the meeting.

It should be pointed out, however, that:

(a) The above observations were gathered coincidentally with an ongoing empirical study of organizational cultures in a manufacturing organization. The point of observation, the forms and time-scale of the observation, and the attention paid to the organizational practices on the roof were conditioned by this fact. I was observing a department meeting called to discuss sensitive matters, and in order to be as unobtrusive as possible I had sat in a peripheral part of the room next to the window, while my work instruments were placed on the floor or used as something to fiddle with distractedly.

(b) The considerations prompted by these observations took the form of a "first impression" rather than careful and rigorous analysis. The observation had been neither continual nor structured; nor had it involved the measurements so pervasive even in qualitative empirical research conducted in organizational settings. I had not counted the workers' hand movements as they stripped the roof, nor did I have any clear idea of how many times they had walked across the roof, how many times two of them had worked together, or how many times assistance had been requested or offered, how much work was progressively made. Nor was it possible for me to restart the observation from scratch. In short, I had no numerical data, but instead impressions, ethical evaluations and aesthetic judgments, which, instead of giving answers, asked questions.

(c) My "first impression" was informed with fear and concern, due partly to the fact that the research group of which I was a member (Research Unit on Cognition, Organizational Learning and Aesthetics) was studying safety practices in diverse organizational contexts, one of which was the building trade.

At this point the readers have sufficient information to try, should they so wish, to "put themselves in my place" and imagine (i) the awkwardness of my situation as an "absent/present observer" of the difficult departmental meeting, and (ii) the conflict caused by my unexpected fascination and interest in the organization observed outside the window as it set about stripping the roof: a second line of research that was entirely extraneous to the first. If the readers do so "put themselves" in my place, they will be in the same position as someone who conducts "imaginary participant observation" (Strati 1999: 11–18)—that is, observation grounded on the ability to immerse oneself imaginatively in an organizational situation and based on the evocative process of knowing organizational life, which characterizes—besides the aesthetic approach—interpretative and introspective streams in "ethnography" (see, e.g., Coffey, Holbrook, and Atkinson 1996; Henley 1998; Walker 1993). They may rely on exclusively intellective reflection but also, by activating their perceptive-sensorial faculties, on aesthetic judgment, emotions, and aesthetic sentiments. If they try, again using their imagination, to "sit" in my place, "looking" out of the window and "feeling" discomfort caused by awareness that the focus of their analysis is not events on the roof, experiencing the aesthetic attraction of what was seen and heard, which implied distracting themselves from previously careful planned research, then they will be in the situation of someone conducting—at the imaginative level, of course—direct and personal observation of the work of that particular organization. By virtue of participant observation conducted through the imagination, the readers "see," "hear," "perceive," and "are aware of" the research process in which they are imaginatively taking part through sensorial faculties rather than intellectual abilities.

The principal and most interesting feature of imaginary participatory observation is the following: if the readers decide to engage in this form of knowledge-gathering, the above description may prompt them to ask questions very different from the ones that I asked. They might not, for example, give particular importance to the workplace safety practices of the three workmen, or they might not be surprised by the agility of their movements as they worked on the roof. They might, for instance, focus on technological innovation and the work practices on the roof, or on organizational communication and the construction of gendered organizational discourses that might mobilize masculinity (Martin 2001) in the context of these practices.

My questions were prompted by my strong reaction to the fact that the three workmen were engaged in organizational practices that literally removed the ground from beneath their feet, and to do so used what I found to be surprising work methods. They worked quickly, as if they had been overcome by a destructive frenzy and drew pleasure from the noise made by the pieces of roof as they hit the ground in the yard below (which obviously were been closed off). What I observed was not slow and deliberate movements but

1. confidence in footwork and posture, and manual dexterity,
2. speed, as if the roof had to be stripped as quickly as possible,
3. the rhythm of the work set by the regular cadence of the pieces of roof crashing into the yard below,
4. the focusing of attention on the task at hand,
5. organizational communication made up of gesticulations and few words,
6. the performance of several tasks, which required changing place on the roof as the work progressed, changing posture according to the operation to perform, moving across the roof to help a workmate.

Now, although some questions had been answered by my observations—for example, how the men coordinated work, which hierarchical practices were in use, how far body expressions were legitimated forms of organizational communication—there was one that was still unanswered: why did the workmen not slip or put a foot wrong? The slope of the roof, the varying nature of the materials ripped free and thrown into the yard, the alternation of individual work and cooperation, and the progressive actualization of stripping the roof—these were aspects which, taken together:

1. enhanced my concern about conceptions of safety and risk in organizations whose business is working on roofs, both dismantling them and constructing, repairing and re-laying them;
2. highlighted that my observations had not produced knowledge about how an organization of this kind could operate.

Conversations on Organizational Learning

When the meeting had finished and we were going off for lunch, I decided to stop for a moment in the yard, where the workmen were now taking their lunch break seated amid the debris from the roof, and ask them my questions: How do you do it? How is it done?

The first reaction was laughter, which may have been due to embarrassment, or to self-satisfaction, or even to scorn at the professor who could not understand. This was followed by an exchange of wisecracks in dialect that I could not follow, and then by an answer from the workman whom I took to be the leader. Stamping his feet, he said that the secret lay in "feeling the roof with your feet": in feeling, that is to say, that your feet are firmly fixed to it. This was not enough, however. You must never make awkward movements that might cause a loss of balance that your legs, even though they were well planted, could not counteract. You had to "look with your ears," because noises were a valuable source of information. You had to watch the others, see what they were doing, what point they had reached, ask how they felt, exchange views and instructions, give a hand if necessary. You needed your hands to work, not to hold onto the roof. It was your legs that kept you on the roof, which you felt firmly "attached to your feet."

During the next few days I again paused to talk to the workmen as they took their lunch break. The topic was always the same, but I changed the questions, asking how one could learn to work on the roof. What was it that one needed to know from the beginning? What was it that you had to be able to do? How could you know what you had to be able to do before you went up on the roof to do it?

"You mustn't be afraid of being up there on the roof," one of the other workmen said; "you mustn't be scared of heights," or of the "open air," or of the "view" up there. But, the foreman insisted, lack of fear "is of little use if you don't feel the roof with your feet" and if "you don't feel yourself nailed to the roof." How do you learn to feel yourself nailed to the roof? "It's something that has to come naturally," answered the foreman, something that "you have to learn the very first time" because afterwards it's too late," at which the others laughed. I saw that the grotesque and the ridiculous—the distinctive features of the aesthetic category of the "comic"—were part of the language-in-use of that roof-stripping and re-laying organization, although they did not extend it to include me as well.

The workmen noticed that I was not amused by the idea that someone who did not know that s/he did not know how to work on a roof might fall and be injured. They therefore began to talk to me seriously about what should be taught to a "male" novice roof-stripper—"you can't expect a woman doing this job." He should be taught to climb up and down ladders like a bear, looking up at the roof, always holding onto the ladder with at least one hand, moving one foot at a time and taking one rung at a time. When he is on the roof, he should not lean with the pitch of the roof, but hold his body so to counteract the slope, almost as if he were "leaning" on the air between him and the roof. He should be taught that there are good, bad, and deceptive handholds to be recognized at sight; that he should test and retest the firmness of handholds because "nothing stands still" on the roof and new handholds must constantly be found; that the roof "makes noises" that should be listened to and interpreted, both to assess the progress of the work and to avoid dangers that cannot be seen but only intuited by listening; that he should always watch what his workmates are doing, both to coordinate the work and to ensure their safety.

Yet these replies still did not thoroughly answer my questions. However precise and however important they may have been for someone learning the job of roof-stripper, the "lessons" described to me by the workmen covered only some aspects of the negotiations characteristic of organizational socialization, which concern as much rules, norms, and forms of organizational authority as the practical modes of task performance, the sense of work activities, the meaning of day-to-day life in the organization, and the management of organizational power relations. They failed to satisfy my questions because, on close consideration, the lessons taught to the male novice were grounded on something that was vague, unexpressed, and unknown.

What is there of the exact and formalized in instructions on how to work on a roof—such as "take care to distinguish and interpret noises that you have not heard before" or "lean on the air between your body and the roof"— when these things have never been done before? The instruction to "feel" as if your body is leaning on the air is only apparently definite; it is instead essentially vague and indeterminate, and so too is the instruction to "feel" as if your feet were nailed to the roof. Moreover, instructions that might appear better defined, on more careful analysis prove to be very unclear. What exactly is meant by using the information acquired by "listening" to the noises given off by the roof? According to one's personal background some of these noises will seem normal, others will seem strange; some will be familiar, others will seem new, maybe alarming: they will "seem" rather than "be." The same applies to the good, bad, and deceptive handholds pointed out by workmates during the initial phase of the novice's socialization, and then subsequently when the handholds change as the work progresses: "see them" is a generic expression, if one excludes cases in which the handholds are those fixed by the workmen for safety reasons. It is not that all the "lessons" that the workmen described to me were of this type. For example, the instructions on how to climb up and down ladders were precise. But much less clear was how the male novice should learn to abandon the bear posture to get off the ladder and onto the roof, and vice versa. Though this may seem a mere detail, the instruction to the novice always to keep watch on his workmates is certainly not: when should he watch them since it cannot be precisely "always" as they said? When he had interrupted his work? What exactly should he "see" when watching them? In this case, too, the lessons given to the novice struck me as generally useful advice, not the explicit formalization of a precisely defined instruction.

I talked to the workmen on a further occasion during their lunch break. They added that not everyone was suited to their work, and that you realized immediately whether or not you were. Once again, there was no lack of the banter typical of the "comic" in organizations: "if it doesn't come naturally to you," you'd better "find another job immediately" because if you wait to see how things turn out, they will turn out badly. But my perplexity was evident to them. How to work on a roof "is taught badly," said the foreman; the fact is that whether you are able to do so is something that "you have to feel yourself." You can't do it if you feel afraid, if you wait for the fear to pass with time, if "you feel that you're in danger" while you're up there. Instead, you should take the work differently, because "there's something beautiful about" working on a roof. And then, you "see immediately" if someone can do the work. When choosing a new worker, you "should watch him on the roof and feel confident" that he will not hurt himself. "You can't take on just anyone" for a job like this; it is "a responsibility" that you have toward everyone: the man himself, his family, your workmates, the business, the trade unions.

The Interweaving Between Aesthetic Understanding and Tacit Knowledge

Aesthetics—or the perceptive-sensorial capacities of people and their faculty of aesthetic judgment—was therefore particularly important as regards:

1. the work on the roof,
2. the decision to go in for that kind of work,
3. teaching someone how to do it,
4. selecting the personnel able to do it.

The statements reported above by the workmen, and especially their leader, show that theirs is work that cannot be done by those who principally perceive it as obliging them to work in a dangerous organizational setting. It can only be done by those who feel safe and who move with confidence, who trust and rely on their workmates and foreman, who feel it a pleasure to do the work because there is something beautiful about working on a roof.

Now, if the readers wish, they may try to imagine themselves in the shoes of someone beginning this kind of work, someone who has done it for some time, or even someone with the responsibilities of the foreman. They may ask whether they have the personal capabilities required by the work, whether they feel able to do it, whether there is some aspect of it that attracts them, whether they would continue to do the work for a certain period of time. On the basis of their imaginations, they may experience (Gabriel, Fineman, and Sims 2000; Sims 1985) some of the sensations that—plausibly—are afforded by the senses of vision, hearing, smell, taste, touch, and by the aesthetic judgment: that is, sensations of aesthetic experience at the imaginative level that do not fulfill the criterion of scientific truth, in the sense that they are not due to experience actually gained by working on the roof, and that for precisely this reason can only fulfill the criterion of plausibility. A wide range of diverse initiatives in organizational settings—plans, project-teams, industrial designs, starting up, to mention a few—are experienced as plausible, or else at the level of fantasy, through the imagination, before it is known whether they can be undertaken and managed. These initiatives may be the result of rigorous rational calculation, but they can be imaginatively experienced through activation of intuition, analogical thinking, sensory capacities, and aesthetic judgment, in order to feel certain sensations beforehand.

Consequently, by activating their aesthetic faculties, the readers may use their imagination to walk across the roof, lean on the air, pay attention to noises, keep an eye on the handholds, monitor what their workmates are doing, rip away some roofing, throw it down into the yard, and hear the crash that it makes. They may assess whether they feel pleasure in doing all these things, whether they find that the work has "something beautiful about it," or whether they find it repellent, whether it gives them the shivers or a sense of vertigo. They may also see if they are able to tell—on the basis of the knowledge that they by now possesses—whether a novice is suited to the job before he/she starts it. When this experiential and knowledge-gathering process has concluded, the reader may be able to say whether they could do the work or, conversely, would find it impossible; or whether, if forced to, they could learn how to do it. In other words, they would know that they knew how to do it, or that they did not know how to do it, or that they knew that they could learn to do it. That is to say, *on the basis of their aesthetic forms of knowing, they would have focused on their tacit knowledge* and become aware that they know how to do the work, although it evades analytical, detailed, and scientifically rigorous description. Trust must be placed in tacit knowledge— awareness of being able to do something even though one is unable to explain how—and not in explicit, formal, and scientific knowledge.

Does this seldom happen in organizations? Does it only apply to manual work? Does it concern activities that require practical experience rather that formal instruction, university education, vocational training? Polanyi points out that it concerns a wide range of organizational settings and meaningful actions by those who work in them:

> The structural kinship of the arts of knowing and doing is indeed such that they are rarely exercised in isolation; we usually meet a blend of the two. Medical diagnosis combines them about equally. To percuss a lung is as much a muscular feat as a delicate discrimination of the sounds elicited. The palpation of a spleen or a kidney combines a skilful kneading of the region with a trained sense for the peculiar feeling of the organ's resistance. It is apposite therefore to include skilful feats among comprehensive entities. (1961, reprinted 1969: 126)

Medicine, in fact, provides an excellent example of an activity that requires years of book study and years of practical experience to gain mastery of abilities both tactile—percussing a lung—and auditory—recognizing the sound produced—that enable the doctor to understand the lung examined and to formulate a diagnosis. We can further develop the medical example. The training that refines the knowledge-gathering sensitivity of the doctor's perceptive and sensory faculties is meant to ensure that all doctors are of equal worth. But nobody would light-heartedly undergo a surgical operation, however routine, in the certainty that, given the training received by all surgeons, one of them is as good as any other. On the contrary, these are situations in which one tends to seek out information, details, tittle-tattle, and gossip in order to place one's confidence in the professional skills of one doctor rather than another. That is to say, the surgeon's "scalpel stroke" is not just the putting into practice of medical knowledge learned from anatomy textbooks or lectures on symptomatology at medical school; nor is it the result of mere medical empiricism.

In order to show the importance of aesthetics and its relationship with tacit knowledge as regards organizational learning, I shall briefly describe the complex features displayed (as a skilled organizational practice) by the scalpel stroke just mentioned—executed with a hand-held scalpel with a rapid and precise motion that imparts pressure and cuts in the direction intended. The action requires concentration, accuracy, dexterity, the right amount of pressure, speed, and certainly not least important, intellective control of the diagnosis. In this process—during which a situated organizational practice is implemented—the relationship between the surgeon and the scalpel, or in other words between the human being and the nonhuman item, is such that the scalpel is not considered in itself, but as an integral part of the body. This is the awareness of the nonhuman element. Polanyi calls it "subsidiary":

> The way we use a hammer or a blind man uses his stick, shows in fact that in both cases we shift outwards the points at which we make contact with the things that we observe as objects outside ourselves. While we rely on a tool or a probe, these are not handled as external objects. We may test the tool for its effectiveness or the probe for its suitability, e.g. in discovering the hidden details of a cavity, but the tool and the probe can never lie in the field of these operations; they remain necessarily on our side of it, forming part of ourselves, the operating persons. (1962: 59)

Subsidiary awareness, which here concerns my description of the skilled act of employing the scalpel, indicates that in relation to the scalpel stroke this nonhuman element is assimilated into the surgeon's existence and thus "missed"—as Latour (1992) puts it. The surgeon makes himself aware of the scalpel with which he is realizing the organizational practice in question, as if it were part of his body, and in particular of his eyes, arm, and hands. To return to Polanyi (1966; reprinted 1969: 148), "when we learn to use a language, or a probe, or a tool, and thus make ourselves aware of these things as we are of our body, we *interiorize* these things and *make ourselves dwell in them.* Such extensions of ourselves develop new faculties in us" that influence our vision of the world and have us experience life in terms of that vision.

Focal awareness, by contrast, is that awareness whereby we see the scalpel as a free-standing nonhuman object: it is newly made, it has a defect, it still has to be sterilized, it is not in its proper place. This is not the awareness of the scalpel-in-use—to employ a term from the phenomenology of science and knowledge (Husserl 1913)—during the operation, given that if the surgeon focused his attention on the scalpel itself, he would remove it from the surgical practice that he is performing: focal awareness and subsidiary awareness, in fact, are "mutually exclusive" (Polanyi 1962: 56).

With reference to my description of skilled surgical practice, the main understanding to be drawn from Polanyi's distinction between focal and subsidiary awareness is that the surgeon learns to know the scalpel by acquiring subsidiary awareness of it. By using the scalpel, he immerses himself in it and integrates it into himself as part of his corporeality. The knowledge thus acquired, therefore, is personal knowledge yielded by one's own personal faculties of sensory perception and aesthetic judgment, and, to return to Polanyi, mainly by tacit knowledge, because—contrary to logical positivism and also, less starkly, neopositivism and postpositivism—it is not possible "to establish all knowledge in terms of explicit relations between sensory data" (1966; reprinted 1969: 156). What explicit relations among sensory data can we establish with regard to the scalpel stroke? Or with regard to feeling oneself attached to the roof while stripping it? And if we are able to establish these explicit relations, will we be able to execute a scalpel stroke or strip a roof? Polanyi addresses the matter by discussing the ability to ride a bicycle:

> Again, from my interrogations of physicists, engineers and bicycle manufacturers, I have come to the conclusion that the principle by which the cyclist keeps his balance is not generally known. The rule observed by the cyclist is this. When he starts falling to the right he turns the handlebars to the right, so that the course of the bicycle is deflected along a curve towards the right. This results in a centrifugal force pushing the cyclist to the left and offsets the gravitational force dragging him down to the right. This manoeuvre presently throws the cyclist out of balance to the left, which he counteracts by turning the handlebars to the left; and so he continues to keep himself in balance by winding along a series of appropriate curvatures. (1962: 49–50)

What the cyclist actually does is this: for every angle out of equilibrium, he adjusts the curvature in inverse proportion to the square of the speed at which he is going, But, one asks, is it on the basis of this explicit knowledge that we can teach someone how to ride a bicycle? Is it really necessary to impart this knowledge to a child, an adult, or even someone getting on in years who wants to learn to ride a bicycle? The answer is "no." It is not by adjusting the curve in ratio to one's imbalance over the square of the speed that one learns this ability. There are a number of other factors involved—Polanyi warns—factors *that are not covered by the rule thus formulated.* Polanyi's conclusion is that the rules of art "can be useful, but they do not determine the practice of an art; they are maxims, which can serve as a guide to an art only if they can be integrated into the practical knowledge of the art. They cannot replace this knowledge" (1962: 50).

If we now return to knowing how to work on a roof, we can discern a number of features of the organization employing the three workmen described above. This organization:

1. relies on the putting-into-use of the workers' personal skills that enable them to "feel attached with their feet to the roof" and thus have their hands free to do the work;
2. recruits workers on the basis of its capacity to assess the abilities of a novice at the moment when he begins to learn and become socialized to organizational practices—that is, during the brief initial phase in which he tries to use his ability to work as a roof stripper;
3. does not provide training that teaches its workers how to "feel attached with their feet to the roof," to "lean on the air" between them and the roof, to recognize handholds and noises—in short, that teaches the skills required to work for the organization;
4. bases its identity in organizational practices that crucially require what Polanyi calls "personal" knowledge: that is, the workers' tacit knowledge which, as we have seen, is closely bound up with aesthetic knowledge if, as regards aesthetics in organizations, one does not consider only the faculty of aesthetic judgment but also people's perceptive and sensorial capacities.

In sum, this organization differs from other organizations by virtue of the fact that it comprises abilities specific to it that cannot be explained analytically and rationally. This raises a theoretical issue and at the same time relates to the debate between aesthetic understanding of organizational life and the search for rational explanation at any price (Strati 1998: 324).

Ron Sanchez, for instance, asserts that "the presumption that "tacit knowledge" is likely to be the only viable source of distinctive competence and competitive advantage is unwarranted" (1997: 169–170), and that "a notion of 'knowledge that is not capable of being articulated' (as distinct from the 'knowledge that is articulable only with difficulty') appears to be epistemologically problematic" (1997: 165). "Real knowledge"—to paraphrase Gherardi and Turner's *Real Men Don't Collect Soft Data* (1987)—therefore has to be "articulable" or, at least, to be "enclosable" in cognitive schemata that let it be known (Gioia and Ford 1995). Or, else, "real knowledge" has to be "includable" in the transitions between identified knowledge modes, such as the individual, collective, tacit, and explicit mode (Baumard 1996; Eng. trans. 1999: 30–31).

Sanchez's above assertion that tacit knowledge is epistemologically problematic, as well as Spender's two-by-two matrix of modes of cognizing—the result of applying the distinction between the explicit or conscious and the implicit or automatic types of knowledge "to both the individual and collective mind" (1997: 33)—illustrates the difficulty of organizational scholars in understanding and appreciating the tacitness and corporeality of personal knowledge. Donaldson (2001: 956–957) shares this difficulty and warns us that the ineffability of tacit knowledge may lead scholars to "a remagification of organizations," and that it constitutes a mystification of the organizational world—and also that this concept is overused, since if people in organizations share ideas "through talking, then those ideas are not ineffable and the knowledge is not tacit."

Aesthetic understanding of organizational life, on the contrary, emphasizes tacitness and corporeality of knowing in practice. It supports Polanyi's philosophical distinction, considering that it is not solely based on expression of knowledge in discourse—that is, on the sayable and the unsayable (Donaldson; Sanchez)—or on the automatic and the conscious (Gioia and Ford; Spender), or on magic and formal rationality (Donaldson). From an aesthetic perspective (Ramirez 2000; Strati 1999), tacit knowledge is a distinctive and specific form of knowing that by both "attempt and organization" lets organizational practices be invented, performed, learned, and taught by the participants in the social construction of organizational life.

But even if one does not share an aesthetic viewpoint, the crucial importance of tacit knowledge in situated learning in organizations as social contexts can be stressed. This is the case of Nonaka and Takeuchi's study (1995), in which they refer to tacit knowledge to depict the organizational structure that enables an organization to create knowledge efficiently and continuously. In their model, the organization does not seek to translate the tacit into the explicit. Rather, it looks for the hypertext "jumps" and "links" by which the tacit and the explicit construct organizational processes of learning and dynamics that facilitate organizational knowledge creation.

The leaps and links that connect tacit and aesthetic knowledge to explicit knowledge highlight the fact that skills practices like those discussed with regard to the roof-laying and -stripping organization may be "nontranslatable," or if preferred "nontransferrable." And their learning does not take place through the formal and institutional practices envisaged by traditional cognitive theory.

On the contrary, the process of organizational learning described by the three workmen highlighted an awareness as regards the organization in question: namely, that the knowledge required to work on a roof "is taught badly" (as the foreman said), and it is acquired through the performance of organizational practices. And the reader's imaginary participant observation may be attracted and mobilized by the uncontainability of their tacit knowledge— the impossibility of saying it—and its specifity—for it is precisely done—all at once.

This relates to the themes discussed by the theory of situated learning and of learning-in-organizing.

Conclusions: Personal Knowledge, Community of Practice, and Learning-in-Organizing

Although the roof-strippers' skills and practices constituted personal knowledge, they should be considered to be artifacts specific and peculiar to the organization for which the men worked. It was in that organizational setting, in fact, that those practices assumed the value and meaning that I have shown. In other words, it was in order to construct their organization collectively that the three workmen activated their capacities of aesthetic knowledge and put their tacit knowledge to use—besides, obviously, their explicit knowledge, although this was less essential to the purposes of the organization. Their practices should be viewed as organizational artifacts, although they were practices that were not implemented by the organization—unless we want to reify personal, tacit, and aesthetic knowledge into the social construct "organization"—but instead pertained to the persons who belonged to it.

What I observed through the window, in fact, was not an organization in action engaged with alacrity and a certain pleasure in dismantling a roof. It was instead the organizational practices of three persons, and my question about "how do you work on a roof" was prompted by seeing those bodies acting, the agility with which they moved, the nonhuman elements with which they interacted, and by my feeling intrigued and distracted by the noise that their individual and collective actions were making. Put otherwise: I did not see the social object "organization," but three persons who were "doing organization," or better, "intellectually *and aesthetically* doing" that specific organization. Consequently, there was no higher entity—the organization— on the one hand, and the three persons on the other. Nor did I observe three persons who had mixed themselves into the organization as if it were an extraneous body. I did not discover the underlying organizational structure widely envisaged by organization scholars and which Karl Weick opposes, emphasizing the metaphorical reality of organizations and arguing that people invent organization and their settings (1977). In short, what I observed were three men engaged in organizational practices on a roof. Hence, learning and organization were not distinct entities to be related to each other or somehow fitted together. Rather, *learning was constitutive of organizing, just as organizing was constitutive of learning:* otherwise what sense would the skills that I observed have had?

The organizational practices that the three workmen enacted bring out views on roofing that delineate a specific community "of practice" (Brown and Duguid 1991; Lave and Wenger 1991; Wenger 1998). Precisely because it was their skills and practices that distinguished the roof-strippers, anyone who wanted to learn how to work on a roof was obliged to engage in complex interactive processes by which he gradually became part of the community, moving from an initially peripheral position to more and more central ones. Participation in communities of this kind is essential for learning, writes Etienne Wenger (2000: 229), since it is in this way that whatever constitutes "competence" is defined in social interactions.

However, it should not be thought that this is a harmonious interactive process; on the contrary, it is negotiative and sometimes conflictual. Max Weber (1922; Eng. trans. 1978: 42) stressed that "coercion of all sorts is a very common thing in even the most intimate of such communal relationships if one party is weaker in character than the other," while Robert Bellah (1997: 388) argues that "a good community is one in which there is argument, even conflict, about the meaning of the shared values and goals, and certainly about how they will be actualized in everyday life," which in our case is that conducted by working on the roof.

For that matter, points out Alessandro Ferrara (1992: liii), in the modern and contemporary context, community has to do with pluralism, and this "inevitably means a community which contains diversity which has not been entirely amalgamated by consensus." This is even more important when one considers the contemporary globalization process and the numerous facets of everyday organizational life in which globalization interrelates with the local cultures and becomes "glocal," as Robertson puts it (1995). Virtual communities (Hine 2000; Jones 1995; Jones 1998; Mantovani 1994; Smith and Kollock 1999; Werry and Mowbray 2001) have emerged in the symbolic-material reality (Castells 1998) of the organizational life characterized by multitemporal landscape of organizational flows that develop in the permanent revolution of information and communication technology. Hence we can self-perceive "glocality" as diversity, multiplicity, and nonintegration (Beck 1997), which are all facets of the sentiment of feeling like a community.

The distinctive feature of a community of practice, besides being observable in terms of organizational practices, is what Weber (1922; Eng. trans. 1978: 40) described with regard to the community: it is a social relation that rests on the subjective *feeling* of shared belonging. A community, in other words, is not a mere instrument (Taylor 1991), and participation in it is not motivated rationally but felt subjectively. It is felt emotionally and aesthetically, and this further indicates the distance between learning-in-organizing and organizational learning understood as the mental process envisaged by traditional cognitive theory. Instead, feeling, both emotional and aesthetic, highlights the mundane and situated nature of organizational learning.

Put in these terms, organizational learning takes place in unusual ways that have been largely ignored by traditional cognitive theory. The latter, argues Fox (1997: 729–731), claims that organizational learning develops as a mental process, and that it consists mainly in acquisition through formal and institutional practices. Learning serves a higher purpose for the organization: it is intended to improve individual practices, starting with the professional practices of specialists in education—like professional educators or the theoreticians of learning—who are the first to undertake the training of people in organizations. This aim is instead opposed by aesthetic knowledge: aesthetic judgment is not end-directed; indeed, it is whatever remains free from every organizational purpose (White 1996: 206).

Moreover, the predominance of the mind and of cognition in organizational knowledge has also been contested by situated learning theory. Of the latter, Fox (1997: 731–733) emphasizes its endeavour to overcome the mind/body dichotomy that both aesthetic understanding of organizational life and Polanyi's concept of tacit knowledge challenge, and to shift learning from the individual mind to the mind/body's relationship with the social practices experienced daily by persons. Set against the individual acquisition is the process that generates knowledge situated in everyday organizational practices constituted by social commitment, intersubjective relations, discursive practices, and the materials with which people interact in order to act. Learning as practice-based theorizing, writes Gherardi (2000: 212), is not in the head and it is not a commodity. The image of learning as the accumulation of items of knowledge—or of the mind as the container for those items—fails to convey learning-in-organizing. Bourdieu, too, emphasizes the performative nature of knowledge in his book on the practical sense (1980).

The equation that relates learning to organizing highlights the former as "situated activity, mediated by conversations, in situations involving human and non-human actors" (Gherardi 1999: 114): that is, both persons and the missing masses discussed by Latour (1992) and constituted by the nonhuman elements with which people interact as they work in organizations and for them. Learning-in-organizing, precisely because it is situated, is less a way of knowing the world than, as Gherardi and Nicolini argue, a way of being in the world (2000: 332) and of putting a community on stage by performing it (2002).

To conclude, in this chapter I have illustrated by referring to an empirical study—where observations are based on studying workmen dismantle a roof—the crucial importance of aesthetic and tacit knowledge and its associated skills for a particular organization, for its success, its profits, its survival. Aesthetics, in fact, closely interweaves with the tacit knowledge of individuals, and they both signal the socially constructed personal way in which people interact to invent, negotiate, and recreate organizational life through practice, taste, and learning. Moreover, the relationship between aesthetic understanding of organizational life and tacit knowledge in relation to situated organizational learning, or learning-in-organizing, further problematizes the logical and rational knowledge of organizational life and cognitivist dominance in organizational learning studies.

Note

I would like to express my gratitude to all the colleagues who discussed the ideas illustrated in this essay at the 16th Egos Colloquium, Helsinki 2000, and at the seminars held at the University of Torino, June 2000, and Uppsala, October 2000. A previous version of this chapter was published as an article in the Italian journal *Studi Organizzativi* 2, 2000.

References

Addison, Joseph. (1712). "The Pleasures of the Imagination." *The Spectator*, June–July.

Baumard, Philippe. (1996). *Organisations déconcertées: La gestion stratégique de la connaissance*. Paris: Masson. Eng. trans.: *Tacit Knowledge in Organizations*. London: Sage, 1999.

Baumgarten, Alexander Gottlieb. (1735). *Meditationes philosophicae de nonnullis ad poema pertinentibus*. Halle in Magdeburgo: Grunert. Eng. trans.: *Reflections on Poetry*, ed. K. Aschenbrenner and W.B. Holter. Berkeley: University of California Press, 1954.

———. (1750–58). *Aesthetica I-II*. Frankfurt am Oder: Kleyb. Photostat: Olms, Hildesheim, 1986.

Beck, Ulrich. (1997). *Was ist Globalisierung? Irrtümer des Globalismus-Antworten auf Globalisierung*. Frankfurt am Main: Suhrkamp Verlag. Eng. trans.: *What Is Globalization?* Oxford: Blackwell, 1999.

Bellah, Robert N. (1997). "The Necessity of Opportunity and Community in a Good Society." *International Sociology* 12(4): 387–393.

Bourdieu, Pierre. (1980). *Le sens pratique*. Paris: Les Éditions de Minuit. Eng. trans.: *The Logic of Practice*. Cambridge: Polity Press, 1990.

Brown, John S., and Duguid, Paul. (1991). "Organizational Learning and Communities of Practice: Toward a Unified View of Working, Learning and Innovation." *Organization Science* 2(1): 40–57.

Carchia, Gianni, and D'Angelo, Paolo, eds. (1999). *Dizionario di estetica*. Roma-Bari: Laterza.

Castells, Manuel. (1998). *End of Millennium*. Malden, MA: Blackwell.

Cazeaux, Clive, ed. (2000). *The Continental Aesthetics Reader*. London: Routledge.

Coffey, Amanda; Holbrook, Beverley; and Atkinson, Paul. (1996). "Qualitative Data Analysis: Technologies and Representations." *Sociological Research Online* 1(1). Reprint 1999 in A. Bryman and R. Burgess, eds., *Qualitative Research I–IV*. London: Sage.

Cook, Scott D.N., and Yanow, Dvora. (1993). "Culture and Organizational Learning." *Journal of Management Inquiry* 2(4): 373–390.

Dean, James W., Jr.; Ottensmeyer, Edward; and Ramirez, Rafael. (1997). "An Aesthetic Perspective on Organizations." In C. Cooper and S. Jackson, eds., *Creating Tomorrow's Organizations: A Handbook for Future Research in Organizational Behavior*, 419–437. Chichester: Wiley.

Dégot, Vincent. (1987). "Portrait of the Manager as an Artist." *Dragon* 2(4): 13–50.

Donaldson, Lex. (2001). "Reflections on Knowledge and Knowledge-Intensive Firms." *Human Relations* 54(7): 955–963.

Ferrara, Alessandro. (1992). "Introduzione." In A. Ferrara, ed., *Comunitarismo e liberalismo*, ix–lvii. Roma: Editori Riuniti.

Fox, Stephen. (1997). "Situated Learning Theory Versus Traditional Cognitive Learning Theory: Why Management Education Should Not Ignore Management Learning." *Systems Practice* 10(6): 727–747.

Gabriel, Yiannis; Fineman, Stephen; and Sims, David. (2000). *Organizing and Organizations*. 2d ed. London: Sage.

Gagliardi, Pasquale. (1996). "Exploring the Aesthetic Side of Organizational Life." In S.R. Clegg, C. Hardy, and W.R. Nord, eds., *Handbook of Organization Studies*, 565–580. London: Sage.

Gherardi, Silvia. (1999). "Learning as Problem-driven or Learning in the Face of Mystery?" *Organization Studies* 20(1): 101–123.

———. (2000). "Practice-based Theorizing on Learning and Knowing in Organizations." Introduction to the Special Issue on Knowing in Practice. *Organization* 7(2): 211–223.

Gherardi, Silvia, and Nicolini, Davide. (2000). "Learning in a Constellation of Interconnected Practices: Canon or Dissonance?" *Journal of Management Studies* 39(4): 419–436.

———. (2002) "To Transfer Is to Transform: The Circulation of Safety Knowledge." *Organization* 7(2): 329–348.

Gherardi, Silvia, and Turner, Barry A. (1987). *Real Men Don't Collect Soft Data*. Trento: Dipartimento di Politica Sociale, Quaderno 13. Partial reprint 1999 in A. Bryman and R. Burgess, eds. *Qualitative Research*, vol. I, 103–118. London: Sage.

Gioia, Dennis, and Ford, Cameron. (1995). "Tacit Knowledge, Self-Communication, and Sensemaking in Organizations." In L. Thayer, ed., *Organization-Communication* 3, 77–96. Norwood, NJ: Ablex.

Hatch, Mary Jo. (1997). *Organization Theory. Modern, Symbolic, and Postmodern Perspectives*. Oxford: Oxford University Press.

Henley, Paul. (1998). "Film-making and Ethnographic Research." In J. Prosser, ed., *Image-based Research*. London: Falmer Press. Reprint 1999 in A. Bryman and R. Burgess, eds., *Qualitative Research*, vol. II, 302–322. London: Sage.

Hine, Christine. (2000). *Virtual Ethnography*. London: Sage.

Husserl, Edmund. [1913] (1950). *Ideen zu einer reinen Phänomenologie und phänomenologischen Philosophie*, ed. M. Biemel. *Husserliana III*. Den Haag: Nijhof.

John, Eileen. (2001). "Art and Knowledge." In B. Gaut and Lopes D. McIver Lopes, eds., *The Routledge Companion to Aesthetics*, 329–340. London: Routledge.

Jones, Michael O.; Moore, Michael D.; and Snyder, Richard C., eds. (1988). *Inside Organizations. Understanding the Human Dimension*. Newbury Park: Sage.

Jones, Quentin. (1998). "Virtual-Communities, Virtual Settlements and Cyber-Archaelogy: A Theoretical Outline." www.ascusc.org/jcmc/vol3/issue3/jones.html.

Jones, Steven G., ed. (1995). *Cybersociety. Computer-mediated Communication and Community*. Thousand Oaks, CA: Sage.

Kant, Immanuel. (1790). *Kritik der Urteilskraft*. In I. Kant, *Werke in zwölf Bänden*, Vol. X. Frankfurt am Main: Suhrkamp, 1968. Eng. trans.: *The Critique of Judgment*. Oxford: Oxford University Press, 1952.

Latour, Bruno. (1992). "Where Are the Missing Masses? Sociology of a Few Mundane Artefacts." In W.E. Bijker, J. Law, eds., *Shaping Technology-Building Society: Studies in Sociotechnical Change*, 225–258. Cambridge, MA: MIT Press.

Lave, Jean, and Wenger, Etienne. (1991). *Situated Learning. Legitimate Peripheral Participation*. Cambridge: Cambridge University Press.

Linstead, Stephen, and Höpfl, Heather, eds. (2000). *The Aesthetics of Organization*. London: Sage.

Mantovani, Giuseppe. (1994). "Is Computer-Mediated Communication Intrinsically Apt to Enhance Democracy in Organizations?" *Human Relations* 47(1): 45–62.

Martin, Patricia Y. (2001). "'Mobilizing Masculinities': Women's Experiences of Men at Work." *Organization* 8(4): 587–618.

Nonaka, Ikujiro, and Takeuchi, Hirotaka. (1995). *The Knowledge-Creating Company. How Japanese Companies Create the Dynamics of Innovation*. Oxford: Oxford University Press.

Pareyson, Luigi. (1954). *Estetica. Teoria della formatività*. Torino: Giappichelli.

Polanyi, Michael. (1961). "Knowing and Being." *Mind* 70(280): 458–470. Reprinted 1969 in M. Polanyi, *Knowing and Being, Essays by Michael Polanyi*, ed. M. Grene, 123–137. Chicago: University of Chicago Press.

———. (1962). *Personal Knowledge. Towards a Post-Critical Philosophy*. 2d ed. London: Routledge and Kegan Paul.

———. (1966). "The Logic of Tacit Inference." *Philosophy* 41: 1–18. Reprinted 1969 in M. Polanyi, *Knowing and Being, Essays by Michael Polanyi*, ed. M. Grene, 138–158. Chicago: University of Chicago Press.

Ramirez, Rafael. (2000). "Why Is Tacit Knowledge Tacit? An Aesthetic Exploration." Paper presented at the Eiasm Workshop on Organising Aesthetics, Certosa di Pontignano, Siena, Italy, May.

Robertson, Roland. (1995). "Glocalization: Time-Space and Homogeneity-Heterogeneity." In M. Featherstone, S. Lash, and R. Robertson, eds., *Global Modernities*, 25–44. London: Sage.

Sanchez, Ron. (1997). "Managing Articulated Knowledge in Competence-based Competition." In R. Sanchez, A. Heene, eds., *Strategic Learning and Knowledge Management*, 163–187. Chichester: Wiley.

Sims, David. (1985). "Fantasies and the Location of Skill." In A. Strati, ed., *The Symbolics of Skill*, 12–27. Trento: Dipartimento di Politica Sociale, Quaderno 5/6.

Smith, Mark A., and Kollock, Peter, eds. (1999). *Communities in Cyberspace*. London: Routledge.

Spender, J.-C. (1998). "The Dynamics of Individual and Organizational Knowledge." In C. Eden, J.-C. Spender, eds., *Managerial and Organizational Cognition: Theory, Methods and Research*, 13–39. London: Sage.

Strati, Antonio. (1992). "Aesthetic Understanding of Organizational Life." *Academy of Management Review* 17(3): 568–581.

———. (1998) "(Mis)understanding Cognition in Organization Studies." *Scandinavian Journal of Management* 14(4): 309–329.

———. (1999). *Organization and Aesthetics*. London: Sage.

———. (2000). *Theory and Method in Organization Studies: Paradigms and Choices*. London: Sage.

Strati, Antonio, and Guillet de Montoux, Pierre, eds. (2002). *Human Relations* 55(7). Special Issue on Organizing Aesthetics.

Taylor, Charles. (1991). *The Malaise of Modernity*. Montreal: McGill-Queen's University Press.

Van Maanen, John. (1995). "Style as Theory." *Organization Science* 6(1): 133–143.

Vico, Giambattista. (1725). *Principi di una scienza nuova*. Naples: Mosca. Eng. trans.: *The New Science of Giambattista Vico*, ed. T.G. Bergin and M.H. Fisch. Ithaca, NY: Cornell University Press, 1968.

Walker, Rob. (1993). "Finding a Silent Voice for the Researcher: Using Photographs in Evaluation and Research." In M. Schratz, ed., *Qualitative Voices*. London: Falmer Press. Reprint 1999 in A. Bryman and R. Burgess, eds., *Qualitative Research*, vol. II, 279–301. London: Sage.

Weber, Max. (1922). *Wirtschaft und Gesellschaft. Grundriss der verstehenden Soziologie*. Tübingen: Mohr. Eng. trans.: *Economy and Society: An Outline of Interpretive Sociology* I–II. Berkeley: University of California Press, 1978.

Weick, Karl. (1977). "Enactment Processes in Organizations." In B.W. Staw, G.R. Salancik, eds., *New Directions in Organizational Behavior*, 267–300. Chicago: St. Clair Press.

Wenger, Etienne. (1998). *Communities of Practice. Learning, Meaning, and Identity*. Cambridge: Cambridge University Press.

———. (2000). "Communities of Practice and Social Learning Systems." *Organization* 7(2): 225–246.

Werry, Chris, and Mowbray, Miranda, eds. (2001). *Online Communities: Commerce, Community Action, and the Virtual University*. Englewood Cliffs, NJ: Prentice-Hall.

White, David A. (1996). "'It's Working Beautifully!' Philosophical Reflections on Aesthetics and Organization Theory." *Organization* 3(2): 195–208.

Young, James O. (2001). *Art and Knowledge*. London: Routledge.

4

Communities of Practice and Social Learning Systems

Etienne Wenger

You probably know that the earth is round and that it is in orbit around the sun. But how do you know this? What does it take? Obviously, it takes a brain in a living body, but it also takes a very complex social, cultural, and historical system, which has accumulated learning over time. People have been studying the skies for centuries to understand our place in the universe. More recently, scientific communities have developed a whole vocabulary, observation methods, concepts, and models, which have been adopted by other communities and have become part of popular thinking in various ways. You have your own relationships to all these communities, and these relationships are what enables you to "know" about the earth's position in the universe. In this sense, knowing is an act of participation in complex "social learning systems."

This essay assumes this view of knowing to consider how organizations depend on social learning systems. First, I outline two aspects of a conceptual framework for understanding social learning systems: a social definition of learning in terms of social *competence* and personal *experience,* and three distinct *modes of belonging* through which we participate in social learning systems: *engagement, imagination*, and *alignment.* Then I look at three structuring elements of social learning systems: *communities of practice, boundary* processes among these communities, and *identities* as shaped by our participation in these systems. About each of these elements I use my conceptual framework to ask three questions: Why focus on it? Which way is up, that is, how to construe progress in this area? And, what is doable, that is, what are elements of design that one can hope to influence? Finally, I argue that organizations are both constituted by and participate in such social learning systems. Their success depends on their ability to design themselves as social learning systems and also to participate in broader learning systems such as an industry, a region, or a consortium.

The conceptual framework I introduce here is intended for organizational design as well as analysis. The questions I ask are meant to guide the inquiry of the researcher as well the actions of the practitioner: what to pay attention to, how to give direction to our initiatives, and where to focus our efforts. As Kurt Lewin used to say, there is nothing as practical as a good theory.

Aspects of a Conceptual Framework

A framework for understanding social learning systems must make it possible to understand learning as a social process. What is learning from a social perspective? And what are the processes by which our learning constitutes social systems and social identities?

A Social Definition of Learning

In a social learning system, competence is historically and socially defined. How to be a physicist or how to understand the position of the earth in the universe is something that scientific communities have established over time. Knowing, therefore, is a matter of displaying competencies defined in social communities. The picture is more complex and dynamic than that, however. Our experience of life and the social standards of competence of our communities are not necessarily, or even usually, congruent. We each experience knowing in our own way. Socially defined competence is always in interplay with our experience. It is in this interplay that learning takes place.

Consider two extreme cases. Sometimes, we are a newcomer. We join a new community. We are a child who cannot speak yet. Or we are new employee. We feel like a bumbling idiot among the sages. We want to learn. We want to apprentice ourselves. We want to become one of them. We feel an urgent need to align our experience with the competence "they" define. Their competence pulls our experience.

Sometimes, it is the other way round. We have been with a community for a long time. We know the ropes. We are thoroughly competent, in our own eyes and in the eyes of our peers. But something happens. We are sent overseas. We go to a conference. We visit another department. We meet a "stranger" with a completely different perspective. Or we just take a long walk or engage in a deep conversation with a friend. Whatever the case may be, we have an experience that opens our eyes to a new way of looking at the world. This experience does not fully fit in the current practice of our home communities. We now see limitations we were not aware of before. We come back to our peers, try to communicate our experience, attempt to explain what we have discovered, so they too can expand their horizon. In the process, we are trying to change how our community defines competence (and we are actually deepening our own experience). We are using our experience to pull our community's competence along.

Whether we are apprentices or pioneers, newcomers or oldtimers, knowing always involves these two components: the *competence* that our communities have established over time (i.e., what it takes to act and be recognized as a competent member), and our ongoing *experience* of the world as a member (in the context of a given community and beyond). Competence and experience can be in various relations to each other—from very congruent to very divergent. As my two examples show, either can shape the other, although usually the process is not completely one-way. But whenever the two are in close tension and either starts pulling the other, learning takes place. Learning so defined is an interplay between social competence and personal experience. It is a dynamic, two-way relationship between people and the social learning systems in which they participate. It combines personal transformation with the evolution of social structures.

Modes of Belonging

Our belonging to social learning systems can take various forms at various levels between local interactions and global participation. To capture these different forms of participation, I will distinguish between three modes of belonging:

• *Engagement:* doing things together, talking, producing artifacts (e.g., helping a colleague with a problem or participating in a meeting). The ways in which we engage with each other and with the world profoundly shape our experience of who we are. We learn what we can do and how the world responds to our actions.

• *Imagination:* constructing an image of ourselves, of our communities, and of the world, in order to orient ourselves, to reflect on our situation, and to explore possibilities (e.g., drawing maps, telling a story, or building a set of possible scenarios to understand one's options). I use imagination here in the sense proposed by Benedict Anderson (1983) to describe nations as communities: it does not connote fantasy as opposed to factuality. Knowing that the earth is round and in orbit around the sun, for instance, is not a fantasy. Yet it does require a serious act of imagination. It requires constructing an image of the universe in which it makes sense to think of ourselves as little stick figures standing on a ball flying through space. Similarly, thinking of ourselves as member of a community such as a nation requires an act of imagination because we cannot engage with all our fellow citizens. These images of the world are essential to our sense of self and to our interpretation of our participation in the social world.

• *Alignment:* making sure that our local activities are sufficiently aligned with other processes that they can be effective beyond our own engagement (e.g., doing a scientific experiment by the book, convincing a colleague to join a cause, or negotiating a division of labor and a work plan for a project). The concept of alignment as used here does not connote a one-way process of submitting to external authority, but a mutual process of coordinating perspectives, interpretations, and actions so that they realize higher goals. Following the scientific method, abiding by a moral code, or discussing important decisions with our spouse can all become very deep aspects of our identities.

Distinguishing between these modes of belonging is useful for two reasons. First, analytically, each mode contributes a different aspect to the formation of social learning systems and personal identities. Engagement, imagination, and alignment usually coexist, and every social learning system involves each to some degree and in some combination. Still, one can dominate and thus give a different quality to a social structure. For instance, a community mostly based on imagination, such as a nation, has a very different quality than a community of practice at work, which is primarily based on engagement. I would in fact argue that these modes of belonging provide a foundation for a typology of communities.

Second, practically, each mode requires a different kind of work. The work of engagement, which requires opportunities for joint activities, is different from the work of imagination, which often requires opportunities for taking some distance from our situation. The demands and effects of these three modes of belonging can be conflicting. Spending time reflecting can detract from engagement, for example. The modes can also be complementary, however. For instance, using imagination to gain a good picture of the context of one's actions can help in fine-tuning alignment because one understands the reasons behind a procedure or an agreement. It is therefore useful to strive to develop these modes of belonging in combination, balancing the limitations of one with the work of another. For instance, reflective periods that activate imagination or boundary interactions that require alignment with other practices around a shared goal could be used to counteract the possible narrowness of engagement (Wenger 1998).

Communities of Practice

Since the beginning of history, human beings have formed communities that share cultural practices reflecting their collective learning: from a tribe around a cave fire, to a medieval guild, to a group of nurses in a ward, to a street gang, to a community of engineers interested in brake design. Participating in these "communities of practice" is essential to our learning. It is at the very core of what makes us human beings capable of meaningful knowing.

Why Focus on Communities?

Communities of practice are the basic building blocks of a social learning system because they are the social "containers" of the competences that make up such a system. By participating in these communities, we define with each other what constitutes competence in a given context: being a reliable doctor, a gifted photographer, a popular student, or an astute poker player. Your company may define your job as processing thirty-three medical claims a day according to certain standards, but the competence required to do this in practice is something you determine with your colleagues as you interact day after day.

Communities of practice define competence by combining three elements (Wenger 1998). First, members are bound together by their collectively developed understanding of what their community is about and they hold each other accountable to this sense of *joint enterprise*. To be competent is to understand the enterprise well enough to be able to contribute to it. Second, members build their community through mutual engagement. They interact with one another, establishing norms and relationships of *mutuality* that reflect these interactions. To be competent is to be able to engage with the community and be trusted as a partner in these interactions. Third, communities of practice have produced a *shared repertoire* of communal resources—language, routines, sensibilities, artifacts, tools, stories, styles, and so forth. To be competent is to have access to this repertoire and to be able to use it appropriately.

Communities of practice grow out of a convergent interplay of competence and experience that involves mutual engagement. They offer an opportunity to negotiate competence through an experience of direct participation. As a consequence, they remain important social units of learning even in the context of much larger systems. These larger systems are constellations of interrelated communities of practice.

Which Way Is Up?

Communities of practice cannot be romanticized. They are born of learning, but they can also learn not to learn. They are the cradles of the human spirit, but they can also be its cages. After all, witch hunts were also community practices. It is useful, therefore, to articulate some dimensions of progress:

• *Enterprise: the level of learning energy.* How much initiative does the community take in keeping learning at the center of its enterprise? A community must show leadership in pushing its development along and maintaining a spirit of inquiry. It must recognize and address gaps in its knowledge as well as remain open to emergent directions and opportunities.

• *Mutuality: the depth of social capital.* How deep is the sense of community generated by mutual engagement over time? People must know each other well enough to know how to interact productively and whom to call for help or advice. They must trust each other, not just personally, but also in their ability to contribute to the enterprise of the community, so that they feel comfortable addressing real problems together and speaking truthfully. Through receiving and giving help, they must gain enough awareness of the richness of the community to expect that their contribution will be reciprocated in some way.

• *Repertoire: the degree of self-awareness.* How self-conscious is the community about the repertoire that it is developing and its effects on its practice? The concepts, language, and tools of a community of practice embody its history and its perspective on the world. Being reflective on its repertoire enables a community to understand on its own state of development from multiple perspectives, reconsider assumptions, patterns and uncover hidden possibilities, and use this self-awareness to move forward.

The three dimensions work together. Without the learning energy of those who take initiative, the community becomes stagnant. Without strong relationships of belonging, it is torn apart. And without the ability to reflect, it becomes hostage to its own history. The work associated with each mode of belonging can contribute to these criteria. Table 4.1 illustrates how the modes of belonging interact with community elements.

What Is Doable?

When designing itself, a community should look at the following elements: events, leadership, connectivity, membership, projects, and artifacts.

Events

You can organize public events that bring the community together. Obviously, these may or may not be attended, but if they are well tuned to the community's sense of its purpose, they will help it develop an identity. A community will have to decide what *type* of activities it needs: formal or informal meetings, problem-solving sessions, or guest speakers. It will also have to consider the *rhythm* of these events given other responsibilities members have: too often

Table 4.1

Community Dimensions

	Enterprise: Learning energy	Mutuality: Social capital	Repertoire: Self-awareness
Engagement	What are the opportunities to negotiate a joint inquiry and address important questions? Do members identify gaps in their knowledge and work together to address them?	What events and interactions weave the community and develop trust? Does this result in an abililty to raise troubling issues during discussions?	To what extent have shared experience, language, artifacts, histories, and methods accumulated over time, and with what potential for further interactions and new meanings?
Imagination	What visions of the potential of the community are guiding the thought of leaders, inspiring participation, and defining a learning agenda? And what picture of the world serves as a context for such visions?	What do people know about each other and about the meanings that participation in the community takes in their lives more broadly?	Are there self-representations that would allow the community to see itself in new ways? Is there a language to talk about the community in a reflective mode?
Alignment	Have members articulated a shared purpose? How widely do they subscribe to it? How accountable do they feel to it? And how distributed is leadership?	What definitions of roles, norms, codes of behavior, shared principles, and negotiated commitments and expectations hold the community together?	What traditions, methods, standards, routines, and frameworks define the practice? Who upholds them? To what extent are they codified? How are they transmitted to new generations?

and people just stop coming, too rare and the community does not gain momentum. This rhythm may also have to change over time or go through cycles.

Leadership

Communities of practice depend on internal leadership, and enabling the leaders to play their role is a way to help the community develop. The role of the "community coordinator" who takes care of the day-to-day work is crucial, but a community needs multiple forms of leadership: thought leaders, networkers, people who document the practice, pioneers, and so forth. These forms of leadership may be concentrated on one or two members or widely distributed, and this will change over time.

Connectivity

Building a community is not just a matter of organizing community events but also of enabling a rich fabric of connectivity among people. This could involve brokering relationships between people who need to talk or between people who need help and people who can offer help. It is also important to make it possible for people to communicate and interact in multiple media.

Membership

A community's membership must have critical mass so that there is interest, but it should not become so wide that the focus of the community is diffuse and participation does not grab people's identities. Including those who are missing can be very helpful in consolidating the legitimacy of the community to itself and in the wider organization. Conversely, realizing that the membership is overextended allows the community to split up into subgroups. Finally, devising processes by which newcomers can become full members helps ensure access for newcomers without diluting the community's focus.

Learning Projects

Communities of practice deepen their mutual commitment when they take responsibility for a learning agenda, which pushes their practice further. Activities toward this goal include exploring the knowledge domain, finding gaps in the community practice, and defining projects to close these gaps. Such learning projects could involve, for instance, assessing some tools, building a generic design, doing a literature search, creating a connection with a university doing research in the area, or simply interviewing some experts to create a beginner's guide.

Artifacts

All communities of practice produce their own set of artifacts: documents, tools, stories, symbols, websites, and the like. A community has to consider what artifacts it needs and who has the energy to produce and maintain them so they will remain useful as the community evolves.

Boundaries

The term *boundary* often has negative connotations because it conveys limitation and lack of access. But the very notion of a community of practice implies the existence of boundary. Unlike the boundaries of organizational units, which are usually well defined because affiliation is officially sanctioned, the boundaries of communities of practice are usually rather fluid. They arise from different enterprises, different ways of engaging with one another, different histories, repertoires, ways of communicating, and capabilities. That these boundaries are often unspoken does not make them less significant. Sit for lunch by a group of high-energy particle physicists and you know about boundary, not because they intend to exclude you, but because you cannot figure out what they are talking about. Shared practice by its very nature creates boundaries.

Yet if you are like me, you will actually enjoy this experience of boundary. There is something disquieting, humbling at times, yet exciting and attractive about such close encounters with the unknown, with the mystery of "otherness": a chance to explore the edge of your competence, learn something entirely new, revisit your little truths, and perhaps expand your horizon.

Why Focus on Boundaries?

Boundaries are important to learning systems for two reasons. They connect communities and they offer learning opportunities in their own right. These learning opportunities are of a different kind than the ones offered by communities. Inside a community, learning takes place because competence and experience need to converge for a community to exist. At the boundaries, competence and experience tend to diverge: a boundary interaction is usually an experience of being exposed to a foreign competence. Such reconfigurations of the relation between competence and experience are an important aspect of learning. If competence and experience are too close, if they always match, not much learning is likely to take place. There are no challenges; the community is losing its dynamism and the practice is in danger of becoming stale. Conversely, if experience and competence are too disconnected, if the distance is too great, not much learning is likely to take place either. Sitting by that group of high-energy particle physicists, you might not learn much because the distance between your own experience and the competence you are confronting is just too great. Mostly what you are learning is that you do not belong.

Learning at boundaries is likely to be maximized for individuals and for communities when experience and competence are in close tension. Achieving a generative tension between them requires:

- something to interact about, some intersection of interest, some activity;
- open engagement with real differences as well as common ground;
- commitment to suspend judgment in order to see the competence of a community on its own terms;
- ways to translate between repertoires so that experience and competence actually interact.

Boundaries are sources of new opportunities as well as potential difficulties. In a learning system, communities and boundaries can be learning assets (and liabilities) in complementary ways.

- *Communities* of practice can steward a critical competence, but they can also become hostage to their history, insular, defensive, closed in, and oriented to their own focus.
- *Boundaries* can create divisions, a source of separation, fragmentation, disconnection, and misunderstanding. Yet they can also be areas of unusual learning, places where perspectives meet and new possibilities arise. Radically new insights often arise at the boundaries between communities. Think of a specialization like psychoneuroimmunology: its very name reflects its birth at the intersection of multiple practices.

In social learning systems, the value of communities and their boundaries are complementary. Deep expertise depends on a convergence between experience and competence, but innovative learning requires their divergence. In either case, you need strong competences to anchor the process. But these competences also need to interact. The learning and innovation potential of a social learning system lies in its configuration of strong core practices and active boundary processes.

Which Way Is Up?

Not all boundary processes create bridges that actually connect practices in deep ways. The actual boundary effects of these processes can be assessed along the following dimensions:

- *Coordination.* Can boundary processes and objects be interpreted in different practices in a way that enables coordinated action? For instance, an elegant design might delight designers but say little to those concerned with manufacturability. Across boundaries, effective actions and use of objects require new levels of coordination. They must accommodate the practices involved without burdening others with the details of one practice and must provide enough standardization that people know how to deal with them locally.

• *Transparency.* Do boundary processes give access to the meanings they have in various practices? Coordination does not imply that boundary processes provide an understanding of the practices involved. For instance, forms like U.S. tax returns enable coordination across boundaries (you know how to fill them out by following instructions line by line), but often afford no windows into the logic they are meant to enforce (following instructions often tells you little about why these calculations are "fair").

• *Negotiability.* Do boundary processes provide a one-way or a two-way connection? For instance, a business process reengineering plan may be very detailed about implementation (coordination) and explicit about its intentions (transparency), but reflect or allow little negotiation between the perspectives involved. Boundary processes can merely reflect relations of power among practices, in which case they are likely to reinforce the boundary rather than bridge it. They will bridge practices to the extent that they make room for multiple voices.

Table 4.2 explores how the three modes of belonging affect these qualities of boundary processes.

What Is Doable?

Boundary processes are crucial to the coherent functioning of social learning systems. A number of elements can be intentionally promoted in an effort to weave these systems more tightly together. Here, I will talk about three types of bridges across boundaries: *people* who act as "brokers" between communities, *artifacts* (things, tools, terms, representations, etc.) that serve as what Star and Griesemer (1989) call "boundary objects," and a variety of forms of *interactions* among people from different communities of practice.

Brokering

Some people act as brokers between communities. They can introduce elements of one practice into another. Although we all do some brokering, my experience is that certain individuals seem to thrive on being brokers: they love to create connections and engage in "import–export," and so would rather stay at the boundaries of many practices than move to the core of any one practice. Brokering can take various forms, including:

Table 4.2

Boundary Dimensions

	Coordination	Transparency	Negotiability
Engagement	What opportunities exist for joint activities, problem solving, and discussions to both surface and resolve differences through action?	Do people provide explanations, coaching, and demonstrations in the context of joint activities to open windows onto each others' practices?	Are joint activities structured in such a way that multiple perspectives can meet and that participants can come to appreciate each other's competences?
Imagination	Do people have enough understanding of their respective perspectives to present issues effectively and anticipate misunderstandings?	What stories, documents, and models are available to build a picture of another practice? What experience will allow people to walk in the other's shoes? Do they listen deeply enough?	Can both sides see themselves as members of an overarching community in which they have common interests and needs?
Alignment	Are instructions, goals, and methods interpretable into action across boundaries?	Are intentions, commitments, norms, and traditions made clear enough to reveal common ground and differences in perspectives and expectations?	Who has a say in negotiating contracts and devising compromises?

- *boundary spanners:* taking care of one specific boundary over time;
- *roamers:* going from place to place, creating connections, and moving knowledge;
- *outposts:* bringing back news from the forefront and exploring new territories;
- *pairs:* often brokering is done through a personal relationship between two people from different communities, and it is really the relationship that acts as a brokering device.

Brokering knowledge is delicate. It requires enough legitimacy to be listened to and enough distance to bring something really new. Because brokers often do not fully belong anywhere and may not contribute directly to any specific outcome, the value they bring can easily be overlooked. Uprootedness, homelessness, marginalization, and organizational invisibility are all occupational hazards of brokering. Developing the boundary infrastructure of a social learning system means paying attention to people who act as brokers. Are they falling through the cracks? Is the value they bring understood? Is there even a language to talk about it? Are there people who are potential brokers but who for some reason do not provide cross-boundary connections?

Boundary Objects

Some objects find their value, not just as artifacts of one practice, but mostly to the extent that they support connections between different practices. Such boundary objects can take multiple forms:

- *Artifacts.* These are tools, documents, or models. For instance, medical records and architectural blueprints play a crucial role in connecting multiple practices (doctors/nurses/insurers, architects/contractors/city planners).
- *Discourses.* A critical boundary object is the existence of a common language that allows people to communicate and negotiate meanings across boundaries. This was an important thrust behind the quality movement, and is typified by the six sigma discourse at Motorola.
- *Processes.* Shared processes, including explicit routines and procedures, allow people to coordinate their actions across boundaries. Business processes, for instance, are not just fixed prescriptive definitions. At their best, they act as boundary objects that allow multiple practices to coordinate their contributions.

Boundary objects do not necessarily bridge across boundaries because they may be misinterpreted or interpreted blindly. Rethinking artifacts and designs in terms of their function as boundary objects often illuminates how they contribute to or hinder the functioning of learning systems. An organizational structure, for instance, is often considered as an overarching umbrella that incorporates multiple parts by specifying their relationships. But in fact, it is more usefully designed as a boundary object intended to enable multiple practices to negotiate their relationships and connect their perspectives.

Boundary Interactions

• *Boundary encounters.* These encounters—visits, discussions, sabbaticals— provide direct exposure to a practice. They can take different forms for different purposes. When one person visits, as in a sabbatical, it is easier to get fully immersed in the practice, but more difficult to bring the implications home because the very immersion into a "foreign" practice tends to isolate you from your peers. GM, for instance, has had difficulty learning from people sent on sabbatical at its more experimental units such as NUMMI and Saturn because their transformed perspectives could not find a place back home. When a delegation of two or more people visits, as in a benchmarking expedition, they might not get as fully immersed, but they can negotiate among themselves the meaning of the boundary interaction for their own practice, and therefore find it easier to bring their learning back home.

• *Boundary practices.* In some cases, a boundary requires so much sustained work that it becomes the topic of a practice of its own. At Xerox, as in many companies, some people are charged with the task of maintaining connections between the R&D lab and the rest of the corporation. They are developing a practice of crossing these boundaries effectively. Of course, the risk of these boundary practices is that they create their own boundaries, which can prevent them from functioning as brokers. It is necessary, therefore, to keep asking how the elements of the boundary practice—its enterprise, its relationships, its repertoire—contribute to creating a bridge and how the community deals with its own boundaries. And sometimes, a new practice in its own right does develop at these boundaries, which is worth paying attention to in its own terms.

• *Peripheries.* Communities often have to take steps to manage their boundaries to serve people who need some service, are curious, or intend to become members. Many communities have found it useful to create some facilities by which outsiders can connect with their practice in peripheral ways. Examples of such facilities include lists of "frequently asked questions," visitor's rooms on websites, open houses, and fairs. Some communities have even established "help desks" to provide access to their expertise in a more efficient way. The idea behind many of these facilities is to provide for some boundary activities without overwhelming the community itself with the task of accommodating outsiders' demands. For newcomers, some communities organize introductory events, mentoring relationships, or even formal apprenticeship systems.

Cross-Disciplinary Projects

In most organizations, members of communities of practice contribute their competence by participating in cross-functional projects and teams that combine the knowledge of multiple practices to get something done. Simultaneous participation in communities of practice and project teams creates learning loops that combine application with capability development. In these double-knit organizations, as Richard McDermott (1999) calls them, the learning and innovation that is inherent in projects is synthesized and disseminated through the home communities of practice of team members. The new knowledge can then be applied and expanded in new projects, and the cycle goes on.

Such a perspective brings up a different way of thinking about these projects. From the standpoint of the task to be accomplished, these projects are cross-disciplinary because they require the contribution of multiple disciplines. But from the perspective of the development of practices, they are boundary projects. Indeed, participating in these kinds of projects exposes practitioners to others in the context of specific tasks that go beyond the purview of any practice. People confront problems that are outside the realm of their competence but that force them to negotiate their own competence with the competences of others. Such projects provide a great way to sustain a creative tension between experience and competence when our participation in a project leverages and nourishes our participation in a community of practice.

Identities

As I said, you probably know that the earth is round and in orbit around the sun. Of course, it is not the flat plate it appears to be at first glance. You actually want to make sure you know this. It is part of your identity as the kind of well-educated adult you probably are if you are reading this article. You may even know that the orbit is not an exact circle, but a slight ellipse. Chances are, however, you do not know the exact distance between the earth and the sun or the precise difference between the apogee and the perigee. This kind of ignorance, your identity can accept without existential angst because your relationship to the communities where such knowledge matters is very peripheral at best.

I am not trying to make you feel self-conscious about your knowledge of astrophysics. There will be no test at the end of this article. (Did I hear a sigh of relief? No, no, you are perfectly OK just knowing the earth is round, and many of our fellow human beings have lived very good lives not even knowing that.) My point is that if knowing is an act of belonging, then our identities are a key structuring element of how we know.

Why Focus on Identity?

Knowing, learning, and sharing knowledge are not abstract things we do for their own sake. They are part of belonging (Eckert 1989). When I was working with claims processors in an insurance company, I noticed that their knowing was interwoven in profound ways with their identities as participants in their community of practice. Their job did not have a high status in the company (nor in their own eyes, for that matter), so they were careful not to be interested in it more than was absolutely necessary. What they knew about their job, what they tried to understand and what they accepted not understanding about the forms they had to fill out, what they shared with each other, all of that was not merely a matter of necessity to get the job done, but it was also a matter of identity. Knowing too much or failing to share a crucial piece of knowledge would be a betrayal of their sense of self and of their community (Wenger 1998).

In the landscape of communities and boundaries in which we live, we identify with some communities strongly and not at all with others. We define who we are by what is familiar and what is foreign, by what we need to know and what we can safely ignore. You are a cello player, but not the conductor who signals your entry, nor the dancer who dances the ballet you are playing, nor the lawyer whom you saw this afternoon about your uncle's estate. We define ourselves by what we are not as well as by what we are, by the communities we do not belong to as well as by the ones we do. These relationships change. We move from community to community. In doing so, we carry a bit of each as we go around. Our identities are not something we can turn on and off. You do not cease to be a parent because you go to work. You do not cease to be a nurse because you step out of the hospital. Multimembership is an inherent aspect of our identities.

Identity is crucial to social learning systems for three reasons. First, our identities combine competence and experience into a way of knowing. They are the key to deciding what matters and what does not, with whom we identify and whom we trust, and with whom we must share what we understand. Second, our ability to deal with boundaries productively depends on our ability to engage and suspend our identities. Learning from our interactions with other practices is not just an intellectual matter of translation. It is also a matter of opening up our identities to other ways of being in the world. Third, our identities are the living vessels in which communities and boundaries become realized as an experience of the world. Whenever we belong to multiple communities, we experience the boundary in a personal way. In the process, we create bridges across communities because in developing our own identities, we deal with these boundaries in ourselves.

Which Way Is Up?

Our identities are not necessarily strong or healthy. Sometimes they are even self-defeating. In fact, a whole self-help industry has flourished by offering advice for building healthy identities (Giddens 1991). Navigating the social landscape defined by communities and their boundaries requires a strong identity. Progress can be described in terms of a few crucial qualities that must coexist to constitute a healthy social identity:

- *Connectedness.* Where are enduring social relationships through which an identity gains social depth? An identity is not an abstract idea or a label, such as a title, an ethnic category, or a personality trait. It is a lived experience of belonging (or not belonging). A strong identity involves deep connections with others through shared histories and experiences, reciprocity, affection, and mutual commitments.
- *Expansiveness.* What are the breadth and scope of an identity? A healthy identity will not be exclusively locally defined. It will involve multimembership and cross multiple boundaries. It will seek a wide range of experiences and be open to new possibilities. It will identify with broad communities that lie beyond direct participation.
- *Effectiveness.* Does an identity enable action and participation? Identity is a vehicle for participating in the social world, but it can also lead to nonparticipation. A healthy identity is socially empowering rather than marginalizing.

There are potential tensions and conflicts between these qualities. How "big" can your identity be and still be engaged as well effective (not merely an abstract kind of identification)? Can you really think globally and act locally, feel like a citizen of the earth without losing your ability to connect with specific communities? Can you live on the internet and still have a good marriage? In other words, it is the combination of these qualities that matters. Table 4.3 explores how each mode of belonging contributes to these three qualities.

Table 4.3

Identity Dimensions

	Connectedness	Expansiveness	Effectiveness
Engagement	Is there a community to engage with? How far back do you go? What kinds of interactions do you have? What do you do together? Do you trust and are you trusted?	Is there enough variety of contexts and identity-forming experiences, such as logging onto the internet and chatting with strangers, going on a blind date, or visiting a foreign country?	Do you have opportunities to develop socially recognized competences by participating in well-established practices? Are your communities ready to embrace your experience into their practices?
Imagination	Do you have good conversations? Do you talk about your deepest aspirations? Do you listen well?	Can you see yourself as a member of large communities, for instance, a world citizen, the heir of long-lived traditions, the pioneer of a world to come?	Do you understand the big picture well enough to act effectively?
Alignment	Do you keep your commitments to your communities? Do uphold uphold their principles? Do you give and receive feedback?	Do you follow guidelines that align your actions with broader purposes, such as saving energy or recycling for the sake of the planet?	Do you know the regimes of accountability by which your ideas, actions, and requests will be judged? Can you convince others of the potential of a new idea?

What Is Doable?

To help identities achieve simultaneously high degrees of local connectedness, global expansiveness, and social effectiveness, here are some design elements to consider:

Home Base

Identity needs a place where a person can experience knowing as a form of social competence. Think of a project-based organization, for instance, where people go from one project to the next, spending a few days in-between on the "available" list. The learning that they do in their projects does not have a social "home," unless they can also belong to a community of practice. In such a community, they are not only recognized as competent for the sake of a project, but their need to develop their competence is part of their belonging. Their professional development and the development of the practice go hand in hand: the identity of the community as it evolves parallels the evolution of their own identity. They can talk with peers who understand the way they look at a problem, who appreciate the potential value of a half-baked idea, and who know where the cutting edge of the practice lies. With such a "home base" people can engage in a diversity of projects and in interactions with other communities without becoming uprooted.

Trajectories

Identity extends in time. It is a trajectory in progress that includes where you have been and where you are going, your history and your aspirations. It brings the past and the future into the experience of the present. Apprentices in traditional apprenticeship, for instance, are not just learning skills, they are exposed to possible futures. By observing and working with journeymen and masters, they develop a sense of trajectory that expands their identity in time (Lave and Wenger 1991). Members of a community embody sets of paradigmatic trajectories that provide material for newcomers to construct their own trajectory through a community and beyond. In the generational encounter between newcomers and established members, the identities of both get expanded. Newcomers gain a sense of history. And oldtimers gain perspective as they revisit their own ways and open future possibilities for others (Wenger 1998).

A good way to develop identities is to open a set of trajectories that lead to possible futures. The engagement of one's identity then incorporates imagination and alignment: envisioning these possible futures and doing what it takes to get there. These trajectories can be of various types. Inbound trajectories invite newcomers into full membership in a community. Peripheral trajectories allow a person to interact with the community without making a commitment to becoming a full member. Outbound trajectories, such as the ones offered by schools, point to forms of participation outside the current communities.

Multimembership

Identity extends in space, across boundaries. It is neither unitary nor fragmented. It is an experience of multimembership, an intersection of many relationships that you hold into the experience of being a person, at once one and multiple. As I said, it is not something we can turn on and off. When we go to work, we do not cease to be parents, and when we go to the theater, we are still an engineer or a waitress. We bring these aspects of our identity to bear to some extent in everything we do. Even though certain aspects of our identities become more salient in different circumstances, it would be an oversimplification to assume that we merely have a multiplicity of separate identities. Such a view would overlook the extent to which our various forms of membership can and do conflict with, influence, complement, and enrich each other. The work that we do in attempts to combine, confront, or reconcile various aspects of our identities has a double effect. It is a source of personal growth. It is also a source of social cohesion because it builds bridges across practices. As a result, our identities shape the social structures we live in. The work of identity constantly reshapes boundaries and reweaves the social fabric of our learning systems.

Combining concurrent forms of membership in multiple communities into one's experience is a way to expand an identity. Of course we only can combine core membership in a limited number of communities, but we can also have more peripheral forms of participation, or even transitory ones, such as visits, sabbaticals, immersion, or one-time projects. Communities that can include in their forms of participation a large portion of the multimembership of their members are more likely to engage their whole identity. If I do not have to pretend that I am not a parent when I am at work, I am more likely to put my heart into what I do.

Fractals

Identity extends across levels. You are having dinner with your family, ensconced in an intense discussion of international politics with your teenagers, living—in the local context of the dinner table—your sense of identification with the global environmental movement. Similarly, you may belong to a local church, but this belonging is usually an expression of your belonging to a religion that includes many other people in many other churches. Engaging at the local level of your church is a way to belong at the broader level of your religion by combining such engagement with imagination (you can picture many other churches with people very much like you expressing similar beliefs, even though you have never met them) and with alignment (in your church you follow rituals that conform with liturgical formats adhered to by all other churches). Note how the three modes of belonging complement each other. Engagement is enriched by the awareness that others share the same beliefs and follow the same guidelines. Conversely, imagining the whole community and understanding the value of its rituals and norms gains concreteness by the ability to engage in a local group.

Combining modes of belonging this way creates "fractal" layers of belonging. More generally, if a community is large, it is a good idea to structure it in layers, as a "fractal" of embedded subcommunities. If a community is large and does not have a fractal structure with local subcommunities in which people can engage actively, then it can easily happen that beyond a small core group various segments of the community feel disconnected. Subcommunities could be defined regionally, as local "chapters" of a global community. Some representatives of these local communities then form a global community among them whose purpose is to connect the local subcommunities into one large global one. This is how some global communities of well engineers have structured their forms of participation at Shell Oil. Subcommunities could be also be defined by subspecialties as engineering communities are at DaimlerChrysler, where engineers can join communities specialized in specific components (e.g., wipers, seats, or dashboards) but clustered into broader communities defined according to systems (e.g., body or powertrain). With such a fractal structure, by belonging to your own subcommunity you experience in a local and direct way your belonging to a much broader community.

Conclusion: Participation in Social Learning Systems

The perspective of a social learning system applies to many of our social institutions: our disciplines, our industries, our economic regions, and our organizations. This view has implications at multiple levels.

- For individuals, this perspective highlights the importance of finding the dynamic set of communities one should belong to—centrally and peripherally—and to fashion a meaningful trajectory through these communities over time.
- For communities of practice, it requires a balance between core and boundary processes, so that the practice is both a strong node in the web of interconnections—an enabler of deep learning in a specific area—and at the same time, highly linked with other parts of the system—a player in systemwide processes of knowledge production, exchange, and transformation.
- For organizations, this perspective implies a need to foster and participate in social learning systems, both inside and outside organizational boundaries. Social learning systems are not defined by, congruent with, or cleanly encompassed in organizations. Organizations can take part

in them; they can foster them; they can leverage them; but they cannot fully own or control them.

This paradox could be bad news because the organizational requirements of social learning systems often run counter to traditional management practices (Wenger and Snyder 2000).The currency of these systems is collegiality, reciprocity, expertise, contributions to the practice, and negotiating a learning agenda, not affiliation to an institution, assigned authority, or commitment to a predefined deliverable. But there is also good news. The knowledge economy will give more primacy to informal systems. In a traditional industrial setting, the formal design of a production system is the primary source of value creation. Think of an assembly line where value derives from the quality of the design of the formal process. Informal processes still exist, but they produce value to the extent that they conform to and serve the formal design. In the knowledge economy, this relationship is inverted. The primary source of value creation lies in informal processes, such as conversations, brainstorming, and pursuing ideas. Formal organizational designs and processes are still important, but they contribute to value creation to the extent that they are in the service of informal processes.

This framework suggests two directions for organizations. On the one hand, they must learn to manage themselves as social learning systems and develop such systems internally. This means:

- giving primacy to the kind of informal learning processes characteristic of communities of practice and designing organizational structures and processes that are in the service of the informal;
- placing a lot of emphasis on the meaningfulness of participation in the organization, on the possibility for building interesting identities, and on community membership as the primary relationship to the organization (Handy 1989);
- organizing for complexity, working to link the various communities that constitute the learning systems in which the organization operates, offering channels, shared discourses, processes, and technology platforms by which local forms of knowledgeability can have global connections and effects, and providing coordination among practices to create complex knowledge beyond the purview of any practice.

With respect to this internal learning system, the learning potential of an organization lies in its configuration of core practices and boundary processes (Wenger 1998)

On the other hand, organizations must learn to participate in broader learning systems in which they are only one of many players. Companies have learned to participate as one of many players in economic markets to sell products and services to customers taken as individual decision-makers. In the knowledge economy, however, they must learn to participate in learning systems as well. Knowledge production is becoming more distributed, complex, and diversified, in disciplines and industries (Gibbons et al. 1994), in regional economies such as Silicon Valley (Saxenian 1996), and among consumers who have the potential of forming communities (Snyder 1999).

In these learning systems, organizations find the talents they need, new ideas, technological developments, best practices, and learning partners. The rules of participation in social learning systems are different than those of product markets. You do not simply compete; in fact, your most threatening competitor may be your best partner when it comes to learning together. If you hoard your knowledge in a social learning system, you quickly appear as taking more than you give, and you will progressively be excluded from the most significant exchanges.

In a knowledge economy, sustained success for any organization will depend not only on effective participation in economic markets, but just as importantly and with many of the same players, on knowing how to participate in broader social learning systems.

References

Anderson, Benedict. (1983). *Imagined Communities*. London: Verso.

Brown, John Seely, and Duguid, Paul. (1999). "Organizing Knowledge." *Reflections* 1(2): 28–44.

Eckert, Penelope. (1989). *Jocks and Burnouts: Social Categories and Identity in the High School*. New York: Teachers' College Press.

Gibbons, Michael; Limoges, Camille; Nowotny, Helga; Schwartzman, Simon; Scott, Peter; and Trow, Martin. (1994). *The New Production of Knowledge: The Dynamics of Science and Research in Contemporary Societies*. London: Sage.

Giddens, Anthony. (1991). *Modernity and Self-identity: Self and Society in the Late Modern Age*. Stanford, CA: Stanford University Press.

Handy, Charles. (1989). *The Age of Unreason*. Cambridge, MA: Harvard Business School Press.

Lave, Jean, and Wenger, Etienne. (1991). *Situated Learning: Legitimate Peripheral Participation*. New York: Cambridge University Press.

McDermott, Richard. (1999). "Learning Across Teams: How to Build Communities of Practice in Team Organizations." *Knowledge Management Review* 8 (May–June): 32–38.

Saxenian, Annalee. (1996). *Regional Advantage: Culture and Competition in Silicon Valley and Route 128*. Cambridge, MA: Harvard University Press.

Snyder, William. (1999). "Organization and World Design: The Gaia's Hypotheses." Submitted to the Academy of Management, Division of Organizations and the Natural Environment, John M. Jermier College of Business, University of South Florida, Tampa.

Star, Susan Leigh, and Griesemer, J. (1989). "Institutional Ecology, 'Translation,' and Boundary Objects: Amateurs and Professionals in Berkeley's Museum of Vertebrate Zoology, 1907–1939." *Social Studies of Science* 19: 387–420. London: Sage.

Wenger, Etienne. (1998). *Communities of Practice: Learning, Meaning, and Identity.* New York: Cambridge University Press.

Wenger, Etienne, and Snyder, William. (2000). "Communities of Practice: The Organizational Frontier." *Harvard Business Review* (January–February): 139–145.

5

Developing Knowing in Practice:
Behind the Scenes of Haute Cuisine

Marie-Léandre Gomez, Isabelle Bouty, and
Carole Drucker-Godard

Introduction

> *These men who presided over the fixing of such feast were
> highly respected, and it was justified because they had to
> combine very different capabilities: genius to invent; knowledge
> to set out; judgment to adapt; shrewdness to discover; firmness
> to be obeyed; and punctuality to be on time.*
> —Brillat-Savarin

This assertion about the famous seventeenth century French chef Vatel shows the admiration of men for great cooks and the range of their "capabilities." Nowadays, we are still fascinated by them and we can also learn more about their practice.

In "grand restaurants," as in many professional organizations, knowing is the keystone to success, and the head chef is the key-person. How can we characterize his knowing in cooking practice, compared to that of other cooks? How is this knowledge built up and leveraged among cooks, among cooks and chefs, among chefs? At an organizational level, how can we explain differences in performance and success between a "grand" and a good restaurant, and between grand restaurants? In this essay we will try to understand the characteristics and differences in knowing in practice.

Using a constructivist approach, we base our analysis on the case study of a French grand restaurant. We analyze knowing in cooking practice and assert that a chef's knowing in practice is dramatically different from that of other cooking team members. We draw on the concept of "habitus" developed by Bourdieu (1980) to explain how tacit and explicit knowledge, physical and cognitive abilities are embedded in practice. We show that cooking practice in a grand restaurant takes place in a specific game whose rules are historically and socially built at a global level and adapted by every grand restaurant as an organization. Chef habitus is highly tacit and embedded in physical activities. It bridges theory and practice, subjective and objective knowledge, technical skills and rules enforcement, knowledge both in body and mind. We assert that the difference between a chef and a good cook is not just a matter of technical ability or predisposition but also a hard-to-pin-down mix of confidence, concentration, and ability to rise to the occasion, which is also socially constructed knowledge. As a matter of fact, great chef habitus is a mix of (1) personal predisposition; (2) knowledge acquired through tough training and repetitive practice; (3) knowledge of the rules integrated and internalized by cooks, and (4) knowledge acquired through reflexive thinking on practice. Last, we suggest that habitus allows improvisation in cooking practice.

Conceptual and Methodological Background

A Constructivist Approach of Knowing

We develop a constructivist perspective on knowledge and we deal with both knowledge and knowing. This position breaks with traditional epistemology, which considers knowledge as an objective representation of the external world, which we possess and use as a tool in action. Although not widespread, our epistemological viewpoint is now shared by various researchers in organizations. Authors such as Blackler (1995), Tsoukas (1996), Sveiby (1996), Spender (1996), Baumard (1996), Von Krogh (1998), Cook and Brown (1999), and Gherardi and Nicolini (2000) have adopted a rather similar perspective, although not always explicitly.

We hold knowledge as closely linked to action and consider it as both the product of a cognitive activity and the process by which it is constructed. "Knowledge is an activity which is best described as the process of knowing [. . .] and knowing an object or an event is to use it by assimilating it to an action scheme" (Von Glaserfelt 1988: 234). We modify our knowledge framework because it does not fit reality. Nevertheless, knowledge is not only a sensitive perception of the world. The source of knowledge is also situated in practical and cognitive activity. According to Piaget (1975), "I know an object only by acting on it and I can't state anything on it before this action." The world exists before knowing it, but we know particular objects through action and during interactions between our environment and us. All the more, when creating new knowledge we build sense out of a new situation and enhance our potential to act in a new situation.

As a consequence, we consider knowledge as heterogeneous, dynamic, contextualized, embodied, and mediatized.

• *Knowledge is heterogeneous:* there is not a unique type of knowledge and knowing. Philosophy since Aristotle, then psychology, sociology, and organization science, suggested various typologies reflecting the variety and heterogeneity of knowledge. For instance, Nonaka and Takeuchi (1995), Spender (1996), Baumard (1996), and Cook and Brown (1999) rely on the distinction between tacit and explicit knowledge drawn by Polanyi (1967). These dimensions are the most common but other authors also distinguish the various cognitive mechanisms for knowing (Hatchuel 1994; Reix 1995; Le Boterf 1994; Durand 2000) or the places where knowledge is embedded (Girod 1995; Blackler 1995).

• *Knowledge and knowing are dynamic:* knowledge evolves as soon as we act. It is continually reconstructed and developed. It is a characteristic of human beings to be permanently assimilating and appropriating knowledge.

• *Knowing is contextual:* being related to action, knowing is strongly linked to the context of the action. It is embedded in time and space. Should the context change, so will knowing. In a traditional cognitivist perspective, the context is considered as a neutral external environment, whereas in a constructivist approach, knowing is inextricably linked to the material and social circumstances in which it is being constructed (Gherardi and Nicolini 2000). In that sense, it is essential to understand how people use these circumstances to act cleverly, not how they apply cognitive structures to particular situations (Nicolini and Meznar 1995).

• *Knowing is embodied:* it overpasses cognitive frames. As Baumard stated, "no doubt the conceited 'I think therefore I am' which made eclipsed the 'I think therefore I do'"(Baumard 1996: 19). He and Nonaka and Takeuchi (1995) attribute to our occidental philosophical inheritance the intellectual position that considers knowledge as purely cognitive, and neglects the physical facet highlighted by oriental culture. Nonaka (1998) introduced the concept of *ba* to explain this physical aspect of knowledge. We consider that knowing is perceptual and involves our senses. In this, we are close to Strati's definition of "aesthetic knowledge" (2000). Describing it as "the form of knowledge that persons acquire by activating the specific capacities of their perceptive-sensorial faculties and aesthetic judgment in the day-to-day lives of organizations," Strati outlines the importance of our five senses in knowing.

• *Knowing is both personal and social:* knowledge is not universal, as each of us knows through his own past knowing and present experience. As Von Krogh puts it, "because knowledge resides in our bodies and is closely tied to our senses and previous experience, we will come to create the world in ways that are unique to ourselves" (1998: 135). However, Polanyi asserted that knowing is also social because we are living in a collective context. Thus knowing takes place in a social context.

Methodological Outcomes

In the first place, the purpose of this research is to identify knowing in practice. Now the question is "how do we do that?" We chose an exploratory approach and used an abductive method (Blaug 1982; Koenig 1993), in order to draw unique theoretical propositions. First of all, and contrary to the precept of the hypothetico-deductive approach, we do not built on predefined hypotheses and do not know what we will discover (Kirk and Miller 1986). Yet it is noteworthy that abduction is different from pure induction. Whereas induction builds on objective observations of reality starting "tabula rasa" (Glaser and Strauss 1984), abduction integrates previous research and theoretical conclusions in a conceptual framework in order to guide data collection analysis. Following Miles and Huberman (1991) and Yin (1989), we believe that deliberately ignoring previous literature can lead to a loss of time and may not produce cumulative results. As Yin (1989) and Eisenhardt (1990) suggest, collecting pertinent data depends on the researcher's familiarity with and understanding of the object under study. Our research process is illustrated in Figure 5.1.

Second, and following Blaug (1982), Koenig (1993), and Strauss and Corbin (1994), we consider that regularities we identify are temporary and can become obsolete. Our aim is to understand a process and identify regularities, not to produce a universal theory. As Koenig (1993) states, these conjectures need to be discussed and tested afterwards.

In this perspective, our research method is largely inspired by the precept of the discovery of "grounded theory" (Glaser and Strauss 1984) and the constant comparison principle. We collected data through case studies (Yin 1989): our cases are the grand restaurants. First of all, there is a lot of information about these restaurants and their chefs in various media, such as gastronomic magazines, Internet, and TV interviews. This provides us with useful secondary data. It allows us to vary the sources of information, to collect data on the history of the organization and to compare it to its competitors, and to prepare the interviews. Second, we conducted direct observation of practices and organization in kitchens before, during and after seating. Last, we also collected information directly through interviews in grand restaurants, with chefs and members of their teams. The interviews lasted between 45 minutes and 90 minutes. We analyzed our data using a collection of predetermined and emerging categories (abduction) and regularly controlled our

Figure 5.1 **An Abductive Research Process**

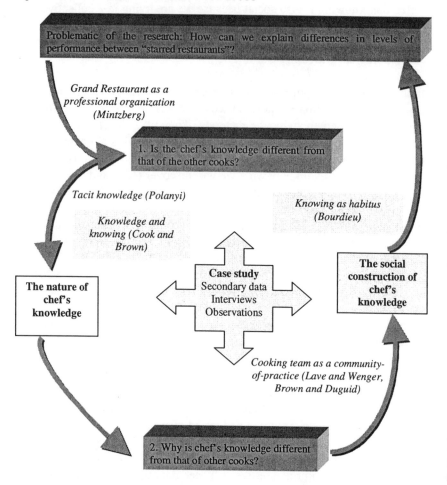

Problematic of the research: How can we explain differences in levels of performance between "starred restaurants"?

Grand Restaurant as a professional organization (Mintzberg)

1. Is the chef's knowledge different from that of the other cooks?

Tacit knowledge (Polanyi)

Knowledge and knowing (Cook and Brown)

Knowing as habitus (Bourdieu)

Case study
Secondary data
Interviews
Observations

The nature of chef's knowledge

The social construction of chef's knowledge

Cooking team as a community-of-practice (Lave and Wenger, Brown and Duguid)

2. Why is chef's knowledge different from that of other cooks?

coding protocol. We also compared tasks in the kitchen in order to identify the differences in knowing, based on our epistemological position that knowing is knowledge in action.

In a constructivist approach, the criteria for validity are quite different from classical criteria: "while these *questions* are appropriate to the naturalistic paradigm, *criteria* as formulated by conventional inquirers are not." (Lincoln and Guba 1985: 218). With regard to the validity of one case study, Yin (1989) asserts that an in-depth analysis of a single case may be valid and contribute to research. From that perspective, our main concerns are credibility, transferability, homogeneity, and confirmability, according to Lincoln and Guba (1985). We thus employed strategies to improve construct validity (Miles and Huberman 1991; Yin 1989). We used multiple sources of evidence (interviews, direct observation, internal and external secondary data) and informants read over their interview reports before we analyzed them. Then we verified that the data we collected in the field relates as closely as possible to the reality we hope to study, with the aim that our instrument provided the best possible representation of the phenomenon being investigated. Thus, we assessed instrument reliability by (1) writing full and precise transcriptions of our interviews, (2) coding raw data obtained both by interviews and documents, and (3) comparing the coding results of the different members of the research team. We described and explained our analysis strategy and the tools used in the analysis to make sure that our results were pertinent and internally coherent. Such careful explanation is a part of validity since it increases the transparency of the process through which results are developed and makes it available for criticism.

The Context of Haute Cuisine and the Grand Restaurant

Haute Cuisine as a Luxury Industry

The context of grand restaurants, organizations composing the field of so-called haute cuisine, is very particular and should be outlined in order to provide a better understanding of the inside practices. Grand restaurants are very selective. Each of them is unique and renowned throughout the world as one among the best. Although we all know the names of some Grand head chefs (Paul Bocuse, Alain Ducasse, Pierre Gagnaire, Gordon Ramsay etc. . . .), only a happy few can afford a meal in their restaurants. They aim to offer creative cuisine, perfect service, exceptional wine, atmosphere, and refinement. Grand restaurants are small and independent organizations, all with a maximum of fifty employees. The main expenses remain human resources, even if wages are rather low. The average ratio is one employee to one customer per seating. Grand restaurants represent the highest level of quality in the cooking industry. They embody excellence. In this section we will present the context of cooking practice in grand restaurants, with the interorganizational and intraorganizational characteristics of that industry.

Performance Evaluation in the Industry

Haute cuisine is a very specific field where profitability is probably not the main criterion to evaluate an organization's performance. Performance is primarily an evaluation of quality by external actors (gastronomic critics).

Haute cuisine is represented by grand restaurants, as defined according to the restaurant's rating by gastronomic guides. Among those guides, the Michelin guide (also called "The Red Guide" because of the color of its cover) is the most important. It is the "arbiter of France's restaurant scene" (Toy 1996). It has been annually rating more than 11,000 restaurants for one hundred years. Michelin's testers are full-time employees of the company. They always act anonymously while eating and pay for their meal. They also systematically visit the kitchen and offices. As a consequence, Michelin's testers have a strong reputation for being serious, demanding, *sans concessions*; their image is one of "fierce independence" (Toy 1996). The Michelin guide grants between zero and three stars to restaurants. Grand restaurants are those awarded three stars. Such an award is never definitive. Restaurants granted stars are systematically visited each year, anonymously of course, by Michelin's testers. Three-star restaurants are tested up to seven times a year each, and some of them have lost a star. According to Joël Robuchon, one of the most famous French chefs, "The Michelin guide is the most important. You can say whatever you want, nothing compares to Michelin. For us, there is nothing above the Michelin three stars." (Nanteau 1999: 75).

Second in order of importance, the GaultMillau guide gives restaurants two ratings consisting of a numerical maximum of 19.5/20 (no one can ever achieve 20/20), and hats (from zero to four [in the U.S. we use stars, i.e., four-star restaurant]). A grand restaurant is one with the maximum rating. According to Michelin and GaultMillau standards, there are fewer than 30 grand restaurants in France today, and fewer than 20 among the other European countries. They can be compared to craftsmen. In those grand restaurants the quest for perfection is continuous, be it in cuisine, wine, service, or seating. Cuisine is a matter of details, precision, and is made on order. Everything is deeply thought about and carefully carried out, and the output is always unique. Yet it is noteworthy that if grand restaurant chefs know each other and reach comparable levels of excellence, they also are really different from each other. Each of them has his own personality and thus his own cuisine.

A Hierarchical Structure in Organizations

The second characteristic to be outlined here is how kitchen work is organized. The organization is nearly the same in all grand restaurants. A hierarchy exists between the different domains in the kitchen (meat, fish, garde-manger, vegetables, and pastry; see Figure 5.2). All kitchen staff (cooks and domain chefs) is under the authority of the Chef A and the sous-chef. When an order reaches the kitchen, the one standing at window announces it.[1] Each domain chef in the kitchen then takes care of the components he or she is concerned with. Once ready (sliced, cooked) each element is brought to the window. There, food items are artistically and immediately assembled to compose the plate. The plate is then vetted and expedited with the other plates of the table to the dining room. Such organization necessitates perfect coordination. This coordination is controlled at the window, where all different elements composing the dishes are supposed to arrive at the same time and warm, although cooking times can be different. The window is also a sanction place. This is where a plate is accepted or rejected for the dining room, according to the judgment of the chef or the sous-chef. The window is the most strategic place in the kitchen. Most of the time the chef stands at the window; he controls and does not cook. If necessary, only the sous-chef can replace the chef and take on this role for the entire seating.

A Crafts Industry Composed by Professional Organizations

The third characteristic of haute cuisine to be outlined is that it remains a craft industry. Cooking is tough and requires lengthy practical training. It appeals to our five senses and is a "learning by doing" profession. Gestures, smells, cooking, and consistencies are to be felt in the first place. Moreover, if technology has brought about many changes to working conditions, they nonetheless remain tough. A cook has to endure the heat near the stove, the fact that kitchens are often cramped, the work schedule, and the nervous pressure during the busiest time. It is exhausting.

As a matter of fact, a grand restaurant is a professional organization, in the way Mintzberg stated it. Knowing in practice is the base of organization, hierarchy, and power. The key actor is the one with the most "knowledge"— the head chef. He is the team's best cook and leader. Customers choose the restaurant because of him; it is "his" cooking style. The head chef is celebrated in newspapers and media, and he may be the owner of the firm.

The Case of a Parisian Grand Restaurant

The Firm History

The case studied is a Parisian restaurant. It employs thirty-seven people (kitchen and service). It was established in Paris at the end of 1996. It is run by Chef A and his wife. Some of the members of the team have been working with Chef A for several years though, in other restaurants. For example, the sous-chef has been working with chef A for more than twenty years.

Restaurant A was rated two stars (Michelin) and 18/20 (GaultMillau) as early as 1997 and became three stars and 19/20 the year after (which is rather spectacular; many two-star restaurants never reach three stars). Prior

Figure 5.2 **Chart of a Grand Restaurant**

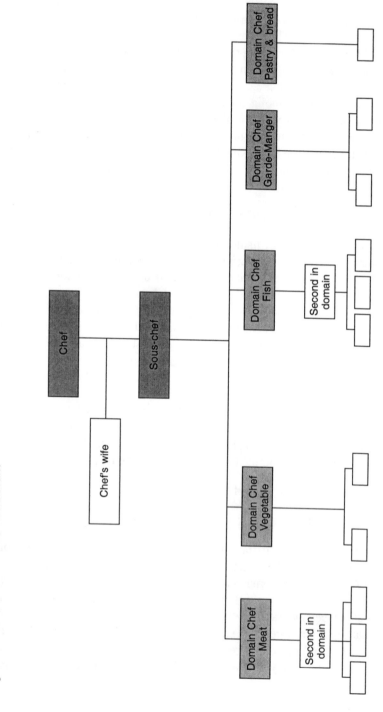

to this restaurant, Chef A ran three other restaurants outside Paris. There, they gradually rose from one star and 12/20 in 1977, to 17/20 in 1980, two stars and 19/20 in 1986, and reached three stars and 19.5/20* in 1993. Financial setbacks drove him to close down his provincial restaurants before seating up in Paris.

Chef A was born 1950 in the center of France. His grandmother and his father ran restaurants and it was soon decided that cooking was going to be his profession: as the eldest, he was chosen to run the family restaurant in his turn. According to Chef A himself, it was not his choice, but a family responsibility. Chef A did not attend any culinary school. As he told us in an interview: "I didn't have money and I didn't want to, I wasn't interested, [. . .] I found it boring."

He began to work in the kitchen when he was very young. Starting with internships and as a member of the kitchen staff, he was trained in various restaurants of different sizes and with different styles, some of them run by great professionals. He only discovered his passion for cooking later on, though, when he found out that his "thing" was in product combinations. As he puts it: "At one time, I discovered that I had a gift which has to do with combinations [. . .] as this occupation seemed really boring to me I needed a good reason to do it [. . .]. I realized, from what people told me, that I was capable at, let's say, going a little bit further than a well done course." Now "it's a love story" he says (Nanteau 1999).

Gastronomy critics define Chef A as "the classmate who had most fun as well as most trouble sitting still" (Wells 1997). His cuisine is "creative," "full of artistry, audacity and richness" (Wells 1997), often surprising, even audacious. On the plate, the mixture of ingredients is complex and the course is really "staged." Chef A plays with contrasting tastes, smells, and consistencies. He builds relationships between ingredients in a course, and between courses in the meal. The menu is vast and complex. The meal is made up of numerous courses (an average of six) accompanied by many surprising *mises en bouche* (bite-sized appetizers) as an introduction. The result is qualified as innovative, multidimensional, even baroque. Chef A's cuisine is frequently compared to modern art. The dishes are "as beautiful as a painting . . . to such a point that one hesitates to touch them" (Nanteau 1999). Gastronomy critics agree that Chef A is in a culinary category all his own. As he puts it himself: "I appropriated things and I have created my own culinary universe."

Backstage at a Grand Restaurant

In order to analyze the collective and dynamic aspects of knowing in practice, we need hereafter to relate a seating as we observed it in Chef A's restaurant.

---

*At the time Gault Millau never awarded a 20/20, considering that cooking could always be improved.

This will provide the reader with a better understanding of cooking practice and highlight the importance of improvisation and coordination.

11:30 A.M.: The seating begins with a team meeting before customers arrive. The headwaiter organizes the daily brief with the dining room staff. Either Chef A or his wife occasionally attends this briefing. Each day a different course is detailed, new ideas are suggested, for example, regarding the cheese board. Waiters must be able to answer every question from clients, whether about the origin of a cheese or the ingredients in a course. During the morning brief the headwaiter also details which particular guests (famous or regular clients) are expected for the seating and where they will be seated.

In the kitchen, work has begun from the early morning. Kitchen staff prepares all the tools and are already cooking long-simmering meals. As we enter this magical place, the atmosphere seems pleasant (cooks talk to each other, explain what they do, clean their cooking space and get it ready, check their instruments), yet we can already fell a tension; the hour before the seating is a very important time. Everybody is busy getting ready: sauces simmer, herbs are being cut, and the temperature in the kitchen is already very high.

Chef A regularly intervenes to control his team's work: "Those vegetables are not sliced finely enough and I want the cut to be round. Watch, I'll show you . . . got it? OK, I don't want to see that happen again." A deep respect for Chef A shows on every face and in the voice of each cook. Cooks call him "Chef." The sous-chef is also in the kitchen since the morning. He too is in charge of controlling the team's work. Everything has to be neat and well organized. All must be ready when the first guests arrive. During this time, the sous-chef might help one cook or another to get ready, but he mainly concentrates on the whole team being prepared for the seating. He also is the one who implicitly indicates to cooks that they should be in position and concentrate, as the first guests are to arrive soon. At this moment everyone checks his clothes and some put on their hats. Silence reigns in the kitchen. It feels like the seating to come is unusual or as if it is the very first one. The tension and the concentration seem so intense that one can hardly believe that the same "scenario" is performed daily.

12:45 P.M.: the first guests arrive. The sous-chef announces the table orders. Each of the cooks involved with the course (an average of four cooks deal with each plate) then says "yes," which means that the orders are taken into account and prepared. A few minutes later the meat chef says: "two minutes at window." All the ingredients of the course have to be cooked in order to be at window simultaneously (in two minutes) and be assembled by the sous-chef.

Chef A enters the kitchen. He informs the kitchen staff that Mr. X (a regular guest) is having a drink at the bar and wishes to have lunch in the restaurant: "What shall we cook for him today? What do you suggest? A sole

Dominique? It's a good idea. And what do you think for an entrée Jacques? OK, you do the Three Courgettes and a sole. Do it well, well. Come on guys, here we go!" Then Chef A decides (it seems a random choice) that today he is going to cook with the meat chef.

1:30 P.M.: It is the busiest time. The dining room is full with 42 clients, 36 of whom arrived nearly at the same time (within the space of 10 minutes). Coordination is spectacular. It is necessary but also very sophisticated. At this moment, domain chefs and their cooks seem to be in another world. They are incredibly and perfectly concentrated and coordinated. The sous-chef orchestrates. We can hear many "yesses" coming from different places in the kitchen but the sous-chef does not get lost. He remembers every order and knows exactly who is supposed to say "yes" and when. He also knows exactly which courses are supposed to arrive at window and when. He has to remember everything while at the same time assembling courses on the plates. In addition, he manages some particular courses (especially fish and poultry) that are expedited to the dining room to be presented and then come back in the kitchen to be boned.

Sometimes a cook asks others to talk in a lower voice so that he can concentrate better. At one point, the sous-chef was busy with something else and a waiter took the plates at window on his own initiative to place them on a tray. The sous-chef became furious: he is the one who controls the plates and decides to place them on a tray; he is the only one who decides if they can be expedited to the dining room. Of course all the guests at a same table must be served at the same time. It is the headwaiter's responsibility to inform the sous-chef if a guest has left the table for a moment.

A moment later something seems to happen with a cook in the meat domain. Chef A reprimands him for having cooked too small a portion of venison. Chef A will then talk about the mistake many times until the end of the seating: "It's the last time I see this kind of thing. I don't understand, I'm here, the chef's here [he talks about the sous-chef], ask us, don't do that alone, it's the last time." As the first orders arrive for dessert, everything calms down and the atmosphere is more relaxed. Those courses do not require the same degree of coordination and are not prepared in the same area (the pastry area is downstairs). Soon Chef A leaves the kitchen for the dining room to visit the guests. At the end of the seating the tidying up is very fast. Two minutes and it's over. The cooks have cleaned up their cooking space; everything is neat and they leave, exhausted.

* * *

At first sight, this observation may be puzzling given the contradictory interpretations it allows. Practice appears to be a mix of perfectly mastered actions, repeated time and time again, and improvisation (when the chef decides at the last moment what will be served to a regular customer, notices the portion of venison, or when he improvises meals during the seating for "carte blanche au chef" orders).[2] It evokes a military structure (with strict rules, organization, and highly coordinated actions, as well as the use of military words) and uncontrolled or unexpected actions (unfortunate initiative of a waiter at window, vegetables sliced too thick). Coordination mechanisms also strike the observer. People look as if they were working on their own, playing their own part, but the practice appears coordinated. Codified signs, glances, and very short but efficient messages ("yes") enable the team to reach a high degree of synchronization. All together and as contradictory as they look, these first remarks tend to confirm that we can not consider knowledge as explicit, verbal, cognitive, and universal.

In the following pages, we analyze knowing in practice with a two-stage approach. We will first detail the tasks and responsibilities of each member of the team as we analyzed them on the basis of observations and interviews. This outlines the characteristics of knowing according to the role of every protagonist in cooking practice and the specificity of chef knowing. Then, we will propose an explanation of differences between actors using the lens of the dialectic habitus–practice conceived by Bourdieu.

Diversity of Knowing in Cooking Practices: From Individual Knowing to Collective Output

How can we describe knowing in cooking practice in a grand restaurant? We base our analysis on the differences of knowing between various areas of practice, and among actors. We will particularly detail the knowing-in-practice characteristics of the key actor of the organization, Chef A, because apart from having a unique culinary style, Chef A is also characterized by his activities in the kitchen.

Chef A's Knowing in Practice

Chef A cooks at every seating. He is characterized by:

- his ability to accomplish any task in the kitchen and interfere in everything;
- his high degree of creativity;
- his managing of kitchen staff;
- his relationship to clients.

Chef A's first characteristic is his ability to accomplish any task in the kitchen. He actively participates in what happens in the kitchen before and during the seating: "In the mornings [after reflection and before cooking] I participate quite extensively [in what happens in the kitchen]. . . . I am in the kitchen around 12:00 P.M. and till 3:00 P.M. I spend the full seating in the kitchen." Chef A considers cooking to be a major part of his role. This is true to the point that, as he states, "Very often, the restaurant is closed when I am not here. . . . This week I have been out three days, and we have called all our clients to inform them I wasn't going to be in the kitchen." The main explanation Chef A gives for his cooking is that apart from the fact that he loves it, he feels it necessary to "leave his mark" on plates: "I really want to leave my mark, what I think about my cuisine. . . . I touch nearly every plate." This means that Chef A *wants* to put his signature on the plates, not that he *has* to do it. It is a matter of will rather than necessity. This also means that some of Chef A's knowledge is purely technical. Chef A was, still is, and wants to remain, a cook. Moreover, achieving his complex cuisine necessitates that he master a wide range of techniques. This mastery emerges as an element of Chef A's key knowledge that he leverages every day when (1) he cooks and (2) he manages his team to give life to his ideas. As he puts it: "Today, I have certainty about the way this or that should be cooked, which might be different depending on the result I want to achieve. There is a method for a particular course, and the same product can be used another way for another idea."

The second distinctive task of Chef A is innovation and creativity. The creation of new courses is a privilege of the chef. Part of his role is reflection about the work being done in the kitchen (current products and courses) and about creativity (new products and courses).

This high degree of creativity is certainly attached to Chef A's particular culinary universe and its complexity. But it is also due to the fact that no one else in the kitchen is able fully to complete this task. Chef A is the only one who can create this particular cuisine, in this particular culinary universe. This does not mean that cooks never have ideas and never participate in the creation of new courses. Rather, it means that only Chef A can create the menu as a whole and regularly introduce new courses in the menu. As Chef A himself states: "Sometimes, on their own initiative, through their own professional experience [cooks] can bring about an idea or a new find. Rarely a new find, but sometimes a particular technique."

In other words, although members of the team can be creative, this remains limited compared to Chef A's creative capacity. This becomes apparent through the creative process. Chef A saves his mornings for such tasks: "In the mornings, . . . I think about my personal work in the kitchen . . . courses, products, processes and creativity." When he has an idea for a new course, he composes a "technical card." Technical cards are then distributed to members of the team, including, of course, the sous-chef. Chef A's technical cards are handwritten. They describe the courses, their style, their own world, and their tone. They are not recipes; they do not codify quantities or cooking times. They instead draw a framework. As Chef A puts it: "There is a technical card . . . which gives them the general outline and we discuss it before they implement it. . . . I give them a framework within which they do whatever they want. They do what they want but the framework is precise. They are not automatons." Starting with the technical card, cooks give life to Chef A's ideas. The result (what is on the plate) is then tasted by Chef A and discussed with the team to adjust it by 95 percent. This is where "innovations" by cooks can enrich the course.

In other words, Chef A has a capacity to express himself in cuisine by creating courses and playing with products. This is one aspect of his key knowledge. He is the source of restaurant A's uniqueness and one of its sources of excellence.

The ability to create new courses and innovate in cuisine would remain sterile if Chef A were not also able to communicate his ideas to his team and manage it success fully. Thus, among the tasks performed by Chef A are communication and team management. This may not be as evident as cooking, but it is as important. In the words of Chef A, "We created a competent group, globally competent, because it's a meal, it's several courses, it's many things, a combination."

In the first place, Chef A communicates his ideas and shares them with the team. He creates his courses on paper and gives his staff the responsibility of cooking them. He uses technical cards as means communication and does not try to show his staff what his idea should look like when implemented. "[The cooks] have the information and they cook and afterwards I adjust. I am not always here [when they cook the new course]." It is noteworthy that technical cards are not recipes at all. They are general descriptions that rather convey the spirit of the courses. In other words, Chef A communicates his ideas while giving his staff autonomy. Cooks have the freedom to cook what they understand to be Chef A's idea, which is significantly different from cooking Chef A's recipe.

Second, Chef A built a team around him to produce his cuisine daily. Usually, he chooses the members of the team according to their cooking skills. During the testing period he observes the cook's technique and his wife observes the cook's ability to integrate into the restaurant's team (human relationships). Afterward they make a decision. One aspect of Chef A's key knowledge appears to be in choosing the members of his kitchen staff and inciting them to stay. Some of the members of the team have been with Chef A for many years. For example, the sous-chef has been working with

Chef A for nearly twenty years. Chef A describes his staff as: "competent and highly motivated and concentrated, concentrated. Their motivation and concentration are above the average, that's clear."

Third, Chef A daily manages and cooks at the same time. While observing what happens in the kitchen during the seating, we noticed that Chef A kept an eye on what was going on around him and regularly interfered to adjust techniques, rations, or plates, for example. He did not "control" in a hierarchical sense though. Rather, Chef A participated and assisted the team in reaching excellence with each plate. One aspect of Chef A's knowing is thus in management. In his own words: "It is important to feel comfortable with people. Some people are really talented but they do not feel comfortable with you [. . .] you know you have to feel people and that they feel comfortable and then it's not about working anymore, it's about who they are."

Lastly, Chef A performs another task: he has a relationship with clients. He regularly comes out of the kitchen to visit the dining room. He is the visible member of his kitchen team and, as such, plays a representative role. Visiting the dinning room is also a means of keeping in touch with the "market," inquiring about what clients did or did not like, why, whether they feel comfortable, what they would like. . . . Such a task requires "business" knowledge, which is totally different from types of knowledge leveraged in the kitchen. This means that Chef A has more than pure technical and artistic competencies. He also runs a business and exhibits "marketing" knowledge.

Sous-chef's Knowing in Practice

The sous-chef is also a key protagonist, particularly in Chef A's restaurant since their working relationship spans so many years. His knowing complements the chef's. He possesses technical mastery and his understanding of Chef A's ideas and culinary universe is so profound that, cooking, he can produce exactly the same result as Chef A. As Chef A puts it, he is "the only one who can accurately reproduce what I do." Chef A and his sous-chef have been working together for nearly twenty years, and they are so much alike that the latter is nearly the twin of the former. Technically they probably are interchangeable cooks. Chef A even goes further and states that "His basic technique is far better than mine."

The main task performed by the sous-chef during the seating is to be at the window. Because Chef A and his sous-chef are such similar cooks, they can (and do) reverse their roles in the kitchen. The sous-chef is the expeditor and stands at the window so that Chef A can cook, contrary to what happens in most grand restaurants, where the head chef stands at the window and the sous-chef cooks. At the window, the sous-chef displays management and technical knowing. He organizes the work in the kitchen during the seating. Specifically, he announces courses to be cooked and launches the cooking. He masters timing so that the different elements that compose a plate are ready at the same time and can be assembled. He is also the one whose word is systematically awaited, before the plate can be expedited to the dining room: he makes sure that plates are complete, perfect, and can be served.

Cooks' Practice: A Technical Knowing in Practice

Other cooks may be head of a domain (meat, fish, garde-manger, pastry), or under the responsibility of a domain chef. Their task is essentially technical, and limited to one area, even if they periodically change domains to expand their knowledge. The kitchen staff is a technical team. Its members' task is to cook in determined domains. As Chef A puts it, "I ask them to be successful with the basics for a start."

As regards these members of the team, knowing in practice is fundamentally technical and very specific (limited to the domain they cook in and those they have cooked in prior to their current position). The team is somehow fragmented because cooks are very specialized. Only Chef A and his sous-chef can organize and coordinate cooks during the busiest time.

This does not mean that the cooks' knowing in practice is minor. Cooks somehow have the responsibility of what is on the plate. They make tangible Chef A's ideas and creations through the leveraging of their technical culinary knowing in practice. Nevertheless, they are only concerned with cooking in their own domain.

Moreover, although they have all reached a certain degree of technical excellence (which enabled them to become members of the kitchen staff of a grand restaurant), cooks do not all seem to have exactly the same knowing in practice. Some of them seem to have a touch, something above pure technique. They seem to have a potential or sensitivity that others do not have. As Chef A puts it: "Some people are incapable of cooking a fish or a meat. They always are off-target. They always just miss the point. It's like playing the piano. There is a touch. You can read Mozart's life and know his scores by heart. Some people will still hit the keys like brutes." As opposed to: "I have one of my cooks here. He doesn't know it yet, but he has a lot of finesse. He's sensitive; he's subtle."

These last quotations point to the fact the technical culinary knowing in practice includes a large amount of mastery closely comparable to that shown in the arts. This knowing is developed through long training. It also is characterized by its intuitive dimension. Culinary art calls for technique as well as for touch and sensitivity. Those last two dimensions probably cannot be elicited and do not seem to be equally shared among cooks.

Table 5.1

Description of Cooking Team Knowing

		Chef A	Sous-chef	Cooks
Creation	New courses	X		
	Technical innovation	X	X	Can
Technique	Window	X	X	
	Cooking within a domain	X	X	X
	Cooking within all domains	X	X	
Business	Communication	X		
	Team management	X	X	
	Relationship to clients	X		

Nevertheless, every cook has to begin at this job. It gives the opportunity to observe and understand the way a grand restaurant is run—that is to say, the rules of the particular game of haute cuisine, as we will explain later.

Synthesis: Differences of Knowing in Cooking Practices

The identified knowing in practice identified here can be summarized in Table 5.1. Chef A's main knowledge is technical (both diversified and specialized at the same time). Chef A also has creative and business knowledge. The sous-chef has comparable technical knowledge but not the creative ability to innovate in the menu and create new courses. The sous-chef also has some business knowledge as regards team management and work organization. In that sense his knowing is more technically oriented than that of Chef A. Lastly, other team members show purely technical knowledge, limited to cooking, even if their practice in the context of a grand restaurant gives them the opportunity to familiarize themselves with this particular context, which is essential to developing knowing in practice at a higher level. Talking about a possible drift if he is away from his restaurant, Chef A points to such differences in knowing in these terms: "I think that the problem lies in a drift, and it's easy to understand. I mean you leave for 10 or 15 days, even a month, I think it wouldn't change a lot of things. Afterwards problems would emerge regarding product renewal, new things, new ideas to implement, little things that are pluses you know." This quotation points to the fact that some specific aspects of Chef A's knowing in practice are key to the restaurant. It also outlines the fact that they seem to be leveraged periodically, as opposed to those of the sous-chef and the cooks, which are leveraged at each seating. Such differences in knowing in practice between kitchen staff, the sous-chef, and Chef A can be represented as an inverted pyramid as seen in Figure 5.3.

Figure 5.3 **The Inverted Pyramid of Differences in Knowing in Practice**

Chef A
- Innovation: courses and menu creation
- Business: management and communication
- Technique: wide, specialized, and subtle competences

Sous-chef
- Business: organization and management
- Technique: wide, specialized, and subtle competences

Kitchen staff
- Technique: specialized competencies, sometimes subtle

How can we explain the differences in knowing among the cooking team? In other words, how is it that the chef has reached that level of performance in practice and other cooks probably never will?

Cooking as a Game: Interpreting Pierre Bourdieu's Logic of Practice

The use of Bourdieu's concepts of habitus and practice appears relevant in order to understand the deep tacitness of knowing, the mixture of rules and improvisation, as well as the observed coordination mechanisms. Understanding the particularity of Chef A's habitus, as opposed to that of others, helps us understand why chefs are chefs, how they reached this high level of excellence.

The Concept of Habitus

As a former rugby player, Bourdieu often uses the game metaphor to convey his sense of social life. By game, he does not mean entertainment, but the practice of a game by a deeply involved athlete, who competes with others and with his own limits. Practice is motivated by serious stakes. Moreover, everyone is convinced he or she is part of a larger system, not only his/her team, but also the game itself, with its rules and participants.

Our practice of a game is conditioned by our habitus, our knowing in practice. Habitus is the knowledge of the game that we previously constructed, and that we reconstruct during the game. Habitus is a "structured structure predisposed to function as a structuring structure" (Bourdieu 1980: 88). As a "structured structure," it is the result of initial capabilities, the enforcement of integrated rules of the game, and knowledge acquired through past experience. Habitus is deeply rooted in our bodies. At first sight it can appear as an automatic "stimulus-answer" scheme. However, Bourdieu insists that it is impossible to dissociate the automatic from the reflexive part of habitus, as well as cognitive from embodied, objective from subjective, theoretical from empirical aspects.

Habitus is also a dynamic concept and a "structuring structure." It is an art of inventing rather than a catalogue of knowledge. It includes all the structures that allow an infinite number of practices, even if these practices are limited in their diversity (because they are constrained by our own capabilities and schemes, and also restricted by the rules of the game). As an art of inventing, habitus allows for improvisation. This is the basis for practice because contexts and situations are highly variable. Even if we can identify recurrent frames and compare situations one with another, we never face exactly the same context twice; thus practice always has to differ. Improvisation is also necessary given the "emergency of practice." While practicing, we have no time for deep thought. Thinking about practice occurs during training, not during performance, be it a football game, a theatrical representation, or a restaurant seating. During practice, actors are completely integrated into the game; they are taken over by the game and practice is focused on the finality of the game. As a matter of fact, actors are not concentrating on what they are doing, but on what they will do. "The one who is taken by the game does not adjust to what he sees but to what he foresees, sending the ball not to where his partner is but where he will be after shooting" (Bourdieu 1980: 157).

How Chefs Reach Such Knowing in Practice: The Importance of the Social Aspects in Habitus Construction

In cooking, as in every practice, habitus is both personal and social. It is personal in that it is a combination of initial capabilities and affinities of the cook, his/her predisposition for this practice, and the way he/she integrates new experience of practice and training. Habitus is social in that it depends on interactions with others in practice, and reflects the original apprenticeship context and the way it was encouraged. Of course, habitus includes technical skills, and not everyone can reach such a level of technical mastery, but it is not enough to explain the degree of excellence in practice reached by chefs. Technical skills are a prerequisite to becoming a chef, but chefs have something more. Examining the social dimension of habitus is helpful to gain a better insight.

First, Bourdieu insists on the importance of the way our environment responds to our first practices. The way others consider our playing this game influences our self-confidence and our involvement. In the field of grand restaurants, this is all the more obvious as cooks, like athletes, have to get involved early in the game. They most often become apprentices between the ages of 13 and 16. A large majority of French three-star cooks were literally "raised" in a catering context, with parents or grandparents being chefs themselves, and thus consider cooking a very serious matter. Some of them even had no choice but to become a chef. As Chef A relates: "I didn't like this job at all, but I did it almost under constraint by my family." Being raised in a "cooking environment" helps a chef to develop some technical skills of course, but it more so it incites him or her to take cooking as a serious game. This is necessary in order to concentrate on practice and then develop a high degree of excellence. This is a prerequisite to developing and improving habitus in the game. According to Chef A, "As in other forms of competition, I think there is the passion for willingness. You need to be psychologically strong." "You need obstinacy," asserts another chef. Chefs want to perfect their cooking, they want to reach a high degree of excellence and work hard to increase the quality of their cuisine. Before reaching three stars, they go through years of eighteen-hour workdays. They even sometimes work at night to increase their skill in one field. Chef A related that he worked "at night because [he] couldn't master chocolate technique."

Second, as they concentrate on practice, chefs and future chefs also develop a reflexive knowing through training and trial-and-error. They spend a large part of their time analyzing their practice. Chef A saves most of his mornings for reflexive thinking. Chef B says: "I like these moments when my mind goes away, they are necessary" Chef B often stays at home, in his own kitchen, to try something new and to experiment. This reflection allows chefs to perfect their meals and also to innovate. It is a time for creation. They found inspiration in their practice, the mix of products, but also in the arts. Chef A is fond of painting, others are fond of music or sculpture. One chef even happens to work with a perfume creator, and tries to interpret fragrances in meals. Chefs remain open to different modes of expression, and also stay aware of the original ideas and different skills of their teams. They stay aware in order to discover the personal pieces of habitus a cook could bring to the practice of the team. Chef A acknowledges: "their initiative, their own professional experience can bring an idea . . . a technique. My sous-chef, who has been working with me for a very long time, has perfected a better technique than I. He can shell crabs incredibly fast." As a matter of fact, they capitalize on every new source of knowing, be it the arts, experiences of other cooks, or their own experience.

Third, the context of chefs' past practice is essential too. Most chefs were trained in France, one of the most renowned countries in the field of haute cuisine. French training schools, tools, utensils, and food products are widely acknowledged as excellent. All this created a favorable context that allowed the field of haute cuisine to develop. This is important, but not sufficient to explain the differences between a good cook and a great chef. Most chefs were trained in famous restaurants where they acquired the best technical skills, but, more importantly, could assimilate the essence of a grand restaurant. That is to say they had the opportunity to learn the rules of haute cuisine technique, to develop an habitus that would fit the standards of the field and lead to the capacity to fulfill the requirements for three Michelin stars. Since the performance is arbitrated by clients and overall by Michelin guide testers, chefs have to be aware of the requirements of these evaluators. Nevertheless, the rules of haute cuisine are not written in books. It is necessary to practice in an environment that fits those rules in order to assimilate them. In grand restaurants, would-be chefs learn about organization, supplies, management, how to decorate a restaurant and a dining room. This is where they acquire what Bourdieu calls a "sense of practice." It is the very tacit and empirical constituent of habitus. It cannot be taught at school, and can only be constructed through practice.

Coordination of Knowing in Practice: Homology Relations Among Actors

In collective practice, actors develop a sense of practice as they mobilize their habitus for action. New modes of coordination arise because actors develop a particular knowing of others' participation in practice, an understanding of other actors, which allows for coordination with few words and few signs. This is what Bourdieu calls "homology relation." It means diversity in homogeneity, and reflects the relations between the habitus of different actors. Cooks, chefs, and apprentices are involved in the same game, under the same rules of the field of haute cuisine. Various habitus are different, but similar enough so that actions in practice are comprehensible to all the participants, who have developed a similar sense of practice. In this perspective, communication during practice remains mainly automatic. Cooks do not need too many words to explain what they do. "Their practice and output are immediately comprehensible by the others, then considered obvious and taken for granted. Habitus allows an economy of intention, not only in production, but also in the interpretation of practices and outputs" (Bourdieu 1980: 97). Repetitiveness of practice, more than the explanation of codes, enables the development of these coordination mechanisms.

In Chef A's restaurant, coordination is based on few words, such as "running?," asked by the sous-chef as soon as he announces a course order. Then, cooks just reply "yes," and the sous-chef announces another course, as if he did not wait for answers (but he does; if a cook happens not to answer, the sous-chef asks him directly). This announcement takes less than three seconds, and another order is announced. During cooking time, coordination is necessary to be sure that all the components of a plate will arrive at the same time at the window. The domain chef primarily responsible for the course (for instance, the fish chef), announces the time left before the main element is ready (for example: "sole, two minutes"). He does not need to list all the components. Everybody knows them. All involved cooks reply "yes, two minutes." Exactly two minutes later, everything arrives at the window. Other orders from the same table also arrive at the same time.

Such synchronization is possible only because of thorough preparation. A seating is comparable to the performance of a play whose coordination is rehearsed both before and then after, as a preparation for the next performance. Cooking practice widely exceeds seating times.

Conclusion

Contributing to the Debate on Knowledge in Organizations

This analysis of cooking practice in a grand restaurant points out the differences among actors, and particularly between a three-star chef and other cooks. We can better understand these differences if we consider that types of knowing are more complex than is often suggested. In a constructivist perspective and on the ground of Bourdieu's concept of habitus in practice, knowing is more than a knowledge that we possess. It could rather be considered as something we do.

The case presented here highlights the complex nature of knowing. Knowing in cooking practice is a mix of personal predisposition, knowledge acquired through tough training and repetitive practice, knowledge of the rules integrated and internalized by cooks, and knowledge acquired through reflexive thinking about practice. As a matter of fact, knowing is a social process. Even if it involves only one individual—the chef, for instance—it takes place in the context of a social practice where the criteria of evaluation are socially and historically constructed and institutionalized.

Cooking knowing is highly tacit, embedded in physical activities, and actually bridges theory and practice, subjective and objective knowing, technical skills and rules enforcement, knowing both in body and mind. The example provided by cooks and chefs illustrates that not all knowledge can be codified in order to be transmitted and, what is more, not all knowledge can be made explicit.

Toward Further Research

We drew our analysis on a single case here. Other cases are under study. Through case comparison, we will try to enrich our analysis. As knowing is difficult to observe and then to discern, multiple observations will allow us to discover unexplored aspects. We can also focus on a new problematic: Do all chefs possess the same knowing scheme? Under which aspects does knowing differ from one organization to another? We will also try to understand the interdependence between the organization and the Chef A. Why can some restaurants stay open while the chef is away whereas others have to close? Moreover, it will be relevant to link our knowing-in-practice analysis to other organizational theory and strategic management approaches, such as knowing networks and communities of practice, in order to analyze the links between three-star chefs and between three-star chefs and their former sous-chefs.

This analysis of knowing may also be extended or partly transferred to many other practices. In particular, we could study practices in other professional organizations where knowledge and knowing are key to the structure of the organization and the whole industry; for example in an orchestra, or a ballet company company, in a surgical team, a consulting firm, or a law firm. For grand restaurants, as for these other organizations, analyzing their knowing in practice is essential to enhancing performance, from the development of optimal practices to their valuation on the market, through the question of "knowing practices" in the community and its effect on the emergence of key actors, such as chefs.

Notes

Direct quotations from Chef A were recorded during author interviews with him. Explanations of kitchen activities and conversations were culled during author observations in the kitchen.

1. The window is the place in the kitchen where plates are assembled and controlled, and from where they are expedited to the tables in the dining room.

2. "Carte blanche au chef" is an order for which the customer trusts the chef to decide the entire composition of the meal according to his inspiration. In some grand restaurants, this can make up 40 percent of the orders.

References

Baumard, P. (1996). *Organisations déconcertées, la gestion stratégique de la connaissance*. Paris: Masson. Eng. trans.: *Tacit Knowledge in Organizations*. London: Sage, 1999.

Blackler, F. (1995). "Knowledge, Knowledge Work and Organizations: An Overview and Interpretation." *Organization Studies* 16(6): 1021–1046.

Blaug, M. (1982). *La Méthodologie économique*. Paris: Economica.

Bourdieu, P. (1980). *Le Sens pratique*. Paris: Les editions de Minuit. Eng. trans.: *The Logic of Practice*. New York: Monthly Review Press, 1989.

Brillat-Savarin, A. (1982). *Physiologie du goût*. Paris: Flammarion.

Cook, D., and Brown, J.S. (1999). "Bridging Epistemologies: The Generative Dance Between Organizational Knowledge and Organizational Knowing." *Organization Science* 10(4): 381–400.

Durand, T. (2000). "L'alchimie de la competence." *Revue française de gestion* (Janvier–Février 2000): 84–102.

Eisenhardt, K.M. (1990). "Building Theories from Case Study Research." *Academy of Management Review* 14(4): 532–550.

GaultMillau (2000). "La cuisine aux créateurs." *GaultMillau Magazine* (October): 22–25.

Gherardi, S. (2000). "Practice-based Theorizing on Learning and Knowing in Organizations: An Introduction." *Organizations* 7(2): 211–223

Gherardi, S., and Nicolini, D. (2000). "To Transfer Is to Transform: The Circulation of Safety Knowledge." *Organization* 7(2): 329–348.

Girod, M. (1995). "La Mémoire organisationnelle." *Revue française de gestion* (September–October): 30–42.

Glaser, J.C., and Strauss, M. (1984). *The Discovery of Grounded Theory: Strategies for Qualitative Research*. Hawthorne, NY: Aldine de Gruyter.

Hatchuel, A. (1994). "Apprentissages collectifs et activités de conception." *Revue française de gestion* (été [summer]): 109–119.

Kirk, J., and Miller, M. (1986). *Reliability and Validity in Qualitative Research*. London: Sage.

Koenig, G. (1993). "Production de la connaissance et constitution des pratiques organisationnelles." *Revue française des ressources humaines* 9: 4–17.

Le Boterf, G. (1994). *De la Compétence, Essai sur un attracteur étrange*. Paris: Les éditions d'organisation.

Leonard, D., and Sensiper, S. (1998). "The Role of Tacit Knowledge in Group Innovation." *California Management Review* 40(3): 112–133.

Lincoln Y., and Guba, E.G. (1985). *Naturalistic Inquiry*. Thousand Oaks, CA: Sage.

Miles, M.B., and Huberman, M.A. (1991). *Qualitative Data Analysis*. Thousand Oaks, CA: Sage.

Nanteau, O. (1999). *Portraits toqués: Enquête chez les trois-étoiles*. Paris: L'archipel.

Nicolini, D., and Meznar, M. (1995). "The Social Construction of Organizational Learning." *Human Relations* 48(7): 727–746.

Nonaka, I. (1998). "The Concept of 'Ba': Building a Foundation for Knowledge Creation." *California Management Review* 40(3): 40–54

Nonaka, I., and Takeuchi, H. (1995). *The Knowledge-Creating Company*. New York: Oxford University Press.

Piaget, J. (1975). "L'Equilibration des structures cognitives." *Etudes d'épistémologie génétique* 33.

Polanyi, M. (1967). *Personal Knowledge: Towards a Post-Critical Philosophy.* New York: Harper Torchbooks.

Reix, R. (1995). "Savoir tacite et savoir formalisé dans l'entreprise." *Revue française de gestion* (September–October): 17–28.

Spender, J.C. (1996). "Making Knowledge the Basis of a Dynamic Theory of the Firm." *Strategic Management Journal* 17: 45–62.

Strati, A. (2000). "Aesthetic, Tacit Knowledge and Organizational Learning." Communication to the 16th Egos Colloquium, Helsinki.

Strauss, A., and Corbin J. (1994). "Grounded Theory Methodology: An Overview." In Denzin N. K., Y.S. Lincoln, eds., *Handbook of Qualitative Research*, 274–285. Thousand Oaks, CA: Sage.

Sveiby, K.E. (1996). "Transfer of Knowledge and the Information Processing Professions." *European Journal of Management* 14(4): 379–388.

Toy, S. (1996) "Little Red Book: The Michelin Guide Has Been the Bible for Restaurants and Hotels in France for Nearly 100 Years." *Wine Spectator,* November 30. Available at www.winespector.com/wine/Archives/Show_Article/0,1275,1023,00 html.

Tsoukas, H. (1996). "The Firm as a Distributed Knowledge System: A Constructionist Perspective." *Strategic Management Journal* 17 (winter, special issue): 11–25.

Von Glaserfelt, E. (1988). *The Construction of Knowledge, Contributions to Conceptual Semantic.* Salinas: Intersystems Publications.

Von Krogh, G. (1998). "Care in Knowledge Creation." *California Management Review* 40(3): 133–153.

Wells, P. (1997). "From the Provinces to Paris, 'Immediate' and Enthusiastic Cuisine." *International Herald Tribune*, January 3, 8.

Yin R. K. (1989). *Case Study Research: Design and Methods.* Applied Social Research Methods Series, vol. 5. Newbury Park, CA: Sage.

6

Organizing Processes in Complex Activity Networks

Frank Blackler, Norman Crump, and Seonaidh McDonald

Introduction

Over the past two decades many organizations in the UK have faced a fast-changing environment as capital has taken a higher surplus of wealth, the government has pulled back from its role as the redistributor of income, and key aspects of the economy have become internationalized. An ideology of enterprise has been promoted by governments, supported by ongoing programs of privatization and deregulation, and by the growing use of information and communication technologies to support flexible systems of production and management. There has, of course, been no shortage of ideas about how managers should respond to such developments. Commentators have emphasized the need to be customer-responsive, to concentrate on niche markets, to reduce staff numbers, to subcontract, and to compete in alliances. Indeed, a wide range of approaches to support these developments has been advocated, including the management of corporate cultures, groupware technologies, the "reengineering" of business processes, the development of flexible workforces, knowledge management, and organizational learning.

This chapter discusses an approach to analyzing practices in a company ("HighTech") that was caught in a period of changes such as these. HighTech is a small player in the global market for electro-optic products. It employs an unusually large percentage of highly qualified engineers. Located over three sites that are distributed across the UK, it produces a range of highly sophisticated products for the defense market, where it has a strong, and long-established, reputation for innovative design engineering. However, with the end of the Cold War the company's top managers found themselves in an increasingly uncertain situation. The way in which the UK government had supported research and development in the defense sector was reorganized along competitive lines. The market for electro-optic products, although still large worldwide, was shrinking. Top management recognized the need to introduce a range of new technologies and working methods to compete more effectively in the short term. Medium term they anticipated that technological developments would undermine the established division of labor between engineering disciplines in the company. Long term it was anticipated that defense-oriented companies in Europe would merge, as was happening in the United States, where the industry was becoming dominated by fewer, larger organizations.

We spent two years at HighTech researching practices retrospectively and in real time.[1] Our initial analysis of the general impetus for change in HighTech was reported in an earlier paper in *Organization* (Blackler, Crump, and McDonald 1999a) where, using an activity theory orientation, we presented a retrospective analysis of changes that have overtaken manufacturing industry over recent years and detailed the changing nature of expertise in HighTech. This chapter develops a different perspective. We begin by reviewing the distinctive nature of activity theory, emphasize its intervention orientation, then develop the approach for organizational analysis. Activity theory interprets practice as activity, explores the links between event and context, and suggests an agenda for interactive social science. It provides a way of analyzing organizations as distributed, decentered, and emergent systems of knowledge. We suggest that the processes of "perspective making," "perspective taking," and "perspective shaping" are central organizing processes in situations where different expert groups must cooperate in the pursuit of multiple, perhaps competing, objectives. Finally, we apply the approach in a study of three contrasting ad hoc teams convened to develop new approaches to business strategy.

Practice as Activity

Recent developments in the theory of practice provided the starting point for our study of HighTech. Interest in the theory of practice is not new (see Ortner 1984) but in recent years a convergence has developed across a range of traditions with a growing interest being shown in processes of sense-making and learning, in theories of situated and distributed cognition, and in the intimate relationships between knowing and doing. Tsoukas (1996) provided an overview of the relevance of such literature to organizational analysis. Commenting on the relationship of knowledge and action he suggested that organizations can be analyzed as knowledge-based systems. He identified two general approaches among theorists who have adopted this perspective: those who seek to distinguish different types of organizational knowledge (e.g., Nonaka and Takeuchi [1995], who distinguish between tacit and explicit knowledge) and those who feature the importance of relationships and the emergent nature of collective competency (e.g., Weick and Roberts [1993], who develop the metaphor of the "collective mind"). Tsoukas emphasized the importance of work in the latter tradition and concluded that the knowledge of an organization is necessarily indeterminate and emergent, that it cannot be controlled centrally (and is thus both distributed and decentred), and that new knowledge partly originates from outside the organization.

The approach to analysis that we describe here, activity theory, enabled us to analyze HighTech as a distributed, emergent, and decentered knowledge system. An activity-theoretical approach to knowing and doing has much in common with contemporary anthropological, ethnomethodological, and actor-network approaches. However, developed as it was from concepts pioneered in a non-Western context (Russian psychology), it offers a distinctive contribution to these matters. Activity theory is, perhaps, best characterized as "functional materialism." It denies the conventional assumption that abilities emerge independently from their historical and cultural settings. Fundamental to the approach is the idea that human capacities develop when, in collaboration with others, people act upon their immediate surroundings.

Activity theory has its origins in Vygotsky's concept of mediation and Leont'ev's concept of activity. Engeström offers a contemporary presentation of their approach[2] in his general model of "activity systems." This features the relations between object-oriented activity, agents, and the community of which they are a part. Objects of activity are partly given and partly emergent. Engeström suggests (a) that the relations between individuals and the object of their activity are mediated by concepts and technologies, (b) that the relationships between the community and the overall object of its activity are mediated by its division of labor, and (c) that the relations between individuals and the communities of which they are a part are mediated by rules and procedures. Such factors comprise an interrelated *bricolage* of material, mental, social, and cultural resources for thought and action.

In his general account of how activities develop Engeström (1987) makes the point that, as well as being systems that support goal attainment, activity systems are *disturbance-producing* systems. Incoherencies, inconsistencies, paradoxes, and tensions are integral elements of activity systems. They become manifest in "disturbances" when, for example, people are evidently interpreting situations in different ways, inherent dilemmas in the overall pattern of activity become clear (Engeström particularly emphasizes the tension between use value and exchange value), or unexpected difficulties emerge in the execution of day-to-day tasks. Engeström argues that relationships within activity systems are made orderly only by the determination people show as they engage with the objects of their activity. As disturbances become evident within and between activity systems, participants may begin to address underlying issues and to create new learning. As people change their situations they change their activities and, simultaneously, they change themselves.

In Table 6.1 we have summarized these points and their implications. Activity theory problematizes (a) what people are doing, (b) how and with whom they are doing it, and (c) how collective learning may occur. It introduces the question (d) how can people shape the contexts that shape their practices? Activity theory also suggests a particular approach to research: (a) practices should be studied as transformative activity, (b) they should be located within a broader analysis of their historical development, and (c) by highlighting disturbances within activity systems researchers can help those they are studying to recognize, reflect upon, and perhaps rebuild their activity systems. Comparisons between activity theory and cognate approaches in the social sciences are outlined in an endnote.[3]

Organizing Processes in Activity Networks

The question arises of how activity theory can be adapted for organizational analysis. One approach might be to analyze particular organizations as activity systems in their own right. However, partly as a result of the complex division of labor that exists in work organizations, participants' understandings of the links between their actions and the overall activity system of which they are a part can become obscured. While a level of internal differentiation between individuals and groups is inevitable in activity systems (of any size), complex organizations can easily become segmented and fragmented.

Differentiation within activity systems does not necessarily lead to fragmentation, of course. Weick and Roberts's (1993) analysis of "heedful organizing" provides an excellent example of how one highly differentiated and complex organization, an aircraft carrier operating in combat conditions, could nonetheless function as a highly integrated and effective activity system. As Weick and Roberts note, essential to the effective operation of the carrier was the vigilant collaboration of key personnel. Nonetheless the overall objects of activity in the situation they describe (such as the launching and recovery of planes) are unusually visible to the members of the system. As a general rule, the overall objects of the activity and patterns of collaboration in complex work organizations are typically much more difficult to see and to represent. They tend to be multiple, only loosely connected, emergent, abstract, and contestable.

Table 6.1

Activity Theory and the Study of Practices

An activity-theory approach to research:	(a) What are people doing?	Issues problematized by activity theory	
		(b) How and with whom are they doing it?	(c) What is the nature of collective learning?
(i) Study the detail of practices.	The "object of activity" is fundamental to activity-theoretical analysis of practices. Objects of activity are partly given and partly anticipated. They are intimately related to the mediating factors through which they are constructed.	Activities are culturally situated and linguistically and technologically mediated. They are enacted in communities and involve a division of labor. Such factors and their interactions are described as "activity systems." This is the unit of analysis used in activity theoretical research.	Activity systems are tension-producing systems. Disturbances within and between activity systems provide the driving force for their development.
(ii) Study practices in the context of their historical development.	Actions are discrete, have clear beginnings and endings, and exist over short time scales. They are goal oriented. "Activities" on the other hand are complex patterns of practice that endure over long time periods. Activities suggest goals and provide motives.	Activities develop over time. As a general trend, activity systems in work organizations appear to be becoming more complex and interdependent, and objects of activity more abstract and emergent.	When activity systems become more improvised and fluid, established priorities and relationships are loosened and may be re-formed.
		(d) How can people shape the contexts that shape their practices?	
(iii) Support the development of the practices that are being studied.	Research can help people become aware of the object of their activity and of the process of object construction.	Research can explore the nature and dynamics of particular activity systems and the trajectory of their development.	Research can trigger discussions about disturbances within and between activity systems and these are, and might be, responded to.

Rather than analyzing organizations as single activity systems, it is more satisfactory, therefore, to analyze them as networks of overlapping activity systems or, for simplicity of expression, as activity networks. The units that make up such networks can be labeled "communities of activity"; such communities can be loosely defined in terms of the extent to which members recognize shared work priorities, work with a common cognitive and technological infrastructure, and support each other's activity. Relations between activity systems bring the (sometimes difficult) issues associated with multidisciplinary work into sharp focus. Collaboration across different systems of activity raises issues concerning priorities, identities, and operational methods as well as questions about relative authority and influence. Horizontal integration across expert communities within an organization can be difficult to achieve, for example, as the shared understandings of activity and the shared infrastructure of activity that make cooperation the norm within particular communities of activity can act as a barrier to close collaboration with outsiders (Dougherty 1992). Vertical integration between communities of practice involves similar problems. A crucial aspect of vertical integration is likely to be the efforts of senior staff to control others and the efforts of junior staff in a hierarchy to represent their activities in such a way that senior managers will allow them necessary resources (Bucciarelli 1996).

Engeström's general model of activity systems reveals the collective infrastructure of expertise within particular activity systems. In Figure 6.1 we have adapted the model to feature core organizing processes within networks of activity. The central triangle in the model represents the elements whose relationships the model is designed to explore: one community of activity, others with which it interacts, and the shared object of their endeavors. In developing an analysis of how their relationships can be described, we have adopted and extended a terminology suggested by Boland and Tenkasi (1995):

1. *Perspective making* refers to the different contributions that different communities of activity bring to the organization. As suggested by activity theory, this involves the management of priorities, infrastructure, and identity. The processes of perspective making support "domain innovations" within particular expert communities.

2. *Perspective taking* refers to relations between communities of activity and involves the management of authority and influence (both horizontally and vertically within an organization's hierarchy), questions of priority and of relative identities. Perspective-taking processes support "boundary innovations" in the relationships between communities.

Figure 6.1   **Organizing Processes in Activity Networks**

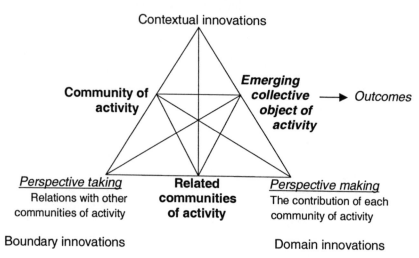

3. *Perspective shaping* refers to assumptions about context, achievements and possibilities. It involves the management of imaginations that underlie frameworks of problem identification, the conceptual resources people bring to their activities, and the facilities they have for reflection. Perspective-shaping processes support "contextual innovations."

HighTech as an Activity Network

This section uses activity-theoretical ideas to develop a general analysis of tensions and interactive complexities in HighTech. Concepts especially relevant to this analysis are: (a) the notion that objects of activity are partly given and partly emergent, and that the process of object construction is intimately related to the activity system participant's work within; (b) the idea that through the concept of the "activity system" expertise can be understood as a collective, heterogeneous phenomenon; and (c) the proposal that cooperative-relations activity networks depend upon the processes of "perspective making," "perspective taking," and "perspective shaping."

Objects of activity are partly given and partly emergent and depend upon key features of the activity systems used by participants. As noted earlier, top management in HighTech had tried, with some success, to steer the organization in new ways. The problems they were addressing were complex, however, and in the highly competitive circumstance that the company faced, their task could be understood to be the achievement of a range of priorities, some of which would be competing (e.g., short-term profit *versus* long-term development; reliance on established strengths *versus* the need to develop new competencies; the need to plan ahead *versus* the need to improvise and experiment, etc.). HighTech had, no doubt, faced competing priorities in the past but, in the highly pressured situation that top management was facing at the time of our study, the difficulty of reconciling these various priorities was much in evidence.

Events at one site that took place over less than a decade illustrate how such tensions were manifesting themselves and how they were being managed. Undertaken first was a major reorganization of manufacturing that included a substantial program of downsizing and a move to a purpose-built, open-plan, and futuristic factory. Immediately afterwards design engineering was also reorganized, moving from a structure based on separate engineering disciplines to the development of multidisciplinary project teams. Next the site was reorganized into decentralized business groups that worked independently (and to some extent competitively) and whose mission was urgently to expand sales. Subsequently a high-level Marketing Division was superimposed on this structure in an effort to shift focus away from short-term sales to long-term customer relations. Shortly afterwards the whole company was reorganized into two cross-site, cross-disciplinary divisions intended to support closer integration and an enhanced ability to innovate.

Looking back over these events it was evident that, rather than focusing attention on multiple goals simultaneously, management addressed first one aspect of the problems they were facing, then another. Thus the focus of their concerns moved from costs, operational control, and integration, to business expansion, then company image and customer relations, and then to the need for integrated and proactive approaches to strategy. At any particular stage in the history of these developments, management pursued its priorities singlemindedly. The manner with which new priorities were imposed over old ones suggested, indeed, that members of the top management group were uneasy with the multifaceted and essentially emergent nature of HighTech's activities. They appeared determined to treat the situation as if it was, or could be made to be, structured and controllable.

Through the concept of "activity system," expertise can be studied as a collective, heterogeneous phenomenon. HighTech had traditionally invested heavily in technological and procedural developments and the top management team recognized the outstanding abilities of a number of the company's staff, some of whom had international reputations in their specialist fields. At the same time, the top team had little appreciation of the importance of group and leadership skills for knowledge management and they found it difficult to accept the idea that resources should be invested in the development of expert communities.

Cooperative relations between communities of activity are mediated by the processes of "perspective making," "perspective taking," and "perspective shaping." As a general rule coordination processes in HighTech were formal, driven by procedures, and often competitive. Evidence of segmentation was evident in the horizontal relations between specialist groups. Relations between the various design engineers seemed generally cooperative, although fragmentation in multidisciplinary teams did occur. Relations across design teams were often distant and competitive, and relations across business groups, and between engineers and the Marketing Division, were sometimes frosty. Relations across the company's three sites could be antagonistic. Moreover (as detailed in Blackler, Crump, and McDonald [1999a] there was evidence of sharp horizontal segmentation with top management distant from, and apparently unsympathetic toward, the felt needs of key specialist groups. Overall, we concluded that the way "perspective making," "perspective taking," and "perspective shaping" processes were managed within the organization was restricting the abilities of expert groups to collaborate vigilantly and to develop what Weick and Roberts (1993) describe as a "collective mind."

The Study of Strategy Development Groups

The imposition of a new cross-site, multidisciplinary divisional structure, referred to above, was introduced toward the end of our time in HighTech. It was decreed from the top with no prior consultation with staff and in the face of clear evidence of its unpopularity. This style of managing structural change was the norm in HighTech. In certain particulars, however, what was being attempted in this instance was novel. A key element in the reorganization was the constitution of cross-site, multidisciplinary groups who were charged to review strategy in key areas of the company's business.

In scale and scope the introduction of the Strategy Development Groups at this time was both innovative and ambitious. Top management intended that the SDGs would stimulate widespread debate and review of the changing circumstances affecting the various facets of the business, provide an opportunity for people from different parts of the company to share and develop opinions about what might be done, and ensure that the views of members of the Executive Board were informed by as wide a range of opinion as possible. Membership of each group was decided by a Steering Committee of three senior members of the Executive Board. They identified relevant individuals from across the organization to represent relevant points of view (technology, sales, marketing, operations), arranged some cross-membership over the groups, and included a "wild card" in each of them (i.e., a member of staff who was not a specialist in the field of operations addressed by that particular group but who, it was hoped, would encourage people to question taken-for-granted assumptions). Sixteen groups were planned, to cover nine business and product areas and seven functional and support areas. They were to be phased in over a period of months. Each was to be chaired by one of the three members of the Steering Committee. Significantly, after the first four months of their operation each of the groups set up in the first wave was required to make a presentation to the full Executive Board.

The groups were of particular interest from a research perspective. First, the mandate for them crystallized many of the uncertainties the company was facing. The development of new business strategies involves a review of incomplete and ambiguous sets of information and the development of new (typically cross-disciplinary) insights into markets and technologies. Second, the purpose and composition of the groups raised the possibility that participants might develop new ways of working together, perhaps relaxing established patterns of authority and influence. Indeed, each of the groups we studied needed to create conditions that would support an effective review of strategies. As we noted above, activity-theoretical ideas suggest that multidisciplinary teams are likely to be difficult to organize effectively. In the context of the various schisms we had observed in HighTech we anticipated that problems that emerged in the teams might quickly become personalized, a development that would itself inhibit further collaboration. To overcome such problems, we surmised, the ad hoc multidisciplinary groups would need rapidly to negotiate the object of their activity and appropriate ways of working.

Research Methods

We followed three of the groups (referred to here as groups A, B, and C) over the first four months of their operation (with, normally, at least one of the authors attending meetings in an observational capacity). The groups were chosen on the basis of the importance of their work to HighTech. Each was chaired by a different manager. The three groups we followed each held around half a dozen extended meetings during the period of the study, with extra meetings and video conferences being held by subgroups of some of the teams. In addition, we maintained ongoing informal contacts with staff

Figure 6.2 **The Analytical Framework**

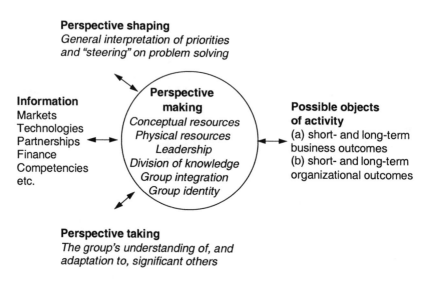

Perspective shaping
*General interpretation of priorities
and "steering" on problem solving*

Information
Markets
Technologies
Partnerships
Finance
Competencies
etc.

**Perspective
making**
*Conceptual resources
Physical resources
Leadership
Division of knowledge
Group integration
Group identity*

**Possible objects
of activity**
(a) short- and long-term
business outcomes
(b) short- and long-term
organizational outcomes

Perspective taking
*The group's understanding of, and
adaptation to, significant others*

over the research period, attended two "away day" meetings for key personnel from one of the new divisions, and kept in contact with the Steering Committee responsible for the overall progress of the exercise. Toward the end of the research period we formally interviewed members of the groups that we had studied.

Utilizing the conceptual approach outlined above, we sought to understand how members of the SDGs constructed and executed their work and to consider how the efforts of such teams might be guided and supported. Central to our work was an attempt to feature the tensions and dilemmas that characterized the activity systems of each of the groups, to examine how they each coped with these tensions, and to represent relevant processes in a way that would make them more manageable. In our summaries of practices within the teams we endeavored to feature the apparent object of each group's activities. We assumed that the way in which such objects were defined and realized would be a result of the general orientation people brought to their work in the team ("perspective shaping" processes), the evolving dynamics of the activity systems of each of the teams (i.e., their "perspective making"), and the ways group members understand and adapt to significant others ("perspective taking" processes). Depending on the approach they developed, the teams might rely on different sources of information (personal impressions, available or researchable data concerning markets, technologies, competitors, and potential partners, etc.). The general framework we used to present these factors is shown in Figure 6.2.

Figure 6.3   **Organizing Processess in Group A**

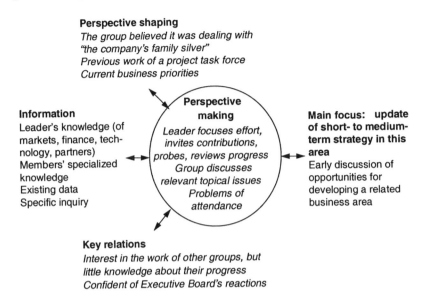

Perspective shaping
*The group believed it was dealing with
"the company's family silver"
Previous work of a project task force
Current business priorities*

Information
Leader's knowledge (of
markets, finance, tech-
nology, partners)
Members' specialized
knowledge
Existing data
Specific inquiry

**Perspective
making**
*Leader focuses effort,
invites contributions,
probes, reviews progress
Group discusses
relevant topical issues
Problems of
attendance*

**Main focus: update
of short- to medium-
term strategy in this
area**
Early discussion of
opportunities for
developing a related
business area

Key relations
*Interest in the work of other groups, but
little knowledge about their progress
Confident of Executive Board's reactions*

Organizing Processes in the Strategy Development Groups

One key finding of our study was how different the three groups were one
from the other. Group A reviewed business opportunities in a core area of the
company's business (members were proud of this) but where technological
advances by competitors presented a threat. The aim of the group's activity
was to update an existing, and well-formed, strategy in this field. The group
was able to draw on the achievements of an earlier project group, and although it had a number of difficult issues to address, it quickly focused its
efforts. The concerns of the group were close to the day-to-day priorities of
group members, and the group acted as an important source of information
exchange. The chairman of the group structured discussions of the complex
details considered by the group, and while he drew from members' knowledge and experience, his own knowledge of technologies, markets, and competitors was itself a major asset for the group. Partly because of the chairman's
reputation and position on the board, the group was confident of a good
reception from the Executive Board at the end of its initial four-month working period. It took time for group members to take note of, and then to begin
to integrate, possible concerns and contributions from staff working in a cognate area. Because of work pressures, most members missed at least some
meetings of the group. These points are summarized in Figure 6.3.

Group B dealt with an area where, it was felt, new opportunities could be created if the company repositioned itself in the marketplace. At the start of its work the group sought to understand the possibilities of such a repositioning; later it sought to develop specific proposals to operationalize the process and to impress the Executive Board. The group brought together representatives from three areas of the organization that, previously, had operated largely independently, although the technologies that underpinned their work were similar. The chairman impressed upon group members the potential value of their diverse backgrounds in considerations of strategic development, stressing the possible advantages of a market repositioning. The group's deliberations moved from discussions about the general desirability of a market repositioning through discussions about ways of representing the full range of relevant products and markets, to presentations to each other of the approaches members had each taken in their own market segments, to the preparation for their submission to the Executive Board. Group members appeared to try hard to contribute to the various meetings of the group. The use of a whiteboard early in their meetings helped provide a "shared space" for their various contributions. Nevertheless, they lacked a shared vocabulary to help them develop a strategic frame of reference (talk tended to remain at the level of products rather than competencies, for example, and the potential advantage of intercompany alliances was only considered late in the series of meetings). By the end of the series of meetings we observed that the identity of the group seemed to be based on the idea that it was "further ahead" than other Strategy Development Groups. As was the case in both the other groups it proved difficult to arrange the meetings to suit all group members and few were able to attend all meetings. The organizing processes of Group B are shown in Figure 6.4.

Group C explored the possibility of developing new business opportunities in nontraditional markets. It is widely recognized at HighTech that the possibilities the group addressed (and which assumed a shift out of defense and into civil markets) were especially difficult to reconcile with the organization's traditional activities. Some members strongly disagreed with each other about the most appropriate way for the group to proceed and, in early meetings, a power struggle developed in the group. Subsequently much of the group's business was conducted in small subgroups convened outside the meetings of the full group. Members united in criticizing the ability of the rest of the company to understand and exploit possible growth opportunities in civil markets. Members were uncertain about what their group's objectives should be taken to be, and the question of how the group should regard its priorities was a continuing issue of concern to members. Drawing

Figure 6.4   **Organizing Processes in Group B**

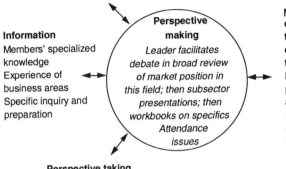

Perspective shaping
The potential importance of a market
repositioning in this area
The value of synthesizing staff contributions
in the development of such a strategy
The group as "further ahead"

Information
Members' specialized
knowledge
Experience of
business areas
Specific inquiry and
preparation

Perspective
making
Leader facilitates
debate in broad review
of market position in
this field; then subsector
presentations; then
workbooks on specifics
Attendance
issues

Mainfocus: (i) detailed
consideration of short-
term options, in context
of (ii) vision of a long-
term repositioning
Discussion of new
procedures to compare
alternative options
Early mention of future
shifts in the balance
of competencies

Perspective taking
Importance of presentation to
executive board is recognized
Limited interest in other groups

from their (extensive) knowledge and experience, group members focused on ways of developing a new decision-making system to vet ideas about possibilities in this area. They did not explore possibilities for adapting specific products that the company had already developed. The group chairman was often absent from meetings (around the time when the group was due to present its ideas to the Executive Board, his resignation from the company was announced). When he was present he dominated the group, apparently raising members' anxiety levels. Criticisms of the board were expressed in meetings of the group; at the same time, the group invested much effort in the development of a strong presentation for the Executive Board. A strong resolve developed for the group to convince the board that significant diversification into the area discussed by the group was highly desirable, and the identity of the group seemed to develop around the idea that they were the hero innovators for HighTech. By the end of the series of meetings group members expressed the feeling that they had reached a consensus on the issues (although that was not our impression as outsiders). One member of the group lobbied key members of the Executive Board in advance of their presentation. In the event, Group C's report was to be received very badly by the board. Figure 6.5 illustrates the group's organizing processes.

Figure 6.5 **Organizing Processes in Group C**

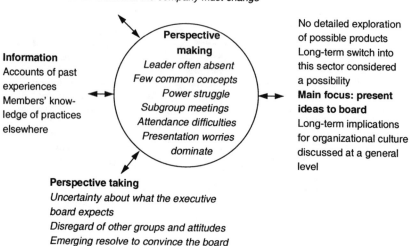

Perspective shaping
This area seen as the company's Cinderella
Task objectives unclear
Growing consensus that the future
will be different and the company must change

Information
Accounts of past
experiences
Members' know-
ledge of practices
elsewhere

Perspective making
Leader often absent
Few common concepts
Power struggle
Subgroup meetings
Attendance difficulties
Presentation worries
dominate

No detailed exploration
of possible products
Long-term switch into
this sector considered
a possibility
**Main focus: present
ideas to board**
Long-term implications
for organizational culture
discussed at a general
level

Perspective taking
Uncertainty about what the executive
board expects
Disregard of other groups and attitudes
Emerging resolve to convince the board

As in our general discussion of HighTech, three ideas from activity theory can be used to explore these dynamics.

Objects of Activity

Objects of activity are partly given and partly emergent, and depend on key features of the activity systems used by participants. The objects of activity of the three groups differed significantly. Group A focused on a difficult series of problems that were, however, familiar both to group members and to top management. It drew from previous research into the issues, was steered competently by its chairman, who was an expert in this area, and members were confident of a good reception from top management. The potential tension between the need to "think big" and produce short-term plans hardly arose; the group quickly focused on operational details. Group B faced a more uncertain task that required the integration of different experiences and perspectives from across the organization to construct a new agenda. The chairman endeavored to structure its meetings to make it possible for shared insights to develop, encouraging members to participate. The group needed to reconcile the need to develop general insights with the production of specific recommendations for short-term action and, in its later meetings, members focused almost exclusively on the production of detailed plans. Group C was uncertain how to approach its activity. The group felt unsupported by top management. Old disagreements between members provided a backlog of rivalry and competition. It might be said that this group was the most innovative of the three, but the group seemed to lose its rudder. Members increasingly focused on their self-image as company heroes. The tension between the need to think broadly and the need to produce short-term plans was resolved entirely in favor of the former.

Expertise

Expertise can be understood as a collective, heterogeneous phenomenon through the concept of the "activity system." Each of the Strategy Development Groups needed rapidly to integrate its diverse membership to reinterpret ambiguous technological and market information and, to a greater or lesser extent, to reimagine aspects of HighTech's future activity. We were interested in the extent to which the demands of the task would be associated with the emergence of new working relationships in the groups. Relations in Group A appeared to follow conventional patterns. Factors such as the relative familiarity of its task, the traditional and expert role of the leader, and the anticipated reaction of the Executive Board help explain this outcome. In contrast, the chair of Group B recognized that if the variety of perspectives in his group was effectively to be combined, the group had rapidly to develop a modus operandi. He encouraged use of a whiteboard to facilitate shared representations of the issues people discussed and, in response to the suggestion from members of the group that people should each summarize relevant experiences, he set time aside for such discussion. The group's agenda raised some difficult issues, not only about the notion of "strategy" (a topic unfamiliar to some), but also questions of business survival, organization, and the very immediate need to impress the Executive Board. The leader endeavored to contain the anxieties such points might have raised, and the group developed what members described as an open pattern of working together. (We were unable to study whether or not this had any "spillover" effects either in the short or the medium term.) Relations in Group C were turbulent in the early and middle stages when uncertainties, anxieties, and personal antipathies were much in evidence. In its attitude toward top management and the rest of the organization alike, the group was to become somewhat deviant. Later, group members focused on the need to manage external relations with the Executive Board and members united in the preparation of what was intended to be a slick and persuasive presentation built around computer-controlled graphics.

Cooperative Relations Between Communities of Activity

These relations are mediated by the processes of "perspective making," "perspective taking," and "perspective shaping." As a result of our study of the groups, we were able to make some specific suggestions to them and to the Executive Board about issues that seemed central to their effective operation. Following the general orientation developed from activity theory, we suggested that tensions and dilemmas in the groups provided a rich source for organizational learning, that strategy development requires organizational development, that the importance of the processes of perspective making, perspective taking, and perspective shaping should be explicitly recognized. We then made specific suggestions about the ways these processes could be managed, which were discussed with members of the Strategy Development Teams.

Conclusions

To summarize the HighTech case: like many organizations operating in global markets, HighTech has faced a complex mix of institutional, technological, and organizational changes. Activities within the company have become more complex and intertwined, established demarcations have been shifting, and priorities have become more uncertain. Traditionally, HighTech had been steered through a mix of project management techniques, professional autonomy, and hierarchical control. Consistent with company tradition, top management's approach to the increasing complexity of HighTech's situation had been to dictate priorities. In the increasingly ambiguous context of the business, however, and in the face of the growing interactive complexity, such arrangements appeared to be inhibiting, rather than supporting, creative and flexible responses. Problems of fragmentation at HighTech become increasingly evident over the period of our study, and members of the Executive Board accepted that their traditional approach needed review, albeit there were sharp disagreements of opinion about what exactly should be done. As part of a major restructuring of the organization, a series of Strategy Development Groups were introduced to reconsider future options and to pioneer new collaborative ways of solving problems.

Social science theories can reveal new facts, but this is unusual. More importantly, social science theories can help people to see situations in new ways and can support the development of new strategies of action. As we have detailed, our approach to studying events in HighTech and its Strategy Development Groups was to theorize practice as historically located activity. We emphasized activity theory's focus on emergent objects and relationships and the interpretation it suggests of expertise as a collective and multifaceted phenomenon. We conceptualized the organization as a network of activity systems suggesting that the core organizing processes within such networks are "perspective making," "perspective taking," and "perspective shaping." Applied to the analysis of HighTech the approach suggested that management's attempts to retain strong central control were misplaced. Applied to the analysis of the SDGs it illuminated ways in which such ad hoc groups could organize themselves more effectively, and it highlighted also the importance of broader cultural and procedural changes.

Earlier we developed Table 6.1 to summarize the distinctive aspects of Engeström's (1987) presentation of activity theory for the analysis of practices. In this Table we highlighted the questions activity theory addresses ("What are people doing?" "How are they doing it and who with?" and "What is the nature of collective learning?") and featured key elements of the orientation. Engeström's approach suggests that three factors are central to the emergence of new activities. These are:

(i) people's understanding of the multifaceted nature of their (collective) expertise;

(ii) their appreciations of the developmental trajectory of their activity system;

(iii) their responses to "disturbances" produced within activity systems.

In Table 6.2 we have developed this account to feature an additional issue that is crucial to the analysis of organizations. This is the question: "How do people relate to others schooled in different communities of activity?" In place of an image of organizations steered by planning and hierarchy, our analysis of self-regulating processes in activity networks provides a way of analyzing organizations as distributed, emergent, and decentered activity networks. Generalizing from the Strategy Development Groups study, Table 6.2 incorporates the idea that three further factors are central to the ongoing self-development of activity networks. These are:

(iv) members' appreciations of the complexity of the overall activity network to which they contribute; in particular, their acknowledgement that the network must achieve complex, perhaps competing, priorities;

(v) their understanding of the adequacy of existing approaches to perspective making, perspective taking, and perspective shaping for the self-regulation of the network;

(vi) the availability of forums for discussion and experimentation that contain the anxieties that can arise when activities, identities, and infrastructures are shifting.

Table 6.2

Activity Theory and Organizational Analysis

An activity-theory approach to organizational research:	(a) What are people doing?	(b) How are they doing it and with whom?	Issues problematized by activity theory	
			(c) How do they relate to others schooled in different communities of activity?	(d) What is the nature of collective learning?
(i) Study the detail of practices.	The "object of activity" is fundamental to activity-theoretical analysis of practices. Objects of activity are partly given and partly anticipated. They are intimately related to the mediating factors through which they are constructed.	Activities are culturally situated and linguistically and technologically mediated. They are enacted in communities and involve a division of labor. Such factors and their interactions are described as "activity systems." This is the unit of analysis used in activity-theoretical research.	A degree of internal differentiation is inevitable in activity systems of any size, but complex organizations can easily become segmented and fragmented. Rather than analyzing organizations as single activity systems, therefore, it is more satisfactory to analyze them as networks of overlapping activity systems.	Activity systems are tension-producing systems. Disturbances within and between activity systems provide the driving force for their development.

(ii) Study practices in the context of their historical development.	Actions are discrete, have clear beginnings and endings, and exist over short time-scales. They are goal oriented. "Activities," on the other hand, are complex patterns of practice that endure over long time periods. Activities suggest goals and provide motives.	Activities develop over time. As a general trend, activity systems in work organizations appear to be becoming more complex and inter-dependent, objects of activity more abstract and emergent, and communities of activity more transient.	Expertise in complex activity networks is (necessarily) distributed, emergent, and "decentered," that is, the course of its development is not, and cannot be, only controlled from the center. Organizing processes in activity networks can be described as "perspective making," "perspective taking" and "perspective shaping."	When activity systems become more improvised and fluid, established priorities and power relationships are loosened and may be reformed. Shifting boundaries in activity networks may produce anxiety and defensiveness.

(e) How can people shape the contexts that shape their practices?

(iii) Support the development of the practices that are being studied.	Research can help people become aware of the object of their activity and of the process of object construction.	Research can explore the origins and dynamics of particular activity systems and networks and the trajectory of their development.	Research can explore the varied nature of activities (and the priorities they imply) in an activity network and the dynamics of perspective making, taking, and shaping.	Research can support a review of current patterns of activity and the infrastructures that support them, and a search for alternatives.

Much scope exists for the further testing, development, and application of these ideas. For example, through its concern with how people achieve their knowing and doing, activity theory avoids divorcing institutional frameworks for action from the detail of everyday life. Analysis of perspective making, taking, and shaping processes therefore need not be confined to the detail of group dynamics (as was the largely the case with our analysis of the Strategy Development Groups). Such analysis could be (indeed, should be) extended to explore also the relevance of broader sociostructural and cultural factors to the understanding of collective work practices, patterns of authority and influence between communities, and participants' assumptions about past achievements and future possibilities.

Note too that our representation of these core organizing processes (see Figure 6.1), would also benefit from further development. Figure 6.1 can be understood as implying that communities of activity within organizations have relatively clear and separate identities. Certainly communities of activity in organizations may have clear identities; demarcations in HighTech had, in the past, been very clearly drawn, for example. But increasingly both in this organization and elsewhere, boundaries between communities of activity are being destabilized and communities are becoming more temporary, fluid, and overlapping. In addition, many traditional occupations, professional associations, and patterns of training and socialization are also undergoing considerable change at the present time. In such circumstances it is important to recognize that not only are activities and activity systems are becoming larger and interpenetrated, but that also the communities through which activities are enacted are themselves changing. Such complex developments are not well understood. Further work is needed to explore the processes through which temporary and fluid communities negotiate, develop, and enact their activities

Finally, further work is needed to explore the utility of the package of ideas introduced here as a guide to intervention and organization development. Given the emphasis activity theory places on emergent objects and relationships, it is likely to be of most interest in the management of complex, unfolding events. The uncertainties associated with developments in contemporary economies, such as those summarized at the start of this chapter and illustrated in more detail by events at HighTech, are a case in point. Changes in familiar systems of knowing and doing are not easy to understand or manage and they may be experienced as threatening. Activity theory offers a rich vein of ideas to understand such events and to inspire new approaches to intervention.

Notes

1. The research reported here was funded by the UK's Economic and Social Research Council as part of their "Innovation Research Programme": Research Grant No. L122251027.

2. The basics of activity theory were provided by Vygotsky in the 1920s and 1930s. Vygotsky was influenced by Marx's suggestion that human nature is not fixed. Marx attributed a key role to productive activity, of course, emphasizing that people need to interact with nature in order to survive and that to do this they collaborate in the conversion of raw materials. At different times and in different societies people inherit different resources and opportunities and, because of this, the nature of human activity expresses itself in different ways. Vygotsky extended the insight. Psychological processes can only be understood through the culturally provided factors through which they are mediated, he pointed out. While Marx emphasized that people alter their environments by the use of tools, Vygotsky developed the insight that people alter themselves through the use of language (Vygotsky 1978, 1986).

Leont'ev was to develop the suggestion that human consciousness is socially created by introducing a level of analysis that, at the time he was working, had not previously featured in either psychological or sociological analysis. While the notion of action gives coherence to related operations, Leont'ev's notion of "activity" provided a way of featuring the coherency of related actions. The conceptions people have of their activities are probably best understood as sociocultural interpretations; such interpretations are developed through involvement and are subsequently imposed on particular circumstances by the participants themselves. Activities imply the motives and goals of participants, Leont'ev suggested. Activities develop through time, stimulated by the tensions that inevitably develop within and between them. Activities provide the link between the individual and society; indeed, Leont'ev argued, societies can be conceptualized as an interlacing pattern of different activities Leont'ev 1978, 1981).

These ideas were to influence critical psychologists in Germany, who studied the relationship between identity and social position (Tolman and Maiers 1991), educationalists in the United States (e.g., Scribner 1986; Brown et al. 1989; Lave and Wenger 1991) whose ideas were to have some influence on organization studies (e.g., Orr 1990; Brown and Duguid 1991; Spender 1988). The analysis presented in this chapter owes more to the work of the Finnish scholar Engeström (1987, 1990), whose writings explicitly sought to modify and develop Leont'ev's version of the Vygotsky tradition. A model of activity systems based on Engeström's general account (see Engeström [1987] discussed by Blackler [1995] and Blackler, Crump, and McDonald [1999a]) is as shown in Figure A.

3. The notion of activity identifies classes of actions in terms of the contexts that people consider appropriate for them. It has similarities with Goffman's (1974) notion of "frames," Schank and Abelson's (1977) notion of "scripts," Strauss's (1978) "social worlds," and Bordieu's (1977) "habitus." Unlike these approaches, however, activity theory features the intimate relations between the factors that mediate activity and the activities themselves.

Activity theory shares the concern of certain recent developments in social theory debated by Knorr-Cetina (1981) to avoid treating individuals as if they can be understood in isolation from their contexts, and the contexts as if they exist in isolation

Figure A

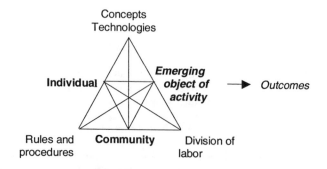

Concepts
Technologies

Individual

Emerging
object of
activity

Outcomes

Rules and   **Community**   Division of
procedures   labor

from individuals. Like Weick's (1977) enactment theory, Giddens's (1984) structuration theory, and Unger's (1987) notion of formative contexts, activity theory interprets social structures as both the production of human activities and the context for them.

Social learning theory (e.g., Wenger 1998) places a heavy emphasis on the importance of identity and community. In contrast, activity theory gives primacy to the outward-looking, transformational nature of collaborative endeavors. Activity theory suggests that collective developments occur when, through their actions, people reinterpret their environment, rebuild their activities, and reconceive of themselves. In this respect the approach has similarities with some psychodynamic approaches to organization (e.g., Hirschhorn 1993), which treat the culture of an organization as something that develops from its primary task. Similarly, activity theory suggests that studies of discourse and influence and studies of values and control should be located within a broader analysis of pragmatic activity (Engeström 1998, 1999).

Like actor network theory, activity theory features the heterogeneous network of factors associated with knowledge, power, and ordering processes. However, the emphasis it places on opportunities for innovation and the development of collective competencies contrasts with the emphasis in most actor network studies on fixed patterns of power and domination (see Miettinen 1999).

Unlike conventional theories of knowledge, which analyze knowledge as something given that novices must internalize, activity theory features the creative aspect of learning and its dependence upon a culturally provided infrastructure (Blackler 1995). Unlike theories that envisage collective learning to be a tension-free process (e.g., Nonaka and Takeuchi 1995) activity theory predicts that periods of tension and unease are a key element in the cycle of collective development (Engeström 1987).

Like action research, activity theory features the value of interactive research methods. Unlike action research, however, the approach is built on an explicit theory of collective development.

4. Suggestions for the organization of Strategy Development Teams are illustrated in Figure B.

References

Blackler, F. (1995). "Knowledge, Knowledge Work and Organization: An Overview and Interpretation." *Organization Studies* 6: 1021–1046.

Blackler, F.; Crump, N., and McDonald, S. (1999a). "Managing Experts and Competing Through Collaboration: An Activity Theoretical Analysis." *Organization: The Interdisciplinary Journal of Organization, Theory and Society* 6(1): 5–31.

Figure B

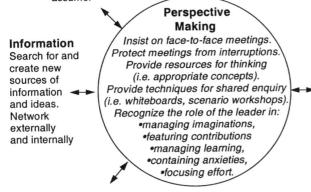

Perspective Shaping
Debate the general sense of direction the group should assume.

Perspective Making
Insist on face-to-face meetings. Protect meetings from interruptions. Provide resources for thinking (i.e. appropriate concepts). Provide techniques for shared enquiry (i.e. whiteboards, scenario workshops). Recognize the role of the leader in:
•managing imaginations,
•featuring contributions
•managing learning,
•containing anxieties,
•focusing effort.

Information
Search for and create new sources of information and ideas. Network externally and internally

Outcomes
Review the full range of objectives the group should address. Acknowledge the tensions between different objectives. Review group process

Perspective Taking
Management to resource the development of new patterns of influence in the Company and to support a culture of information exchange. Strategy Groups to share ideas and experiences

————. (1999b). "Organizational Learning and Organizational Forgetting: Lessons from a High-Technology Organization." In J. Burgoyne, M. Easterby-Smith, and L. Araujo, eds. *Organizational Learning: Theory and Practice.* London: Sage.

Boland, R.J., and Tenkasi, R. (1995). "Perspective Making and Perspective Taking in Communities of Knowing." *Organization Science* 6(4): 350–372.

Bourdieu, P. (1977). *Outline of a Theory of Practice.* Cambridge: Cambridge University Press

Brown, J. S., and Duguid, P. (1991). "Organizational Learning and Communities-of-Practice: Toward a Unified View of Working, Learning, and Innovation." *Organization Science* 2(1): 40–56.

Brown , J.S.; Collins, A.; and Duguid, P. (1989). "Situated Cognition and the Culture of Learning." *Educational Researcher* (January–February): 32–42.

Bucciarelli, L.L. (1996). *Designing Engineers.* Cambridge, MA: MIT Press.

Dougherty, D. (1992). "Interpretive Barriers to Successful Product Innovation in Firms." *Organization Science* 3(2): 179–202.

Engeström, Y. (1987). *Learning by Expanding: An Activity Theoretical Approach to Developmental Research.* Helsinki: Orienta-Konsultit.

————. (1990). *Learning, Working and Imagining: Twelve Studies in Activity Theory.* Helsinki: Orienta-Konsultit.

————. (1998). "Three Theses on Teams." Paper presented to the Critical Management Studies Workshop at the Annual Meeting of the Academy of Management, San Diego, August.

————. (1999). "Communication, Discourse and Activity." *The Communication Review.*

Giddens, A. (1984). *The Constitution of Society: Outline of a Theory of Structuration.* Cambridge: Polity Press.

Goffman, I. (1974). *Frame Analysis: An Essay on the Organization of Experience.* New York: Harper and Row.

Hirschhorn, L. (1993). *The Workplace Within.* Cambridge MA: MIT Press.

Knorr-Cetina, K. (1981). "Introduction: The Micro-sociological Challenge of Macro-sociology: Towards a Reconstruction of Social Theory and Methodology." In K. Knorr-Cetina and A. Cicourel, eds., *Advances in Social Theory and Methodology: Towards an Integration of Micro- and Macro-Sociologies.* London: Routledge and Kegan Paul.

Lave, J., and Wenger, E. (1991). *Situated Learning: Legitimate Peripheral Participation.* Cambridge: Cambridge University Press.

Leont'ev, A.N. (1978). *Activity, Consciousness and Personality.* Englewood Cliffs: Prentice-Hall.

———. (1981). *Problems of the Development of the Mind.* Moscow: Progress Publishers.

Miettinen, R. (1999). "The Riddle of Things: Activity Theory and Actor-Network Theory as Approaches to Studying Innovations." *Mind, Culture and Activity.*

Nonaka, I., and Takeuchi, H. (1995). *The Knowledge Creating Company.* Oxford: University of Oxford Press.

Orr, J. (1990). "Sharing Knowledge and Celebrating Identity: War Stories and Community Memory in a Service Culture." In D. Middleton and D. Edwards, eds., *Collective Remembering,* 169–189. London: Sage.

Ortner, S. (1984). "Theory in Anthropology Since the 60s." *Comparative Studies in Society and History* 26(1): 126–166.

Schank, R., and Abelson, R. (1977). *Scripts, Plans, Goals and Understanding.* Hillsdale: Lawrence Erlbaum.

Scribner, S. (1986). "Thinking in Action: Some Characteristics of Practical Thought." In R. Sternberg and R. Wagner, eds., *Practical Intelligence: Nature, Origins and Competence in the Everday World.* Cambridge: Cambridge University Press.

Spender, J.C. (1988). "Pluralist Epistemology and the Knowledge-based Theory of the Firm." *Organization: The Interdisciplinary Journal of Organization, Theory and Society* 5(2): 233–256.

Strauss, A. (1978). "A Social World Perspective." *Studies in Symbolic Interaction* 1: 119–128.

Tolman, C., and Maiers, W. (1991). *Critical Psychology: Contributions to an Historical Science of the Subject.* Cambridge: Cambridge University Press.

Tsoukas, H. (1996). "The Firm as a Distributed Knowledge System: A Constructionist Approach." *Strategic Management Journal* 17: 11–25.

Unger, R. (1987). *False Necessity: Anti-necessitarian Social Theory in the Service of Radical Democracy.* Cambridge: Cambridge University Press.

Vygotsky, L. (1978). *Mind in Society.* Cambridge MA: Harvard University Press.

———. (1986). *Thought and Language.* Cambridge MA: MIT Press.

Weick, K.E. (1977). *The Social Psychology of Organizing.* Reading, MA: Addison Wesley.

Weick, K.E., and Roberts, K.H. (1993). "Collective Mind in Organizations-heedful Interrelating on Flight Decks." *Administrative Science Quarterly* 38(3): 357–381.

Wenger, E. (1998). *Communities of Practice: Learning, Meaning and Identity.* Cambridge: Cambridge University Press.

7

Spatial and Temporal Expansion of the Object as a Challenge for Reorganizing Work

Yrjö Engeström, Anne Puonti, and Laura Seppänen

Introduction: Objects in Expansion

In theories of postmodernity, the notion of *compression* of time and space has become widely accepted. As Harvey (1989: 240) put it, "space appears to shrink to a 'global village' of telecommunications" and "time horizons shorten to the point where the present is all there is." In his account of changes in work organizations, Sennett (1999: 22–27) continues the compression argument and declares that today's work settings operate on the principle of "no long term." According to Sennett (1999: 25), this "short-term capitalism" corrodes the character: "'No long term' means keep moving, don't commit yourself, and don't sacrifice."

While there is plenty of evidence for compression in our everyday experience, authors such as May and Thrift (2001) have good reason to warn for underdeveloped analyses behind claims that only see compression and shrinkage in our spatio-temporal worlds.

To some considerable extent, this under-development is a consequence of too heavy an emphasis being placed upon developments in transport and communication technologies and not enough upon developments elsewhere both in the field of technology (or what we prefer to call the domain of instruments and devices) as well as across a number of the other domains through which the experience of TimeSpace is rendered. When these more numerous developments are considered, and the connections between each traced, the picture is less of any simple acceleration in the pace of life or experience of spatial "collapse" than of a far more complex restructuring in the nature and experience of time and space. . . . With these changes space is seen to both expand and contract, time horizons to both foreshorten but also to extend, time itself to both speed up but also slow down and even to move in different directions. (May and Thrift 2001: 10)

We agree with May and Thrift that transport and communication technologies are an insufficient basis for analysis. Beyond that, we maintain that technologies and instruments in general, separated from the objects upon which they are used, are an equally insufficient basis. We argue that a new, more interesting insight into the developmental dynamics of timing and spacing in work organizations can indeed be gained if we shift the focus of analysis onto the *objects* of work. We suggest that the ongoing historical transformations in objects of work are best conceptualized as *expansion* rather than compression.

In cultural-historical activity theory, human conduct is seen as object-oriented activity. Leont'ev (1978: 52) pointed out that the concept of object is already implicitly contained in the very concept of activity; there is no such thing as objectless activity. An object is both something given and something projected, anticipated and constructed. An entity of the outside world becomes an object of activity as it meets a human need. This meeting is "an extraordinary act" (Leont'ev 1978: 54). In this constructed, need-related capacity, the object gains motivating force that gives shape and direction to activity. The object determines the horizon of possible actions.

The subject constructs the object, "singles out those properties that prove to be essential for developing social practice," using mediating cognitive artifacts that function as "forms of expression of cognitive norms, standards, and object-hypothesis existing outside the given individual" (Lektorsky 1984: 137). In other words, objects are constructed and invested with meaning by means of cultural tools. Such mediating tools operate not separately but in complex constellations we call *instrumentalities*. Emerging new objects call for and generate new instrumentalities.

Our activity-theoretical concept of object is related to Knorr-Cetina's recent work (1997, 1999; see also Latour 1996; Rheinberger 1997; and Daston 2000 for related arguments). Knorr-Cetina (1997: 9) makes the bold claim that "objects serve as centering and integrating devices for regimes of expertise that transcend an expert's lifetime and create the collective conventions and the moral order communitarians are concerned about." Her contribution is a call for serious attention to objects of work as sources of new kinds of motivation and sociality. The problem in her work is its relatively weak historicity. Knorr-Cetina distinguishes between "technical objects" and "epistemic objects." The latter are typical to scientific work and expert-like work in general. They are openended "processes and projections rather than definitive things" (Knorr-Cetina 1997: 12), implying a radical expansion of the temporal and spatial dimensions of work. But the emerging characteristics of such epistemic objects of expert work are left very vague.

Stepping into the realm of management and organization studies is helpful in opening up the historical and practical landscape of objects of work. Victor and Boynton (1998) suggest that we can examine the evolution of work in capitalism as a succession of five major types: craft, mass production, process enhancement, mass customization, and co-configuration. The last one of the five, co-configuration, is particularly interesting from the point of view of the spatio-temporal expansion of the object.

> When a firm does co-configuration work, it creates a product that can learn and adapt, but it also builds an ongoing relationship between each customer–product pair and the company. Doing mass customization requires designing the product at least once for each customer. This design process requires the company to sense and respond to the individual customer's needs. But co-configuration work takes this relationship up one level—it brings the value of an intelligent and "adapting" product. The company then continues to work with this customer-product pair to make the product more responsive to each user. In this way, the customization work becomes continuous.
>
> . . .
>
> Unlike previous work, co-configuration never results in a "finished" product. Instead, a living, growing network develops between customer, product, and company. (Victor and Boynton 1998: 195)

A hallmark of co-configuration is "customer intelligence." To achieve it, a company will have to continuously configure its products and services in interaction with the customer. Victor and Boynton (1998: 197) name medical devices and computer software systems as two leading industries where co-configuration is being implemented. They emphasize that co-configuration is more than just smart, adaptive products.

> The application of configuration intelligence to the product creates a system of customer, product or service, and company. The complex of interactions among all three, as a product or service adapts and responds to the changing needs of the customer, is the underlying, dynamic source of value. . . . With the organization of work under co-configuration, the customer becomes, in a sense, a real partner with the producer. (Victor and Boynton 1998: 198–199)

Victor and Boynton focus on customer-intelligent products, such as sophisticated digital hearing aids, as examples of co-configuration. It is more difficult, but equally important, to determine what kinds of services and administrative products might be "customer-intelligent" and co-configurational.

Standardized services and administrative decisions delivered on the spot do not qualify. But what about trajectories of complex investigations of economic crimes produced collaboratively by the police, the tax officials, and the prosecutors? Or multiyear crop rotation trajectories for organic vegetable farms produced collaboratively by advisors and farmers? Or long-term care trajectories of chronically ill patients produced collaboratively by primary care health centers, hospitals, and patients?

These are relatively novel objects of work. The very notion of trajectory is an attempt to interweave the temporal and the socio-spatial, as it "refers to a course of action but also embraces the interaction of multiple actors and contingencies that may be unanticipated and not entirely manageable" (Strauss 1993: 53). We claim that compared to their predecessors, the objects we just listed are expanded both spatially and temporally. In the following three case studies, we trace the objects and their expansion in economic crime investigations, in organic vegetable farming, and in the medical care of chronic patients with multiple illnesses.

The creation, mastery, and maintenance of such expanded objects is a demanding and contradictory challenge to the parties involved. Expanded objects require and generate, and are constructed by means of, novel mediating instrumentalities. In each of the three cases, we will examine the new instrumentalities as they emerge in interaction with the new objects. In each case, we will discuss only selected examples of the new instruments; an examination of their full variety and complexity is not possible within the constraints of this chapter.

Case 1: Expansion of the Object in the Investigation of Economic Crimes

A "traditional" crime, such as robbery or homicide, always takes place at a certain time and place. Economic crime, or white-collar crime as it is often called, is much more complex: it is often committed over an extended period of time, and nobody can point to an exact time at which the boundary between legal and illegal was crossed. Nor can an exact place for a white-collar crime be appointed: the perpetrator may have a permanent residence in one location, the company domicile may reside somewhere else, and company property may even be located in other countries (see, e.g., Geis, Meier, and Salinger 1995). In addition to the difficulties in placing this kind of a crime in time and place, it often requires a lot of work to show that there is a crime in the first place—economic crime often toys with the thin line between legal and illegal.

The investigation of economic crimes has initially followed the investiga-

Figure 7.1   **A Sequential Model of White-Collar Crime Investigation**

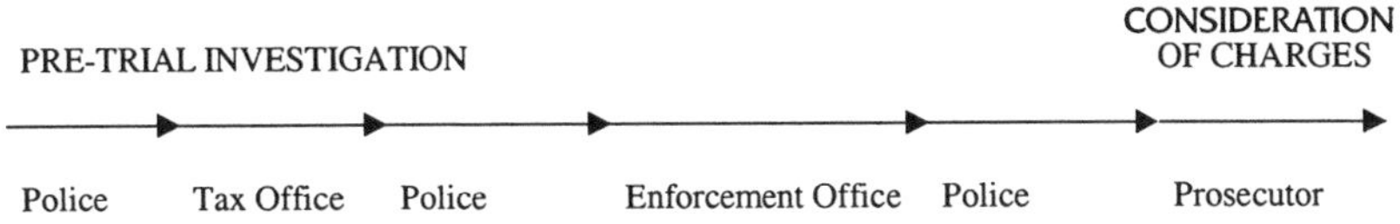

PRE-TRIAL INVESTIGATION

CONSIDERATION
OF CHARGES

Police   Tax Office   Police   Enforcement Office   Police   Prosecutor

Source: Puonti, in press.

tion lines of more traditional types of crime—local police departments investigating and asking for assistance from other police departments and agencies when needed. The traditional model of investigation may be compared to a track relay: each agency takes care of its own part of the investigation, often sequentially and passing the baton through documents without personal contact. A simplified example of a tax-crime investigation according to the traditional mass-crime model is presented in Figure 7.1.

However, it is practically impossible to investigate temporally and spatially distributed economic crimes without collaboration between agencies. Investigation may be started at one police department and then moved to another. As the crime does not obey the boundaries between different authorities either, collaboration is needed also between the police, the tax authority, the enforcement authority, and the prosecutor as the most regular partners. They have to find new ways of collaboration to fight this type of crime efficiently. A parallel model of collaboration between Finnish authorities has been promoted in efforts to control white-collar crime. In Figure 7.2, the horizontal arrows represent movement in time and the vertical arrows represent interaction between the participants.

In the ideal model, investigation starts with a stakeholder meeting in which the goals, resources, timetables, and actions are preliminarily negotiated and agreed upon. The investigation often culminates in a collaborative house search, which is the crucial tool for getting information about the criminal activity.

The parallel model of investigation increases interaction between organizations but it is also changing radically the dimensions of time and space for the participants. These dimensions have to be understood in a new way: the police officers, tax inspectors, enforcement officers, and prosecutor need to form a collaborative community that is involved in the case for the whole period of pre-trial investigation. No longer will the investigation involve each agency separately and sequentially in its turn.

A key challenge in economic crime investigation is the complexity of the crimes themselves and the multiple aspects one crime may include. No one has been able to provide a generally valid definition of white-collar crime,

Figure 7.2 **Parallel Model of White-Collar Crime Investigation**

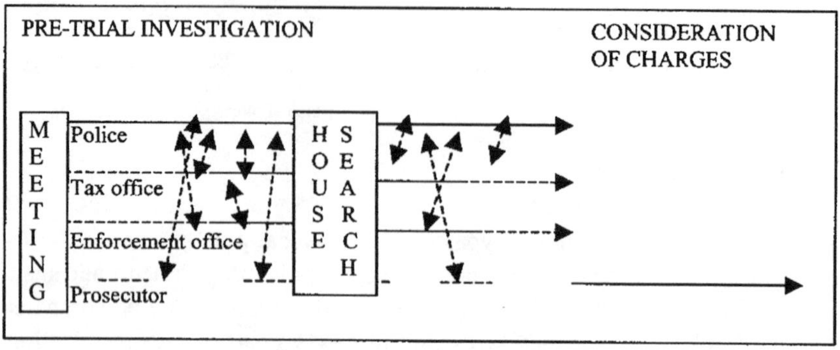

and even if one could be reached, crime itself changes all the time (see, e.g., Friedrichs 1996: 5–7; Laitinen and Virta 1998: 11–14). The authorities should also stress different sides of the crime and its investigation, and they have to negotiate the priorities. Is it more important to recover the criminally gained profit or to get the perpetrator to prosecution? Is it more important to stop the criminal activity or to ensure that the creditors will get their money back? The emphasis in economic crime investigation has lately been on the restoration of criminally gained profit to stop criminal activity more efficiently. It has been claimed that the restoration of criminally gained profit could form a common goal for the authorities. In practice, the crime and its investigation must be constructed separately in each investigation process, and the goals have to be negotiated among the participants.

Temporal Expansion of the Object in Economic Crime Investigation

A specific feature of economic crime is its temporal fragmentation. It is difficult to say when a crime was committed; in the reports of offense the time is often marked according to accounting periods such as "between 5/1/1996 and 4/30/1997 and between 5/1/1997 and 4/30/1998." The crime itself may consist of short-term actions spread over a long period of time, often several years. Economic crime is also carefully planned: for example, the operating periods of criminal companies are so limited that the rigidly reacting authorities would not be able to notice the crime until the company has been terminated and the operations and property moved on to the next company.

The investigation of a traditional crime normally starts after the crime is committed and a report of an offense is made. The new challenge that has come along with economic crimes is to find real-time evidence of an ongoing crime. This is necessary in order to retrive the criminally gained property from the perpetrator and thereby stop the criminal activity permanently. This often leads to a long period of intelligence and information gathering before the active pre-trial investigation.

The object of economic crime investigation is not a standardized item but a complex entity that is both spatially and temporally different from the object of traditional crime investigation. The investigators of so-called mass crimes are facing a situation where their main problem is the vast number of cases under investigation. They often have a workload that seems quantitatively impossible to handle.

Excerpt 1

There [in the previous work context of mass crime investigation] the volume was totally different. The number of cases may well have varied between 50 and 150. . . . You'd have 150 cases and you'd have to remember and know what and who are there [in the case], whom to interrogate, and you even should investigate a little. . . . You couldn't just watch around for a couple of days because new stuff [cases] kept fluxing in. . . . There's the problem that the rhythm was so tough, you had to go fast all the time, clients kept coming in and phones kept ringing, and new cases coming in, it's exhausting.

In economic crime investigation, the number of cases per investigator is radically smaller but the quality of the cases requires a new kind of case management. The work of one of the economic crime investigators we followed was blocked because all four cases he had under investigation were awaiting for the output of another stakeholder in the case (prosecutor, tax inspector, accounting specialist). One of the cases was particularly frustrating for him because the tax inspectors had promised to give a preliminary tax inspection report in a couple of weeks and it was remarkably delayed. The tax inspectors were tied up with other work commitments and the start of the inspection was postponed several times. Each day, the police officer was expecting the reports to be finished. This waiting was nothing new to him. When asked about the future, he said laconically: "The same pattern again. We'll be waiting for the tax authority again."

In this case, the delay of the preliminary tax-inspection reports from the originally promised "a couple of weeks" to four months triggered a series of postponements. When the preliminary reports were finished, the police, the enforcement officer, and the tax inspectors had so many commitments due to other cases, holidays, and training courses that a mutually acceptable time for a house search could not be found in the spring, and it was postponed until the fall. In the fall, another complex crime case engaged the police officers, the tax inspectors, and the enforcement officers at the unit to the extent that, finally, the house search was conducted more than a year later than originally planned.

The new kind of object, temporally fragmented and extended, forces the authorities to try to synchronize their activities. However, this is not easy because the object is not a standard one but different in each investigation. Synchronization problems often emerge in economic crime investigation as the rhythms of different participants need to be merged into one investigation trajectory. Successful synchronization requires an increase in the negotiations across organizations—an expansion in the socio-spatial dimension.

Socio-Spatial Expansion of the Object in Economic Crime Investigation

The socio-spatial expansion of the object in economic crime investigation means that any participating actor needs to see the crime not as an entity in and of itself but as *an entity continuously constructed by the multiple investigating agencies.* The fact that the agencies participating in collaborative investigation processes are normally located physically far from each other does not facilitate this shift. The authorities have tried to resolve this problem and, at the same time, span the organizational boundaries by placing tax inspectors and enforcement officers as liaisons at police departments. It is expected that sharing a place will create a space for interaction that facilitates collaboration and makes it easier to find mutually accepted ways of working and synchrony between organizations.

In one of the cases we followed, the different orientations of the police and the tax office clashed despite the fact that a tax inspector (T1) was permanently located at the police department (Puonti 2003). In the starting phase of an investigation, the police emphasized the essential elements of the crime and finding of the evidence; the tax authorities emphasized the debiting of taxes. The police also seemed to emphasize the stake of the actual perpetrator, the actual owner of the investigated companies, and address the criminal liability toward him. They did not seem to be interested in the individual employees as much as the tax inspectors, who wanted to get the unpaid taxes from individual workers as well.

In this case, interestingly, it could be seen how the tax inspector also acted as a boundary spanner between the two authorities, attempting to facilitate collaboration between them. In the meetings, he supported both the police and the tax inspectors with his comments: he seemed to jump over the organizational boundary, back and forth if necessary. In the following example the role of the tax inspector (T1) as a boundary spanner in a meeting between police officers (P) and tax inspectors (T) stands out. During the meeting, the police explained how ideal a situation it would be if the tax authority were able to make a report of an offense to empower the pre-trial investigation. The tax inspectors were skeptical and stressed the high threshold for making an offense report. Yet, in the following excerpt, which occurred a few minutes later, the tax inspector working at the police department (T1) anticipated erroneously the statement of another tax inspector (T2).

Excerpt 2

P1   So, based on the current knowledge, if you already can suspect . . .

P   Yes that would be it.

P1   . . . something about the present [companies], that would be the best situation, that's what we'd like to have an estimation about.

T2   Preferably, preferably we'd like to have such information about the new companies so that we can immediately . . .

T1   Make a report of an offense, yes, report of an offense.

T2   . . . act on them. If we start to investigate the tails [old companies], well then, the further [back] we go, the harder it is to inspect [new] activities that are shifted elsewhere.

Here T1 seemed to try to support T2, but anticipated his thoughts erroneously. The anticipatory comment turned out to be an utterance that supported the police, not the tax inspector.

Often the attempts of boundary spanners remain individual, isolated attempts. It is difficult to actually span the boundary without tools that are more effective than mere speech. The obscurity and complexity of economic crime may require exceptionally efficient tools: common discursive tools such as those used in the meeting described above may work in other situations, but in this case they led to the formation of a splintered object of work. The police and the tax inspectors are in fact "the makers" of the crime during the investigation process. In a way, they become integral parts of the object they construct. To grasp this, they need a repertoire of self-reflective and dialogical instruments.

Toward a New Instrumentality of Economic Crime Investigation

When the object of work, the crime itself, is obscure and messy, it is often necessary to construct a representation of the object that one can concretely point to. The investigation process is also embodied in a vast influx of information, mainly paperwork. Compressing information in an easily conceivable form is a means of managing the information. One commonly used tool among the investigators is to turn the information into graphic form.

A graphic depiction used in white-collar crime investigation (Figure 7.3) translates thinking into a tangible artifact, a map, that is basically a manifestation of the socio-spatial relations within the object of work. Such a map serves to enhance communication and guide it toward relevant relations instead of irrelevant details.

Graphic depictions such as Figure 7.3 are normally drafted by an assistant and distributed to all participants. In this respect, they are different from many other kinds of models that are jointly constructed by the investigators or researchers themselves (Lynch 1985). However, their construction and use are not standardized.

A graphic depiction was used in two out of the three cases we followed. In the first case, the main investigator told the interviewer that the case was so simple that no depictions were needed. In the second case, a depiction was produced by the tax office. Despite this, it was criticized by the tax inspectors for being unfinished and sketchy. It had practically no relevance in the investigation process. It was distributed to the participants but no shared use was observed.

In the third case, several types and versions of graphic representations were used to depict the case, the most important ones being charts showing the flow of money between companies and a time line of the life span of the numerous companies under investigation. These were included in the house search plan that was distributed to all participants and used in a variety of ways by them. In the interviews made after the house search, some stated that these graphic figures had been very important in finding out what the case was about, while others said that they already knew everything that was in them and that they did not need those depictions anymore.

The parallel model of economic crime investigation (recall Figure 7.2 above) is also a shift toward a project-like model of work. Planning the investigation is often a long, time-consuming phase that is not materialized in a clear form. The police officers we interviewed talked a lot about an investigation plan, but none of them was able to show one on paper. When asked about the investigation plan, some of the investigators showed us a plan ("notes" or "coordinates") made for the house search. Others told us that the plan was in their head, not on paper. No shared investigation plan was documented in the three cases followed. However, in all three cases, a partial plan (a house search plan) was made and distributed to all participating before the house search.

What makes planning in white-collar crime investigation difficult is that the crime is typically obscure, information is hard to gain, and new information may change the plans suddenly several times during the investigation. Thus, the plan should be flexible and enable quick changes.

Figure 7.3 A 3-sized Graphic Depiction of a Network of Companies Suspected of White-Collar Crime

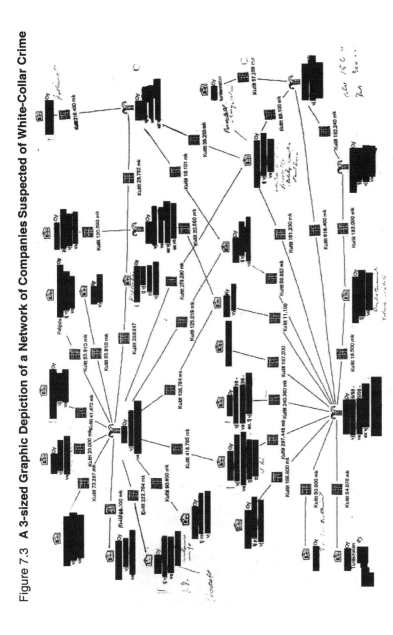

Note: The figure illustrates the flow of money between the companies under suspicion. It was used in an actual economic crime case (names are blackened by the researcher for confidentiality).

The need for a more encompassing investigation plan and documentation of the decisions made was recognized in one of the cases followed. There was a misunderstanding between the tax inspectors and the police officers about the timing of the specifications to the tax inspection report. This frustrated the police. After acknowledging the different views of the police and the tax inspectors concerning the tax-inspection report, the police officer in charge formulated the task as follows.

Excerpt 3

[I]n the future, in the projects I lead, we'll keep a record of all the meetings between the authorities that are held in connection with an actual case, and all the participants will get a copy. That's how we'll make sure that everybody involved in the project knows what each and every person is committed to.

Finally, members of the unit designed a whole new tool, a Project Plan. The Project Plan (Table 7.1) is a document that includes information on the general background of the case, goals, schedules, methods, division of labor, resources and risk analysis, and how the exchange of information is to be handled between the participants, the clients, and the media. One purpose of the plan was to facilitate collaboration between the authorities. Subsequently, the Project Plan was tested in real cases.

The Project Plan is a tool designed and used by practitioners in order to make visible and manage the temporal movement of the object. The project plan and the map of the object (such as that shown in Figure 7.3) are together a rudimentary new instrumentality for mastering the expanded object of economic crime investigation. What is interesting in this case is that both of these tools were constructed from the bottom up by practitioners involved in specific cases. In this case, the new representational tools were not so much drivers of change and groundbreakers for a new object. They were local adaptations to an object that had already expanded beyond the customary skills, tools, and interaction patterns of the practitioners.

Case 2: Mastering Crop Rotation in Organic Vegetable Farming

Environmental issues have increased public concern and support for alternative and sustainable agriculture, among which organic farming is an established and growing sector. The market expansion also favors organic agriculture in Europe and worldwide. However, learning organic farming is not easy. Many of the natural processes farmers are facing take longer to

Table 7.1

Project Plan Template Designed by a Police Unit

General information
Background of the case

Planning
Primary goals (e.g., business prohibition, getting the cases revealed during the investigation to be investigated, etc.)

Coordination
Schedule (starting the operations, proceeding, etc.)

Methods (intelligence methods, coercive means, tax inspections, etc.)

Division of labor between authorities/resources available (main investigators, inspectors, enforcement, officers in charge, who is doing what, who is involved in each phase, etc.)

Risk analysis
What can go wrong, how to avoid failures (taking the changing operational environment into account, failure of coordination, reaching people, making backups)

Flow of information
Exchange of information between authorities (contact persons, reachability)

Contacts between authorities and suspects

Contacts to the media (officer in charge responsible for the release of information, but communications are negotiated in order to gain best possible effect and right timing)

Feedback occasion (trying to learn collaboratively by reflecting on the experiences at the time of finishing the case)

Note: Translated into English by the authors.

deal with than the one-year production cycle, which is important in terms of marketing and economics. Organic nutrient mineralization, plant diseases, soil structure, and perennial weeds are examples of these natural processes. In organic farming, where synthetic pesticides and industrialized fertilizers are not used, a long-term time perspective is needed for production management. The concept of sustainability, often present in actual debates on the use of natural resources, implicitly contains the time dimension.

The object of an activity is historically formed and situationally reconstructed. To understand the changing object of organic vegetable farming, two historical dimensions are helpful, namely (1) "entrepreneurship and customer-orientedness," and (2) "sustainability in resource use" (Seppänen 2000). With the help of these two dimensions, four types of objects in organic farming may be identified (Figure 7.4).

Figure 7.4 **Four Types of Object Construction in Organic Vegetable Farming**

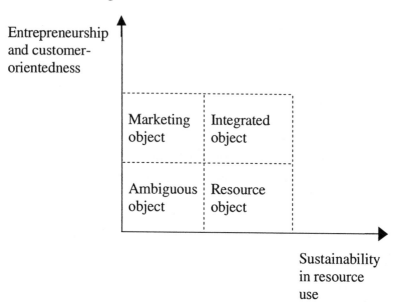

Entrepreneurship
and customer-
orientedness

Marketing object	Integrated object
Ambiguous object	Resource object

Sustainability
in resource
use

1. The ambiguous object is represented by farmers oriented neither toward sustainable use of natural resources nor toward customers. The time dimension in their planning is short, consisting mainly of the one-year productional cycle.

2. The resource object is represented by farmers mainly concerned about the maintenance and improvement of natural resources, such as soil fertility. Crop rotation is considered as an essential element in this. A prolonged time perspective, important in planning and implementing crop rotation, corresponds to the old peasant time conception that spans over generations. The linkage of production to the market does not play an important role.

3. The marketing object is represented by farmers who emphasize economics and entrepreneurship. Customers and products are of importance to these farmers. The time perspective is short. Ecological uses of resources, such as crop rotation, are seen as rules that limit marketing possibilities. In broad terms, the starting point of the Kola organic vegetable farm examined in the following account represents this type of object construction.

4. The integrated object is represented by farmers for whom the sustainability of resource use is not at odds with, but an integral part

of, marketing the products. Crop rotation brings continuity to production and quality to the products. The time perspective is long, allowing simultaneously quick actions in the short run. Here, the concept "organic" is of central importance, referring to the constitution of an organized whole between natural resources, farming, and consumers.

Temporal Expansion of the Object in Organic Farming

The temporal dimension in specialized agriculture varies according to type of production. Production of milk or beef, or perennial crops, proceeds in long cycles of various years, while chicken production and some forms of greenhouse growing have many production cycles per year. In arable farming, such as that of cereals or vegetables, a common productional unit is a growing season, starting in the spring with the sowing time and ending in the fall with harvesting and gaining the income from the yield. The necessary time perspective in organic farming was expressed by an advisor as follows.

Excerpt 4
An organic farmer must always look ahead over at least one year when choosing, for instance, crops for the next growing season, while in the conventional production, solutions can be made for one growing season only.

The key question for the farmer is: "What and how shall I (as a farmer) cultivate this year, so that I can succeed in farming in the coming years as well?" Part of the economic benefit that accumulates this year will be realized in later cash crop production years.

The following case data were collected at an organic vegetable farm, Kola, which earlier produced flowering annuals in greenhouses in a market- and business-oriented manner. While these features are also needed in the new activity of organic vegetable farming, the two forms of production differ in their temporal cyclicity and control of production. In the greenhouses, the Kolas had had three production seasons per year. The greenhouse plants were sown or planted and grown according to ready-made standardized procedures in the well-regulated conditions of the greenhouse. After selling the flowers, the greenhouse tables were cleaned, waiting empty until the next production season started again.

The new activity of the Kolas, organic vegetable farming, is different. The cultivation techniques are not standardized because it is a new type of production and because organic farming techniques vary according to the local conditions of field and farm. The farm fields do not wait empty; they have a complex life of their own that has to be anticipated. Therefore, organic vegetable production requires a time perspective covering many years and production seasons. And despite the anticipation, risks remain. Besides a long time perspective, improvisation and quick action are needed as well. The temporal expansion in organic farming is not only a linear extension of time: it also includes changes in short-term farming. The time dimension acquires a new quality.

The instrument that mediates the time dimension of organic farming is *crop rotation*. It is one of the major strategies in sustainable agriculture and organic farming (Altieri and Rosset 1996: 11). In planning the crop rotation, a sequence of crops is formed that would benefit the yields and sustain the farming system. A successful crop rotation plan makes all the elements of the farming activity fit together. In crop rotation, the time dimension is combined with the localization of the fields through the activity of the farmers.

On organic farms without animal husbandry, crop rotations often include *green manures*. This means that nitrogen-fixing legumes, such as clover of vetch, are sown together with grasses for fertilization and soil improvement purposes. Green manures do not produce income in the year they are sown. Staying in the temporal frame of one year, spending land and resources for green manures does not make sense. The use of green manures becomes understandable only in the longer perspective, where growing them is turned into financial benefit during the next or later years. The long-term challenge is therefore present in fields with green manures. Green manures change the annual time perspective as well. Organic vegetable farmers have to allocate their time, taking care not only of changing conditions of vegetable fields but also of those of green manures in their everyday practice.

Crop rotation also has an institutional and administrative meaning. Having at least a five-year crop rotation plan, accepted by experts, is a precondition for passing inspection as an organic producer. All organic farms are inspected once a year during the growing season.

Toward a New Instrumentality in Organic Farming

For five years, the Kola enterprise produced both greenhouse flowers and organic vegetables. Greenhouse production was finished in 1997. The trajectory under analysis in this chapter, in 1998, was the first production season to depend economically on only organic vegetable farming. The Kolas wanted to cultivate larger acreages with vegetables than before, and therefore they needed a new crop rotation. This was constructed together with an advisor and one of the researchers in March 1998.

In the planning of the crop rotation, the advisor first mapped the state of the art of the Kola farming activity by asking questions about the machinery,

Table 7.2

Crop Sequence as a Representation of a Crop Rotation

1. Green manure
2. Green manure
3. Vegetables
4. Root vegetables
5. Green manure
6. Vegetables

hired labor, yield levels, income, and so forth. Then a new crop sequence was designed. The advisor argued for the benefits of perennial green manures, while the farmers preferred annual green manures and a larger acreage with vegetables. The outcome, a six-year crop rotation, was a compromise between these views (Table 7.2).

After this, the field plots were divided into six 'rotational turns' that corresponded to a six-year rotation sequence. This was meant to balance out, in the course of the years, the ratio between vegetables and green manure. A map of the fields was an important spatial tool in doing this (Figure 7.5).

After the rotational turns were done, the advisor entered the field plots and their acreages into an Excel spreadsheet, specifically designed by advisors in organic farming. The crops of the coming season of 1998 were planned in rough outline. Taking into consideration the history of each field, the rotation sequence was placed rather mechanically on each turn. The outcome of the planning meeting was a table that included all the field plots and their crops for the following five years (Table 7.3).

Unfortunately, the growing season of 1998 was extremely bad, with too much rain. The Kolas had to work hard and got very tired. In the beginning of August during an organic inspection, the farmer walked through all the fields together with the inspector. Table 7.4, first column on the left, shows the route of the organic inspection. At the same time, it shows how the crop rotation, planned in March, was implemented in the fields.

To master the expanding object of organic farming, it is crucial that the farmers construct and conceptualize their crop rotation by crossing the borders of annual production seasons, either to the previous season or to the following year(s) (Seppänen and Koskimies 2002). We may call this "farming across the years." The inspection discussion is not particularly good for showing the situated improvisation aspect of the time dimension of everyday farming practice. But it shows quite well to what extent and how the time perspective that extends beyond one year is put into words and dealt with (Table 7.4). The speech across the years, present in the inspection discussion, is part of the instrumentality in expanding the object.

Figure 7.5   **Map of Kola Fields Used in Planning the Crop Rotation**

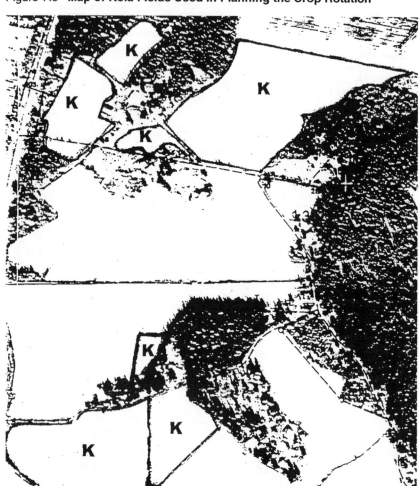

In Table 7.4, columns B to D show the numbers of turns of talk where farming across the years appears. Column A represents speech about that particular growing season. For our analysis, the shaded columns B and C are most important as they represent turns of talk that deal with the management of the fields.

Column B represents those parts of the data where the boundary between years was crossed, but what happened in the past or will happen in the future was not linked with the ongoing growing season. A very common topic in

Table 7.3

Outcome of the Planning Simplified

Rotation turns	1997	1998	1999	2000	2001	2002
1.	Perennial green manure	Vegetables	Root vegetables	Annual green manure	Vegetables	Perennial green manure
2.	Root vegetables	Annual green manure	Vegetables	Perennial green manure	Perennial green manure	Vegetables
3.	Perennial green manure	Perennial green manure	Vegetables	Root vegetables	Annual green manure	Vegetables
4.	Vegetables/ green manure	Vegetables	Perennial green manure	Perennial green manure	Vegetables	Root vegetables
5.	Vegetables/ green manure	Vegetables	Annual green manure	Vegetables	Perennial green manure	Perennial green manure
6.	Vegetables	Perennial green manure	Perennial green manure	Vegetables	Annual green manure	Vegetables

Note: Crop rotation for the next five years for the fields of the Kola farm (the rented fields are in white, the farmers' own fields in gray boxes).

Table 7.4

Turns of Talk in the Organic Inspection Discussion on the Kola Farm, 1998

| | Now | Speech across the years | | |
Place	A. Ongoing 1998	B. no link to "now"	C. With a link to "now"	D. Other than field management
1. Home		103		
2. On the way to the field	45		5	
Field 3: Carrot	174	11		1
Field 4: Carrot and red beet	99			
Field 5: Onion	103		30	
Field 6: Various	132			2
Field 7: Red clover and ryegrass	142	11	5	
Field 8: Berries	145	14	8	15
Field 9: Potato	171			
Field 10: Storage and packing hall	286			
11. On the way to hired fields	85	2		
Field 12: Potato and swede	66	9		
Field 13: Vetch and ryegrass	51	4	2	13
Field 14: Carrot	44	2		
Field 15: Leek and potato	66	4	2	
16. On the way to next field	90			
Field 17: Fallow	40		11	
Field 18: Red clover and timothy	35	11	9	
19. On the way home	217	3		9
20. Home	1,358	14	45	
Altogether 3,687 turns	3,525 turns 95.6%	85 turns 2.3%	72 turns 1.9%	85 turns 2.3%

this category was the preceding crop, either asked about by the inspector ("What was growing in this field last year?") or told about by the farmer. Often this was followed by the farmer's stating how the preceding crop grew or by a discussion of the fertilizing aspect of the crop.

Column C represents those pieces of data where the speech across years was indeed connected to the "now" situation of the growing season. Both the inspector and the farmer expressed these linkages, showing that farming across the years was actually being constructed, at least to some extent.

The nutrient questions especially were dealt with across the years. The nutrients were connected to plant growth and environmental administrative regulations. However, in other production issues, such as the weed couch grass, repeatedly addressed by the farmer, the annual boundaries were not crossed at all. It seems that the nutrients and their leaching were constructed as an important environmental and political question that rolled over other aspects of production, such as the weeds. Another topic across the years was the crop sequence (recall Table 7.2), which appeared both as a list, detached from the fields, and as a temporal narrative about specific fields. The need for a new Kola crop rotation plan made the Kolas contact an advisor from the local rural advisory center. Our data on the interactions between the farmers and the advisor clearly show that a crop rotation plan was not dictated either by the farmers or by the advisor. The new crop rotation plan was, most of all, the result of a common construction process between the farmers, an advisor, and the researcher.

After having checked the crop rotation plan, the advisor sent it back to the farmers and asked whether they wanted to change something in it. The Kolas did not want to change anything. So, in May 1998, the advisor sent the plan to the regional Rural Department office. All changes in crop rotation plans had to be submitted to Rural Departments within regional Employment and Economic Development Centers. The role of the Rural Department was to confirm all changes made to crop rotation plans (Heinonen and Kieksi 1998).

Organic farming, in 1998, was entitled to special aid within the Finnish agri-environmental scheme. Therefore, it was bound to other regulations, especially to the agri-environmental scheme and to other subsidy programs as well. By the end of May, farmers were to fulfill an annual production plan in order to obtain either EU-level or national subsidies. The annual production plan included what crops were cultivated on each field plot, and what type of subsidy was applied for with regard to each field. According to the inspector of the Kola farm, production plans were to match to the long-term rotation plans. This was important from the point of view of subsidies. In May 1998, the Kolas made their annual production plan in accordance to the new crop rotation.

During the Kola inspection, the inspection documents were filled at home. First, the inspector wrote on document forms the actual crops in 1998 of each field plot. Later, she filled in the question on the inspection documents about the crop rotation (Table 7.2).

In September 1998, the inspection documents were presented at a meeting of an 'organic board.' Besides the Rural Department as a coordinator, the board consisted of representatives of farmers, advisors, the Union for Organic Farming, consumers' association, the provincial state office (food control officer), and trade. Also, fourteen organic inspectors were present at the meeting. The Kolas needed the approval of the organic board to be able to sell their products with the organic label. The inspection document of the Kola farm did not have any notes on defects, and it was accepted without discussion.

The regulation in each of the subsidy programs, such as Common Agricultural Policy, agri-environmental scheme, and so on, are based on their own logic. In practice, farmers have to coordinate all these different regulations in their farming activity. Because of the rainy summer in 1998, the Kolas also had to find out the rules for the compensation of crop failure. For the Kolas all this meant many open questions and uncertainty about what they were allowed to do in their fields. In the spring, the Kolas participated in an educational event organized by administrators for farmers about the subsidy schemes. In addition, many phone calls had to be made to local and regional agricultural offices during spring and summer. And despite all this, uncertainty remained about what was allowed or forbidden. An excerpt from the field notes clarifies this. The researcher had just returned from fields 13 and 14, and Maria Kola asked how they looked.

Excerpt 5
Researcher: I would mow the dense couch grass in the northern part of field 14, in order to avoid seeding of the weeds and to weaken the couch grass at least a bit.
Kai Kola: You could mow it with a field chopper, but do you need some sort of permission for that?
Maria Kola: I do not want any inspector to stand here for the whole day, I don't agree with applying any permissions.
Researcher: I don't know about permissions, I know what would be wise to do. . . .
(Field note, July 30, 1998)

Excerpt 5 shows how uncertainty about administrative regulations prevented the Kolas from quickly acting according to the necessity in the field. In October 1998, there was another discussion about the couch grass problem, and about how to continue farming next year.

Excerpt 6
Maria: We have been thinking, then, we did sow the clover grass to [field 18], but the rotations will all be confused. We cannot follow them. After last summer. We have to get a permission for that. And most probably we will. . . .

Excerpt 6 demonstrates how Maria had started to see permission as means toward mastering crop rotation. Applying for permission was no longer something to be avoided at any cost. To the contrary, there was confidence in one's ability to use it: "And most probably we will." The crop rotation plan as a formal requirement forced the farmers to expand their object in terms of the social space of advisory and administrative agencies, rules, and subsidies.

Looking back at the four types of object construction depicted in Figure

7.4, we perhaps somewhat idealistically assumed that within the integrated object, "the concept 'organic' refers to the constitution of an organized whole between natural resources, farming, and consumers." In light of the analysis we just presented, it seems appropriate to say that on the road toward the integrated object, advisory and administrative agencies, rules, and subsidies will be woven into the farmers' construction of their object. At the same time, the bureaucracy around crop rotation plans may also become an obstacle to the farmers' learning to rely on their own experiences and flexibly replanning their own land use.

The instrumentality of crop rotation planning tools was not constructed by the practitioners; it was largely given from above, partly even as a formal administrative requirement. But the templates were turned into active tools in negotiations between the farmers, the advisor, and the researcher. In this sense, the representational tools played a quite decisive role in pulling the farmers into the unfamiliar terrain of temporal and socio-spatial expansion.

Case 3: Expansion of the Object in Medical Care for Chronic Patients with Multiple Illnesses

In 1999 in the city of Helsinki in Finland, 3.3 percent of medical patients used 49.3 percent of the city's annual health care expenditure and 15.5 percent of patients used 78.2 percent of the expenditure. The latter figure corresponds to the well-known 20/80 rule of thumb in health care—meaning that approximately 20 percent of the patients use approximately 80 percent of the resources (*Helsingin terveydenhuollon kuntaprofiili* 2001: 37).

Many of those who use a large portion of resources are chronic patients with multiple illnesses. Their care is difficult to plan and keep under control, both for themselves and for their caregivers. They embody the fact that objects of medical work have changed dramatically after the Second World War. As infectious and parasitic diseases have increasingly come under control, the prevalence of chronic illnesses has increased. Chronic illnesses include cancers, cardiovascular illnesses, renal diseases, respiratory diseases, diabetes, arthritis, and severe allergies, among others. These illnesses require what Wiener, Fagerhaugh, Strauss, and Suczek (1984: 14) call "halfway technologies," that is, medical interventions applied after the fact in an attempt to compensate for the incapacitating effects of disease whose course one is unable to do much about.

> That these illnesses cannot be "cured" but must be "managed" makes them different in many respects from acute illnesses, the model around which health care was traditionally built. A brief look at the salient qualities of

chronic illness makes the differences apparent. Chronic illnesses are uncertain: their phases are unpredictable as to intensity, duration, and degree of incapacity. Chronic illnesses are episodic: acute flare-ups are followed by remissions, in many ways restricting a "normal" life. Chronic illnesses require large palliative efforts: symptomatic relief (from pain, dizziness, nausea, etc.) is often as necessary as the overall progress of treatment. Chronic illnesses are often multiple: long-term breakdown of one organ or physical system leads to involvement of others. One fact becomes obvious: halfway technologies are not only prolonging life but are stretching out the illness trajectories. By trajectories we mean not just the physical course of illness but all the work that patients, staff, and kin do to deal with the illness, and all the social/psychological consequences that encircle the illness course. . . ." (Wiener, Fagerhaugh, Strauss, and Suczek 1984: 14–15)

One of the consequences is that patients move constantly between home and various caregivers.

They cycle through the hospital, then go to the clinic or doctor's office, return home, go back to the hospital during acute episodes, and again back to their homes. The problems of coordinating the care given in the hospital, clinic, and home become immense. (Wiener, Fagerhaugh, Strauss, and Suczek 1984: 15)

The authors conclude that the inability to cope with chronic illness stems largely from the "standard categorical-disease perspective" dominant in industrialized countries. This perspective directs public attention and allocation of funds to the fight against specific illnesses, such as heart disease, cancer, or HIV/AIDS. But it also feeds competition and fragmentation among health specialists and specialties, and diverts attention away from the organization of collaborative care around actual human beings typically suffering not just from a single, well-bounded disease but from a complex bundle of illnesses and symptoms (Wiener, Fagerhaugh, Strauss, and Suczek 1984: 35)

A chronically ill patient typically becomes an object for a number of physicians, each viewing the patient from the perspective of his or her own specialty. Each specialty tends to assert the primacy of its own interest, and to lose its interest when the main responsibility is assigned to another specialty.

Primary-care physicians . . . become the mediators between specialists. Since they are less specialized than the consultants, they are not likely to be able to assert their interest in the patient as a totality. Nor are they able to defend the interests of the patient in the face of more knowledgeable and prestigious specialists.

. . .

This phenomenon within medicine is likely to result in what physicians call "Ping-Ponging" the patient. The patient is the Ping-Pong ball, and the players may be a group of specialists who bounce a patient from one to the other. They may hope that a satisfactory diagnosis will emerge that transcends the individual specialties of the collected assemblage of individuals and specialists. The injunction of colleagueship may result in all other consultants allowing one to "test" his diagnosis before the others, who will have their turn in due course. In the meantime, the effect of continuous tests, diagnostic procedures, and examinations may be as painful and as life threatening as the disease itself. (Bensman and Lilienfeld 1991: 219)

The multiple nature of chronic illness further complicates the issue.

The plurality of specialists are all likely to be attracted to the symptom or condition that takes on a primacy because of their own specialty. And so multiple and often conflicting treatments are prescribed. The drugs used may also counteract one another, or produce negative synergistic effects. (Bensman and Lilienfeld 1991: 220)

The following analysis is based on an ongoing longitudinal intervention study aimed at constructing a collaborative and negotiated practices of care between primary care and specialized hospital care in the city of Helsinki (see Engeström, Engeström, and Vähäaho 1999; Engeström, in press; Kerosuo 2001).

Temporal Expansion of the Object in the Care of Chronic Patients with Multiple Illnesses

The traditional object of medical work, as it is practically defined and bounded both in hospitals and in primary care, is the patient visit or "care episode." In other words, the object is temporally and socio-spatially bounded to a single continuous episode or encounter of physical presence of the patient. Administratively, such a unit has been reasonably easy to standardize. With the increasing prominence of multiple chronic illness requiring long-term continuity of care, however, this unit is breaking down.

In our project in Helsinki, we conduct so-called laboratory sessions with practitioners from both primary care and specialized hospital care, each session centered on a particular chronic patient who is also present in the session. For each session, one of the physicians engaged in the care of the patient prepares a preliminary analysis of the problems and possible solutions in the joint management of the patient's care, to be presented at the laboratory session. For such analyses, the physician is asked to discuss with the patient and with other caregivers possible gaps and miscoordinations of care, using past patient records as reference. The expansion of the temporal dimension of the object regularly comes up.

For the first laboratory session in 2001, a chief physician of rheumatology at the university hospital prepared the analysis of a patient case. At the session, the physician reported on the analysis.

Excerpt 7
Laboratory session #1, 2001
Chief rheumatologist: When we discussed with Lisa [the primary care general practitioner responsible for the patient] there at the primary care health center, then—and it shows of course in the patient records, it does not say that medication has been changed, the dosage of M [name of medication] has been increased, no information about that has been sent to the health center. And one can think that of course it should be sent. But no, that is not done. And probably nobody among us there is completely free of this sin. That for me is perhaps the biggest issue. Because this has been repeated many times over the years, that medication has actually been changed or something like that, which without question, when I now begin to look at it, plain common sense says that a copy of the patient record should in this case be sent to the patient's primary care personal physician. But it has not been sent, and a number of these occurrences have accumulated.

The crucial point in excerpt 7 is the expression "Because this has been repeated *many times over the years,* that medication has actually been changed or something like that. . . " The preparation of the analysis for the laboratory session forced the physician to expand the time perspective on the patient's care trajectory and led to a critical revelation. Here the time perspective expanded into the past. A little later in the laboratory session, an expansion into the future was expressed.

Excerpt 8
Laboratory session #1, 2001
Primary care administrator physician: Even though I am a representative of primary care, I still think that specialized hospital care really doesn't necessarily have to do all these things over such a long duration, particularly because the Helsinki health centers do have their own outpatient clinics and systems both for the distribution of aid equipment and with regard to rehabilitation.

The administrator physician was expressing her worry about patients becoming tied to specialized hospital care for long periods, without any end in sight. Her point was that the specialized care "doesn't necessarily have to do all these things *over such a long duration,*" implying that specialized care should involve primary care in long-term care plans for chronic patients such as the one discussed in the session.

Socio-Spatial Expansion of the Object in the Care of Chronic Patients with Multiple Illnesses

The patient visit or care episode as a traditional way of bounding the object of medical care compresses the patient and the illness into the spatially closed box of what happens and is observed inside the walls of the doctor's office or the clinic. As chronic patients increasingly drift between multiple caregiver locations, the closed notion of the object breaks down.

This is regularly witnessed as the physician conducts the analysis of a patient case. To understand the patient's care, the physician has to seek out the different caregivers who contribute to the care trajectory. The chief rheumatology physician discussed above realized that he had to seek out and meet the patient's primary care general practitioner if he wanted to understand the whole picture of the patient's care. Thus, he took the highly unusual step of physically transporting himself from his hospital clinic to the primary care health center to visit the general practitioner. A member of our research group interviewed the two physicians on the spot immediately after their meeting.

> Excerpt 9
> Interview at the health center in preparation for laboratory session #1, 2001
> Researcher: Well, what did you have in mind primarily, what did you want to clarify here?
> Chief rheumatologist: Specifically this patient's care relationship with the health center, about which I don't know very much. There are illnesses here for which the patient has been entirely in the care of the health center, and there are mentionings about them in there [in the patient records]. And we went through them, and we concluded that at least from my point of view it feels good, that this is the way it should be. Then we pondered this, which was already taken up in my meeting with the patient, this back injury and its care. And we decided that we will work it out, through here, and we will interview the patient in a bit more structured way. So we'll look into what it is all about.

The physician's point about back injury refers to a recent accident in which the patient fell and broke a vertebra. The injury was treated in a hospital emergency room but to the doctor's dismay, the patient was quickly released, sent home, and directed to the rheumatology clinic for the continuation of care—without consulting with the rheumatologists. The identification and negotiated mending of such ruptures between spatially distributed caregivers is a central part of the socio-spatial expansion of the object in this case.

Toward a New Instrumentality in the Care of Chronic Patients with Multiple Illnesses

In the course of the laboratory meetings, the participating practitioners and our research group together designed new instruments aimed at facilitating the collaborative representation and negotiation of the patient's trajectory of care. The idea is that the new instruments are used jointly by the patient and the key caregivers.

To represent the most important caregiver connections of the patient, we constructed a one-page document called the *care map*. Figure 7.6 is a repro-duction (translated into English) of the care map constructed by the chief rheumatologist in collaboration with the patient and the primary care general practitioner of the case discussed above. Figure 7.7 is a version of the same representation, constructed by the rheumatologist to point out the three cru-cial ruptures he had found in the coordination of the patient's care between the different caregivers.

At the laboratory session, the chief rheumatologist explained the third rupture in Figure 7.7 as follows.

Excerpt 10
Laboratory session #1, 2001
Chief rheumatologist: Point three is such, like we heard on the video clip, this was the most inappropriate event. And as I understood it, this event happened such that as the vertebra was broken and a hard back pain en-sued, and you [referring to the patient] were at the city emergency hospital, and they took the attitude that since there is nothing that can be surgically treated, they gave you a prescription for pain killers and told you that it'll probably heal by resting at home. But the pains were severe, and the pa-tient could not manage at home. There was no home help service, and she had to come again. And then she was moved to the city's primary-level hospital and stayed there for some time for treatment. And I got such a strong feeling here that, as we continued to discuss this, and half a year had passed, that one could still clearly see that this matter caused a lot of anger. This was, if we think what does not work, this was the topmost issue from the recent years. I succeeded in meeting the surgeon who saw her [at the city emergency hospital]. But then the physician had changed in the middle of the care, which happens in emergency medicine, and another physician

Figure 7.6 **Care Map of a Patient, Presented by the Chief Rheumatologist**

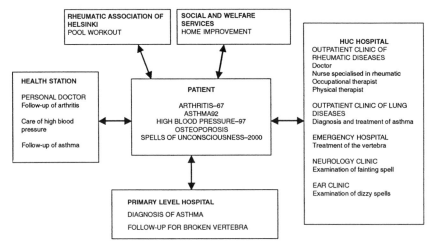

was in charge of her til the end. And I was not able to meet this second physician, not even talk to him/her. And then those medical records did not in any way reveal [this], they gave the impression that everything went as it was supposed to.

Excerpt 10 demonstrates how a dialogical, negotiated construction of communicative representations of the patient's care led to the identification of serious gaps in the socio-spatial network of care (the patient characterized such a gap as "being in a void"). It also led to the temporally expansive realization that experiences of such gaps can have long-term effects: "and *half a year had passed,* that one could *still clearly see* that this matter caused a lot of anger." Finally, it led to the critical realization that existing official documentation of care can completely ignore such problems: "those medical records did not in any way reveal [this], they gave the impression that everything went as it was supposed to."

Along with the care maps shown in Figures 7.6 and 7.7, the practitioners found *care calendars* to be very useful instruments for dealing with the expanding object of their work. The care calendar basically lists in temporal order all the important past and current events and contacts in the patient's care trajectory. The events are listed in a condensed form, typically on one or two pages. But the condensed form is constructed and updated jointly by the patient and the physicians, aiming at a capturing not only events deemed significant from the official point of view but also those considered significant by the patient. An example of a care calendar, again produced by the

Figure 7.7   **Care Map with Ruptures of Care Coordination, Presented by the Chief Rheumatologist**

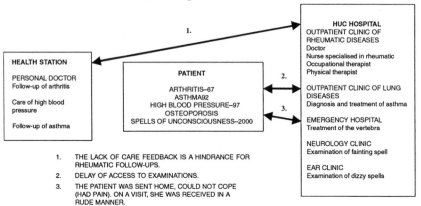

chief rheumatologist together with the patient and the general practitioner, is depicted in Table 7.5.

Neither the care map nor the care calendar was particularly complete or accurate in the form in which they were first presented by the chief rheumatologist at the laboratory session. Their point was to facilitate joint examination, remembering, interpretation, and revision, not to present some sort of an authorized true depiction of reality.

The instruments depicted in Figures 7.6 and 7.7 and Table 7.5 are not in themselves dramatically original or powerful representations. What is novel about them is that they were produced and meant to be used by all the key parties involved in the patient's care, including the patient herself. Thus, they became vehicles of critical reflection and joint planning.

In this case, the basic templates for the instruments were worked out by researchers and practitioners over a series of intervention sessions. As the templates were put into use and filled with content by practitioners, they were themselves molded and reconfigured to fit the particular case and circumstances. The practitioners test and twist these instruments as potential groundbreakers and spearheads toward grasping the temporally and spatially expanded object of care trajectory.

Conclusions

At the beginning of this chapter, we challenged the prevalent notion of the overwhelming compression of time and space in postmodernity, or new capitalism. Our claim is that compression appears as the sole dominant tendency

Table 7.5

Care Calendar of a Patient, Presented by the Chief Rheumatologist

Diagnosis or problem	Care contact
Rheumatoid arthritis, 1967	Helsinki University Central Hospital, 1997—Surgical Hospital; several rheumatic orthopedic operations, including wrist arthrodeses fusion and left hip arthroplasty
Hypertension, 1997	Care and follow-up at patient's own primary care health center
Spell of unconsciousness, June 2000	Helsinki University Central Hospital's Neurology Clinic, 2000
Osteoporosis vertebra fracture	City Emergency Hospital, June 2000
Asthma	Outpatient clinic for pulmonary disease, continuation of care at patient's own primary care health center

only when one fails to examine carefully what is happening in and around the objects of work. In Table 7.6, we summarize our findings concerning the transformation of the object in the three cases examined above.

When we talk about the object, we need to distinguish between the generalized object of the historically evolving activity system (compare G.H. Mead's [1934] "generalized other") and the specific object as it appears to a particular subject, at a given moment, in a given action. The particular crime facing the police investigator, the particular fields and crops facing the farmers, the particular patient facing the physician here and now do not neatly fall into either the generalized category of the "old object" or that of the "new object" as defined in Table 7.6. The particular, situationally constructed objects are unstable mixtures and partial manifestations of the generalized objects.

Objects do not appear, take shape, and become stabilized without instrumentalities. It is curious that in much of the recent work on objects (e.g., Knorr-Cetina 1997) there is very little talk about instruments. Correspondingly, recent work on the evolution of cognitive instrumentalities (e.g., Renfrew and Scarre 1998) tends to omit the objects on which instruments are used and which give rise to the instruments in the first place.

The notion of expansion is crucial to our argument (Engeström 1987). We distinguish expansion from mere quantitative increase or extension. For us, expansion is qualitative transformation and reorganization of the object. On

Table 7.6

Transformation of the Object in the Three Cases

	Old object	New object	Spatial expansion	Temporal expansion	Examples of emerging instrumentality
Case 1	Economic crime treated as single-act mass crime	Ongoing economic crime that contains multiple acts	Multiple locations of crime, multiple agencies	Long-term crime, long-term parallel investigation	Map of flow of money between companies; project plan
Case 2	Marketing object; one growing season	Integrated object; multiple seasons	Fields with green manures; advisory and administrative agencies	Farming across the years	Crop rotation plan; speech across the years
Case 3	Patient visit or care episode	Trajectory of care	Multiple inter-connected caregivers	Multiple years of care, past and future	Care map; care calendar

the other hand, expansion does not imply an abrupt break with the past or a once-and-for-all replacement of the existing object with a totally new one. Expansion both transcends and retains previous layers of the object. Expansion is not limited to the dimensions of time and space. It opens up and problematizes also the ideological-ethical dimension of power and responsibility and the systemic-developmental dimension that connects individual everyday actions to collective and historical transformations (see Engeström 2001; Hasu 2000).

But how do we explain simultaneous compression and expansion? It is useful to think of development in terms of multiple, partially interconnected, partially independent timelines (Scribner 1985). Hutchins (1995, p. 372) presents this idea with the help of a cube. The cube is a moment of human practice. In the cube, three divergent timelines cross each other: the relatively "slowly" progressing historical development of the practice, the somewhat more dense development of the individual practitioners, and the very dense moment-by-moment progression of the conduct of the activity. If we take the point of view of an individual in his or her career among and through multiple practices, compression of time and space is obvious. If we take the point of view of a given collective practice in its historical evolution, we see lots of recent indications of expansion of objects.

In other words, the question is: How do individuals experiencing compression in their careers grasp and deal with expansion of objects in collective practices? This question is more interesting and less pessimistic than lamenting compression or searching for enclaves where compression has not yet hit.

The temporal expansion of objects in our three cases seems to call for a remediation of the long-term and the instantaneous. The investigators of economic crimes, the organic farmers, and the medical practitioners and their chronic patients were all in the process of combining long-term planning and quick reacting to poorly predictable changes and contingencies in the lives of their objects. In each case, the practitioners had to construct plans and historical records that represented events spanning several years in time. But the trajectories of their objects also included surprise moves and emergencies. In musical terminology, with expanding objects, time needs to be both *composed* and *improvised* (on improvisation, see Barrett 1998; Weick 1998). While improvisation is quick, it is above all *rhythmically focused*. As Kessler, Bierly, and Gopalakrishnan (2001) and Leifer, O'Connoer, and Rice (2001) show, it is crucial to distinguish between rhythmically focused speed and mechanically forced haste.

The socio-spatial expansion of objects in our three cases seems to call for a remediation of place and space. The space of information flows needs to be crossed by means of concrete *trails* between places (for the concept of trails, see Cussins 1992). When tax inspectors and enforcement officers are placed as liaisons at police departments (such as tax inspector T1 in excerpt 2), they make trails between local agencies. The same is true of the organic farmers participating in educational events organized by administrators for farmers about the subsidy schemes or making phone calls to local and regional agricultural offices. And it certainly applies to the chief rheumatologist making a visit to the primary care health center, as well as to the rheumatologist, the primary care general practitioner, and the patient attending a laboratory meeting.

In all these cases, there were flesh-and-blood human subjects moving in space from one place to another and establishing trails that could be followed again, both by those subjects and others. Trails make an *emergent knowable terrain*, as if built from below. In the midst of all the fuzz about boundless spaces of flows, perhaps it is time to look closely at the formation of such terrains.

References

Altieri, M., and Rosset, P. (1996). "Agroecology and the Conversion of Large-scale Conventional Systems to Sustainable Management." *International Journal of Environmental Studies* 50: 165–185.

Barrett, F.J. (1998). "Creativity and Improvisation in Jazz and Organizations: Implications for Organizational Learning." *Organization Science* 9: 605–622.

Bensman, J., and Lilienfeld, R. (1991). *Craft and Consciousness: Occupational Technique and the Development of World Images.* 2d ed. New York: Aldine de Gruyter.

Cussins, A. (1992). "Content, Embodiment and Objectivity: The Theory of Cognitive Trails." *Mind* 101: 651–688.

Daston, L., ed. (2000). *Biographies of Scientific Objects.* Chicago: University of Chicago Press.

Engeström, Y. (1987). *Learning by Expanding: An Activity-Theoretical Approach to Developmental Research.* Helsinki: Orienta-Konsultit.

———. (2001). "Making Expansive Decisions: An Activity-Theoretical Study of Practitioners Building Collaborative Medical Care for Children." In C.M. Allwood and M. Selart, eds., *Decision Making: Social and Creative Dimensions*, 281–301. Dordrecht: Kluwer.

———. (in press). *Collaborative Expertise: Expansive Learning in Medical Work.* Cambridge: Cambridge University Press.

Engeström, Y.; Engeström, R.; and Vähäaho, T. (1999). "When the Center Does Not Hold: The Importance of Knotworking." In S. Chaiklin, M. Hedegaard, and U.J. Jensen, eds., *Activity Theory and Social Practice.* Aarhus: Aarhus University Press.

Friedrichs, D.O. (1996). *Trusted Criminals: White-collar Crime in Contemporary Society.* Cambridge: Wadsworth.

Geis, G.; Meier, R.F.; and Salinger, L.M. (1995). "Introduction." In G. Geis, R.F. Meier, and L.M. Salinger, eds., *White-collar crime: Classic and Contemporary Views*, 1–19. New York. Free Press.

Harvey, D. (1989). *The Condition of Postmodernity: An Enquiry into the Origins of Cultural Change*. Oxford: Basil Blackwell.

Hasu, M. (2000). "Blind Men and the Elephant: Implementation of a New Artifact as an Expansive Possibility." *Outlines: Critical Social Studies* 2: 5–41.

Heinonen, S., and Kieksi, J. *Luonnonmukaisen maataloustuo-tannon valvanta 1998—tarkastajan käsikirja* [Control of Organic Agricultural Production—Manual for Inspectors]. Loimaa: Kasvintuotannon tarkastuskeskus (in Finnish).

"Helsingin terveydenhuollon kuntaprofiili" (The Municipal Profile of Helsinki Health Care). *City of Helsinki Urban Facts Statistics 2001*, 10. Helsinki: City of Helsinki Urban Facts (in Finnish).

Hutchins, E. (1995). *Cognition in the Wild*. Cambridge, MA: MIT Press.

Kerosuo, H. (2001). "Boundary Encounters as a Place for Learning and Development at Work." *Outlines: Critical Social Studies* 3: 53–65.

Kessler, E.H.; Bierly, P.E.; and Gopalakrishnan, S. (2001). "Vasa Syndrome: Insights from a 17th-Century New-Product Disaster." *The Academy of Management Executive* 15(3): 80–91.

Knorr-Cetina, K. (1997). "Sociality with Objects: Social Relations in Postsocial Knowledge Societies." *Theory, Culture & Society* 14(4): 1–30.

———. (1999). *Epistemic Cultures: How the Sciences Make Knowledge*. Cambridge, MA: Harvard University Press.

Laitinen, A., and Virta, E. (1998). *Talousrikokset: Teoria ja käytäntö* (Economic Crimes: Theory and Practice). Helsinki: Edita (in Finnish).

Latour, B. (1996). "On Interobjectivity." *Mind, Culture and Activity* 3: 228–245.

Leifer, R.; O'Connoer, G.C.; and Rice, M. (2001). "Implementing Radical Innovation in Mature Firms: The Role of Hubs." *The Academy of Management Executive* 15(3): 102–113.

Lektorsky, V.A. (1984). *Subject, Object, Cognition*. Moscow: Progress.

Leont'ev, A.N. (1978). *Activity, Consciousness, and Personality*. Englewood Cliffs: Prentice-Hall.

Lynch, M. (1985). "Discipline and the Material Form of Images: An Analysis of Scientific Visibility." *Social Studies of Science* 15: 37–66.

May, J., and Thrift, N. (2001). "Introduction." In J. May and N. Thrift, eds., *TimeSpace: Geographies of Temporality*, 1–46. London: Routledge.

Mead, G.H. (1934). *Mind, Self and Society*. Chicago: University of Chicago Press.

Puonti, A. (2003). "Collaboration as Learning Challenge: Constructing a Common Understanding Between Police Officers and Tax Inspectors." *Police Practice and Research* 4(2): 131–147.

———. (in press). "Searching for Synchrony. Negotiating Schedules Across Organizations Involved in Investigating Crime." *Public Management Review*.

Renfrew, C., and Scarre, C., eds. (1998). *Cognition and Material Culture: The Archaeology of Symbolic Storage*. Cambridge: McDonald Institute for Archeological Research.

Rheinberger, H-J. (1997). *Toward a History of Epistemic Things: Synthesizing Proteins in the Test Tube*. Stanford: Stanford University Press.

Scribner, S. (1985). "Vygotsky's Uses of History." In J.V. Wertsch, ed., *Culture, Communication, and Cognition: Vygotskian Perspectives*, 119–161. Cambridge: Cambridge University Press.

Sennett, R. (1999). *The Corrosion of Character: The Personal Consequences of Work in the New Capitalism*. New York: Norton.

Seppänen, L. (2000). "Creating Fools for Farmers' Learning: An Application of Developmental Work Research." *Agricultural Systems* 73: 129–145.

Seppänen, L., and Koskimies, H. (2002). "Activity Theoretical View on Crop Rotation Planning in Organic Vegetable Farming." Paper presented at the Fourth European Symposium on European Farming and Rural Systems Research and Extension, Volos, Greece, April 3–7, 2000.

Strauss, A. (1993). *Continual Permutations of Action*. New York: Aldine de Gruyter.

Victor, B., and Boynton, A.C. (1998). *Invented Here: Maximizing Your Organization's Internal Growth and Profitability*. Boston: Harvard Business School Press.

Weick, K.E. (1998). "Improvisation as a Mindset for Organizational Analysis." *Organization Science* 9: 543–555.

Wiener, C.; Fagerhaugh, S.; Strauss, A.; and Suczek, B. (1984). "What Price Chronic Illness?" In A.L. Strauss, ed., *Where Medicine Fails*. 4th ed., 5–38. New Brunswick: Transaction Books.

8

Organizing Alignment: The Case of Bridge-Building

Lucy Suchman

> *Each one of us is an* arrangement. *That arrangement is more
> or less fragile. There are ordering processes which keep
> (or fail to keep) that arrangement on the road. And some of
> those processes, though precious few, are partially under our
> control some of the time.*
> —John Law

> *[P]lanners (and others engaged in planning) should think of
> themselves as characters in a larger story that they are helping
> to construct, and . . . they should strive to act in a manner that
> is consistent with the characters invoked by their story.
> Planning is persuasive storytelling about the future, and
> competing stories abound.*
> —James Throgmorton

This chapter is meant as a contribution to the development of ethnographi-
cally based, practice-oriented approaches to the study of organizational knowing and acting.[1] That involves, among other things, heeding the call for a
shift from a focus on the universal, the general, and the timeless to an interest in the local, the particular, and the timely (Toulmin 1990: 186). Taking
the work of civil engineering done within a large state agency as a case in
point, my starting place is a view of engineering as knowing and acting from
particular positionings at particular times, within a network of relations that
must be simultaneously elaborated and contained. If building stable artifacts
involves the accomplishment of alignments across heterogeneous human and
nonhuman elements, my emphasis here is on the work of bridge-building as
persuasive performances that both rely upon and reflexively constitute the
elements to be aligned.

Knowledge and Action Respecified

Recent practice-based theorizing includes a reconceptualization of knowledge and action as located in "ecologies" of social-material relations (Fujimura 1996; Star 1995). These relations are not given by nature, but are the product of ongoing practices of what John Law has termed "heterogeneous engineering" (Law 1987; 1994; see also Suchman and Trigg 1993). Both "ecologies" and "engineering" in this context are meant to break down received oppositions of nature and society on the one hand, and society and technology on the other, drawing attention instead to the diverse discursive and material, human and artifactual elements that must be assembled in the construction of stable organizations and artifacts. The intellectual traditions that underwrite these reconceptualizations (symbolic interactionism, actor-network theory, cultural anthropology, ethnomethodology) view knowing and acting as always and necessarily embodied, and therefore as located in particular historically and culturally constituted settings. The generality of knowledges, in this view, comes not from their contextual disembedding but from the extent and stability of relevant social-material relations.

My own approach to the topic of organizational knowing and acting is most deeply influenced by the alternate sociology developed by Harold Garfinkel and his colleagues known as ethnomethodology (Garfinkel 1996). Michael Lynch characterizes a central contribution of ethnomethodology as "respecifying the central topics in epistemology by identifying them as commonplace discursive and practical activities" (1992: 5, fn 9). Consistent with that project, the focus in the present study is less on what engineers "know" than on how they talk among themselves and with relevant others, how they translate their own embodied courses of action into written accounts and other materializations, and how they assess the meaning and adequacy of materials created by others (see also Lynch 1992: 232, fn 1). At issue here is not knowledge as a self-standing body of propositions, but identities and modes of action established through ongoing, specifically situated moments of lived work, located in and accountable to particular historical, discursive, and material circumstances.

Within organizational settings there is an intimate relation between forms of discursive and material practice, and action's rational accountability. Learning how to be a competent organization member involves learning how to translate one's experience, through acknowledged forms of speaking, writing and other productions, as observably intelligible and rational organizational action (see also Gherardi 1998: 376; Gherardi et al. 1998: 274). Demonstrations of competence are inseparable, in this sense, from artful compliance with various professional and technological disciplines, reflexively constituted through those same demonstrations. At the same time, artful compliance necessarily involves endless small forms of practical "subversion," taken up in the name of getting the work of the organization done.

Modes of Sociotechnical Ordering

In *Organizing Modernity*, John Law writes of relations between social order and modes of ordering:

> Perhaps there is ordering, but there is certainly no order. This is because . . . orders are never complete. Instead they are more or less precarious and partial accomplishments that may be overturned. They are, in short, better seen as verbs rather than nouns. (1994: 1)

If we take the liberty of substituting "knowing," "acting," or "organizing" and their nominal equivalents for "ordering" and "order," I believe that this passage reads equally well. An organization, in this view, is made up of multiple occasions and multiple forms of ordering. What Law terms modes of ordering are "contingent but not idiosyncratic" patternings that we can impute to social/material networks, that support comparisons across them (1994: 95). The focus is on organizations as ongoing performances involving heterogeneous modes of action and materialization, both of which must be actively affiliated and aligned across a range of often unruly contingencies.

Law's "relational materialism" takes materials as central to social ordering. At the same time, materials are not given in the natural order of things but are themselves products or effects generated reflexively in and through networks. That is, materials are not simply more and less durable in themselves, but rather some network configurations generate effects that last longer (through their faithful and ongoing reproduction) than others. Somewhat paradoxically, power and size on this view are achieved in part through deletions. So, for example, the translation of a "large organization" involves, among other things and for that moment, deletion of many, partial, fragmented, local and contingent orderings. Similarly, in the case considered here, the creation of "a bridge" involves the translation of a painstaking arrangement of myriad human and nonhuman elements as a single engineering artifact.

Modes of organizational ordering include the generation of particular places in which monitoring, reflection, and decision-making are said to take place. Wherever they occur, organizational decisions are made through the assembly of what Law calls "docile and tractable materials":

> These materials *represent* all sorts of events spread out through time and space. They *juxtapose* what would otherwise have been separate. They *summarize* what might have been said in a great many words or figures. And

they *homogenize* what would otherwise have been performed and embodied in a variety of different materials and a range of modes of expression. These are the materials . . . [t]hat produce organization. (1994: 158)

These ordering materializations are central to organizational knowing and action. At the same time they are also organizationally accountable:

[Organization members] don't just select between the myriad bits and pieces that happen to be lying around and shake them up together in a bag to form a picture. Neither do they invent such bits and pieces, *de novo*. Instead, the components of the picture are *built up*. With difficulty. Often painfully. On the basis of what is already being performed out there. (155)

Given this view of organizing, organizational ethnography constitutes a kind of second-order accounting made up of the juxtaposition and alignment of organization members' stories with those drawn from, and accountable to, the ethnographers' own. What Law terms "modest sociologies" are characterized by an incompleteness without any promise of remedy by further analysis, however much might be added. This is not to deny that our studies can be deepened and extended: on the contrary, it is to assume that they *always* can be. But just as organizations are openended performances, deepening and extending an analysis is not to be mistaken for completing it.

Building a Bridge as Processes of Sociotechnical Ordering

Bridge-building is a canonical example of heterogeneous engineering.[2] For the past two years my colleagues and I have been engaged in ethnographic research on the design of a bridge scheduled for completion by the year 2004.[3] Bridges are designed rarely in comparison with roadways and other surface structures, being costly projects that once built last from at least thirty to in some cases hundreds of years. In the area where our project is located, six toll bridges have been built and no new bridges are planned. At the same time, the area is threatened with earthquakes. In response to the critical problems experienced in the last major earthquake, the state government has set aside substantial funds for "seismic retrofitting" of existing toll bridges.

One of the area's toll bridges is actually a pair of old trestle bridges that connect the north and south shores of a relatively narrow strait. Charged with ensuring the safety of these bridges, engineers at the State Department of Transportation (called here "The Department") have argued that while one of the bridges can indeed be retrofitted, the other is sufficiently old— dating from 1927—so as to be both unsafe and uneconomical to try to reenforce it. Instead, they have proposed "replacement as a retrofit strategy." In this way they propose to direct funds for retrofitting to a new bridge-building project.

At the same time, it is a bit misleading to say that the engineers are engaged in designing a bridge, if what we imagine by that is the design of the structure itself. In this case the bridge design as such is outsourced to a specialist design firm, with Department engineers responsible for oversight. But it also turns out that the bridge itself represents a small fraction of the entire project relative to the highway approaches and interchanges that tie the bridge into the landmasses that it connects. And while the design of the bridge structure is contracted out, Department engineers maintain responsibility for the bridge alignments (that is, for deciding just where the bridge will be located and anchored) and for the design of all connecting roadways. Moreover, it is here that many of the complexities of civil engineering work actually lie.

I have looked elsewhere at the work of engineering design as a technical practice involving writing and reading within the electronic spaces of computer-aided design (CAD) technologies and across a variety of paper-based documents (Suchman 1999). These practices of design—what engineers themselves consider to be identifying of their work—are in turn embedded in an extended network of organizational activities of sense-making, persuasion, and accountability. My focus here will be on these latter activities, considered by engineers themselves to be somewhat peripheral, but also clearly essential, to the "real" work of design. These activities provided the object of the first approximately eighteen months of our study, insofar as the object of the engineering work during that time was the production of a document, the Environmental Impact Statement (EIS), a legal prerequisite to moving forward on design and construction of the bridge itself.

Along with the eventual arrangement of materials into the structure of a bridge, historian of engineering Henry Petroski points to the critical place of documents like the EIS in modern engineering practice:

> In the association [in the mid-nineteenth century] of bridge building with drawing and calculation and written argument before any construction was started, a new era was begun. From then on, the grandest dreams could be articulated and tested on paper, and thereby communicated to those who would have to approve, support, finance, and assist in designing a project that could eventually take years, if not decades, of planning and construction. . . . (1995: 12)

I want to look here at the production of the EIS itself as a process of sociotechnical ordering. As described by the project manager:

> The EIS involves a document, and a process, that is described by federal regulation as a tool for decision-making. Through the environmental process we can compare the benefit and disadvantages of the project alternatives. (video prepared for public hearing of 2/27/97)

The assumed efficacy of techniques and technologies of ordering seems a foundational premise for very large projects like bridge-building. As an observer, one is constantly struck by the thought "This is simply too complicated logistically, technically, and politically; too hard; too much work; too unstable, etc." But one is equally struck by the recognition that such thoughts are simply not options (or at least not options very often) for practitioners committed to the project. The question then becomes how, as a practical matter (rather than only as a matter of faith, although I think it must remain that as well), do they do it?

(Re)producing a Stable Alignment of Elements

I have suggested above that, like an organization, a bridge can be viewed as an arrangement of more and less effectively stabilized material and social relations. Most obviously, of course, the stability of a bridge is a matter of its materiality, based in principles and practices of structural engineering. This material stability is inseparable, however, from the networks of social practice—of design, construction, maintenance, and use—that must be put into place and maintained in order to make a bridge-building project possible, and to sustain the resulting artifact over time.

Highway projects, of which bridge projects are a part,[4] impinge on multiple locales, each with its own constituency of interested actors. Counties, cities, right-of-ways, and environmentally protected areas come along with local politicians, citizens' groups, private property owners, and public interest agencies. Public funding means that each of these constituencies claims some legitimate voice. Project members routinely deal with what Callon (1991) has termed "punctualized" organizational actors (see Table 8.1). These actors appear, however, always specifically—in the form of a letter, a mayor, a local politician, an irate citizen. So they are at once generalized *and* specific others to be dealt with. A county supervisor campaigning on the issue of public transportation, a militant group of hikers and cyclists, a new endangered species listed, a new clean air act can each send the Department back to the drawing board of redesign and renegotiation.

Human and nonhuman actors pose multiple, often conflicting, demands. The Delta smelt, for example, is a small fish, a protected species whose habitat would be disrupted by the Department's proposed construction plans.

Table 8.1

Partial Enumeration of Relevant Actors

Federal/State agency	County/region	City	Department	Other
Federal Highway Administration (FHWA)	Two county board of supervisors	Two cities on north and south shores	Department headquarters	Delta smelt
Governor	Conservation and Development Committee	Southtown Improvement Association	District	Harvest mouse
State Transportion Improvement Program (TIP)	Metropolitan Transportation Committee (MTC)	Mayor of Northtown	Toll bridges	Hazardous waste
Environmental Impact Statement (EIS)	Regional Transportation Plan (RTP)	Homeowners	Structures	C&H Sugar
Federal Emergency Management Agency (FEMA)			Design	Railroad
State Historic Pres. Office (SHPO)			Bridge replacement project	Right-of-way
Fish and Wildlife				Utilities
Coast Guard				
Army Corps				

Assigned as spokesperson for the smelt, the Fish and Wildlife Agency requires the Department to "mitigate" the disruption of habitat by creating comparable wetlands at another location. This leads in turn to extended negotiations with various regional and local agencies and property owners in the search for an alternate locale. The location identified for mitigation on further investigation turns out to be home to another privileged nonhuman, the Harvest mouse, which at present ranges freely over a salt marsh that under the mitigation plan would be turned to wetlands through the construction of sloughs. This play of interests and constraints is replicated across a myriad of actors.

Alignment Work as Persuasive Storytelling

To see more specifically just what is involved in aligning human and nonhuman actors, we can take up the problem of selecting a "preferred alternative" among various possible design options. While the phrase "preferred alternative" evokes an individual-rational process of human choice among a set of logical possibilities, closer inspection reveals multiple actors and preferences, defined in relation to a set of possibilities delineated within the professional community of civil engineering and by the practicalities of this particular project. The problem from the point of view of project members becomes less how to select an alternative than how to delimit a field of alternatives and to organize their effective presentation to relevant others.

In the summer of 1996, four alternative bridge types were being presented to the public as options: truss, suspension, cable-stayed, and steel-arched designs. A consulting firm was engaged by the Department to study each of the four options and to make a recommendation to the District Structures department, which would in turn provide a recommendation to the project manager.[5] She would then take the recommendation to District Management, who would in turn pass it along for final decision by the department director. The project manager pointed out to the team, however, that the director himself was not likely to have a strong opinion on the matter. The latter was more likely to come within the local District. It was District Management who would need to be persuaded, in other words, of whatever the team believed to be the best option.

Basic considerations from an engineering standpoint centered on the constructability of the bridge, and its ongoing maintenance requirements. As of the summer, the senior engineer on the project reported that while he tended to prefer the arch design, his mind changed from week to week. The arch seemed to him more "muscular," more "stocky," and was also the quickest structure to build. On the other hand, arch bridges were also reputed to be very tricky to put in place, in particular during the "raising," a critical and vulnerable time during which the bridge is minimally anchored and highly susceptible to winds. On this basis the district structures engineer expected the recommendation on constructability to be for a suspension bridge, a well-established and reliable bridge type from a construction point of view.

I am interested in viewing the choice of a "preferred alternative" less as a decision than as an effect of enormous work on the part of Department engineers, "more or less successfully hidden behind an appearance of ordered simplicity" (Law 1994: 5). The ordering work in this case includes most obviously production of the Environmental Impact Statement with its drawings, analyses, tables, conclusions, and recommendations. But it includes as well a series of related performances by Department engineers, supported by various human and material allies.

Engineering projects are divided into three "phases," named project approval (centered on approval of the EIS), design, and construction. Project engineers during the approval phase of a project face encounters with a diverse range of other actors. These encounters take them across the boundaries of "normal discourse" within their own professional community into the terrain of other more and less powerful rhetorics (see Throgmorton 1996). Along with the design of plans, engineers are frequently engaged during this phase with the creation of what they term "artwork"—that is, renderings of proposed highway and bridge designs created not as instructions for building but as illustrations.

Urban planner James Throgmorton has argued for a view of planning as "persuasive and constitutive storytelling about the future" (1996: 5). He suggests that an extended process of organizing like that involved in bridge construction involves participants living within and through stories told among themselves and to relevant others (2). The point is not that engineers simply "make up" these stories, but rather that they are authors who actively construct views of future events for others (266). In this sense, Throgmorton urges us to abandon either the modernist ideal of planning as a neutral and objective search for universal truths, or the contrasting allocation of planning to the realm of "politics run amok." Instead, he suggests, we should "embrace the idea that planning is scientific *and* political, technical *and* persuasive, and that the 'tools' planners use act as tropes (persuasive figures of speech and argument) in the planning stories that they tell" (5).

Public Persuasions

A critical constituency for the Project Team comprised the citizens living in two towns located on either side of the bridge. Federal law requires that a draft version of the Environmental Impact Statement be made available for public comment, and that any comments in turn be responded to in the Statement's final version. This extension of the actor network to include public commentary is contained through the designation of a sixty-day public comment period. As described by the project manager:

> Following the close of the public comment period, [the Department] and the Federal Highway Administration will evaluate all of the information compiled for all of the alternatives, consider all of the comments received, and identify the preferred alternative. (video prepared for public hearing, February 27, 1997)

To meet this requirement, a series of meetings was held during the approval phase of the project at central locations in each of the two affected towns. At these meetings, residents were presented with a (somewhat overwhelming) set of informational displays about critical aspects of the project as the Department defined them, including noise and air quality, right-of-way, traffic, and the various bridge alternatives. Attendees were invited to visit the displays, each of which was staffed by relevant representatives from the Department. The meetings were facilitated by a consulting public relations firm specializing in community involvement.[6] After a half-hour or so of browsing among the displays, the meetings were called to order and the agenda described. The project manager then gave an overview of the project, and the senior engineer described the various bridge replacement alternatives. The audience was then allowed to ask questions, which were fielded by the Department member with the most expertise in the area. Finally, participants were invited to visit the displays for as long as they liked, and to pose more questions to Department staff.

The bridge alternatives were presented to the public in the form of "visual simulations," assembled photomontages that placed computer-generated images of the various bridge alternatives against a photographic image of the surrounding environment. Each bridge alternative was shown from three points of view: a "community" viewpoint (i.e., how the bridge would appear from a known location on the shoreline), an aerial view, and a "motorists" view. In addition, a scale model was commissioned from a consulting firm in Chicago for use at the public meetings to help visualize the project plans.

Having taken pains to present all of the options to the local citizenry, the problem for the Department subsequently became how to get those that they considered least workable or desirable *off* the table. While a matrix of logical alternatives is one way of making a problem manageable, the apparent comparability of the options belies the fact that from the Department's point of view some are more sensible than others. Most obviously, one of the options considered and rejected by the Department was the so-called "no-build" option, which would have retrofitted the existing 1927 bridge rather than building a new one. This option had been rejected at the time that we began our project in the summer of 1996, but as of September of that year the citizens of the two adjoining towns were still interested in the question of whether the 1927 bridge might be retrofit instead of replaced. One particularly active member of the local Town Improvement Association stated that "the focus of this project is too narrow," in that the no-build option appeared already to have been ruled out. The option favored by the Improvement Association as well as other local citizens who turned out for a series of community meetings held in the fall of 1996 was to retrofit the old bridge to last until around the year 2010 when, they argued, the area's rapid transit system would be ready to reach as far north as the straits. At that time, the Department should build a single new bridge with four lanes of traffic in each direction and room for public transit. The response from the Department to this proposal consisted of facts and figures regarding the state of the 1927 bridge, the costs of retrofitting it, the limits to the level of safety that could ever be achieved, and the impracticality in terms of cost and disruption of replacing both existing bridges with a single new bridge. Among those local citizens who accepted the need for replacement, many still favored the "truss" bridge type, basically replicating the existing bridge and its 1958 companion. There again the Department responded with an accounting of the prohibitive costs of maintenance of that particular bridge type.

At a public meeting in December of 1996, all four bridge types were shown, but it was explained that the arch and truss options had been discounted, the former because of high construction costs, the latter high maintenance costs.[7] Of the two remaining options, the cable-stayed would be cheaper to build, but would require a center pier, potentially obstructing the shipping channel, where the suspension option would not. But the citizens remained concerned primarily about the aesthetics of two nonmatching bridges placed side by side across the straits. Why, they asked, keep the 1958 steel truss bridge if its maintenance costs were so high? Why not build two new bridges, or one larger one? The Department member speaking for Structures explained that despite their similar appearances there were actually differences in construction between the two existing bridges that meant greater maintenance costs for the older one. Nonetheless, the discussion led to one member of the audience asking "Are you really taking our input?" To this the public relations consultant replied that in fact citizen opinions were mixed (more so, presumably, than they appeared at the meeting), that all the alternatives would be included in the Environmental Impact Statement, that citizens' opinions would be recorded and weighed against costs, opinions of various policymakers, and so forth.

In February of 1997 a public hearing was held as part of the Department's solicitation of public comments on the EIS. In a videotape prepared for the hearing, five design options were described by the Department:

- no-build option
- retrofit and rehabilitation
- replacement on a Western alignment
- replacement on an Eastern alignment
- replacement on a Center alignment.

The senior engineer explained how this field had been delineated as follows:

> Five principal alternatives survived preliminary engineering and environ-
> mental screening, and were carried forward for the detailed analysis in the
> Draft EIS. (video prepared for public hearing of 2/27/97)

Along with these options, the Department was still considering four different bridge types, and several alternative designs for the interchanges on the
bridge's south side. Given this already delimited field, an outstanding problem was how to move the "no-build" and "retrofit" alternatives, which the
project engineers had felt obliged to keep onstage throughout the environmental process, into the wings. In the videotape, the senior engineer explained that
the "no-build" option did not in fact meet the designated purpose of the project;
that is, to extend the lifespan of the highway at its crossing over the straits. The
"Retrofit and Rehabilitation" alternative was described as follows:

> The retrofit alternative would extend the [1927] bridge's useful life by
> about another thirty years, after which there would be a rapid increase in
> maintenance needs and costs. Once again the State would face the prospect
> of another costly retrofit and rehabilitation, or even closure of this struc-
> ture. (video prepared for public hearing of 2/27/97)

In contrast, the West Bridge Alternative was identified as having a projected
life of 100 years or more, and as meeting all seismic and traffic safety standards. It was publicly characterized as "currently [the Department's] most
desirable alternative" (ibid.). The East Alignment, it was explained, would
involve potential displacement of an existing sugar plant, with corresponding costs for acquisition of right-of-way, and would require relocation of the
toll plaza on the bridge's north side. The Center Alignment was characterized as "particularly challenging from a construction standpoint," as construction on the new bridge would have to be orchestrated in a relatively
constrained space between the existing bridges.

The "preferred alternative" was finally selected by the Department in June
of 1997.[8] The decision was made by the Structures division at state headquarters, on advice of specialist consultants hired to assess the cable-stayed
and suspension bridge alternatives. The alternative chosen was a suspension
bridge. The rationale for choosing the suspension bridge was that it had good
seismic responsiveness, no center pier to obstruct shipping in the channel, a
well-known construction process and therefore less risk, good aesthetics,
and was more environmentally friendly (in part due to the decreased risk of
a shipping collision).

Orders of Stabilization

As of December 1996, as far as the senior project engineer was concerned, there were really only two options for the bridge design: either a suspension or cable-stayed bridge type, built on a West Alignment. Yet at public hearings in February of 1997 the full range of options were still being presented. Why? This apparent dissumulation was tied in part to the tension between the requirements of project management on the one hand, and those of public involvement on the other. More specifically, the project was being conducted under a seismic retrofit program that involved an accelerated time schedule for analysis, bidding, design, mitigation, permit acquisition, and other necessary activities. This accelerated schedule conflicted with the prescribed process for public review and commentary. The latter required preparation of the Draft Environmental Impact Statement, a period of public commentary, completion of the Final Statement, and FHWA approval, all in advance of moving forward on design. Yet in order to meet the accelerated construction schedule, these processes had to be run in parallel.[9] This acceleration, combined with the fact that members of the Project Team were deeply immersed and implicated in the project on a daily basis, meant that they had moved well ahead of the local citizens in their considerations of the space of alternative design options.

My story about selection of the "preferred alternative" should not be heard as an ideal decision process corrupted, but rather as illustrative of the inevitably hybrid, practical, political, technical, contested, negotiated, and situationally specific character of organizing a large modern project. Engineers are at once, albeit differently at different moments, technical experts, politicians, and advocates for a particular point of view (Throgmorton 1996: 40). In the production of an Environmental Impact Statement, sense-making and persuasion are subtly and inextricably intertwined. Authorship entails both an obligation to make an extremely complex set of considerations comprehensible to the public *and* a great deal of structural and rhetorical power. On the one hand, the report has somehow systematically to present the environmental considerations for a logical space comprising four bridge types, three alternative alignments, and several interchange options. At the same time, at the point that the report is completed, the Department members have already engaged in extensive activities of sense-making and discussion among themselves, leading them to have effectively discounted a number of the alternatives and to have some favorites, or at least a strong set of considerations and arguments, with respect to those that remain. In presenting the Statement, then, they must adjudicate the requirement for a balanced treatment of the options with an interest in guiding their audience's attention away from those alternatives that in their view seem unworkable and toward those areas that they see as genuinely open for debate.

This story of bridge-building points as well to the multiplicity of perspectives involved in such large modern projects. A view of artifact construction as heterogeneous engineering emphasizes issues of stabilization of human and nonhuman networks as central. Along with the contingencies of this process as seen from the perspective of engineers, however, one can catch glimpses of other perspectives, collected generally under the heading of "residents" or "citizens." In a real sense there are at least two different artifacts at issue, with associated networks of stabilization, that must somehow be aligned. Project engineers are immersed in a history and daily order of professional practice and practical exigencies. Their orientation is to moving the project forward according to the order of phases and timetables, toward the production of an artifact within budget and with appropriate projections of maintainability and durability. Residents, on the other hand, are working on a different order of stabilization: that of their daily lives. The time frame of the project to them represents a period of disruptions to be minimized, while the artifact that is the object of that activity is something that they will, quite literally, have to live with long after the project is completed. These two different "stabilizations"—of artifact, careers, professional networks on the one hand, and of daily life, property, and so forth on the other—comprise different, only partially intersecting fields of knowing and acting.

The problem that the case reveals, then, is twofold. First, engineers face other constituencies, most notably local residents, for whom a bridge represents a substantially different, domestic rather than professional object, and who are oriented along different lines of stabilization (see also Verran 1998). As Throgmorton points out, while modernist planning assumes a common system of values among affected actors, this is clearly not the case. Traffic flow or neighborhood quiet, access to distant communities or quality of life in local ones—these and myriad other issues reveal differences that cannot be resolved through analysis. Second, persuasive resources are unevenly distributed across actor networks. The challenge is how to deal effectively with historically constituted accumulations of discursive power in which, as in the case discussed here, engineering discourses speak more loudly than those of citizens. Can those resources be redistributed so as to make the field of discussion and debate a more "level" one? And if so, can stabilization still be achieved? The answers to these questions are less a matter of principle than of science *and* politics, technology *and* persuasion.

Conclusion

The construct of *heterogeneous engineering* is meant to underscore the extent to which the work of technology construction is, to a significant degree, also the work of organizing. Particularly in the case of a large modern project like that of bridge-building, an interest in engineering in this sense necessitates building a figurative bridge between the fields of technology and organization studies. While drawing on a somewhat different collection of resources for theorizing than those employed in other contributions to this issue, the analysis offered here shares a commitment to a view of knowing and acting in organizations as always and irremediably a *contingent* process. So, for example, the metaphor of "organizational learning," as Gherardi defines it, "stands as a valid alternative to the image of the rational organization, because it depicts an organization grappling not only with trial and error but also with the ambiguity of interpretative processes, of experience, of history, of conflict, and of power" (1998: 374). Similarly, the emphasis across these perspectives is less on the structures and functions of organizations as represented by organization members or analysts, than on the practical performances through which the work of organizing gets done. Representations of the organization in this view stand not as explanations for organizational action but as products of, and resources for, organization members' own ongoing (re)production and transformation of what it is that the organization comprises or could be. Accounts of the organization in this respect are part of everyday reasoning and acting in organizational life and, as such, are part of our subject matter as researchers.

As a state agency, the Department of Transportation is simultaneously a jurisdictional and a professional bureaucracy (see Gherardi 1998: 376), charged with developing highways and bridges according to rules of law and of civil engineering. And indeed, organization members demonstrate a strong orientation both to legal procedures and to conventions of professional engineering practice. They do so, however, not in the mode of implementation but of ongoing reconciliation, persuasion, negotiation, and management of the persistent contradictions and uncertainties endemic to any actual engineering project. The results are arrangements of social and material elements that, aligned well, can be effectively performed as stable artifacts that support the movement of people and goods through time and space. The sustainable reproduction of such enduring alignments, through processes of organizing as much as of construction, is the stuff of which bridges are made.

Notes

1. In contrast to other contributions to this issue that take "learning" as a central construct and develop its sociality, my own work has been oriented to questions framed not in terms of learning but in terms of socially constituted practice. Nonetheless, I assume learning in the sense developed by Lave and Wenger (1991), Lave (1993), and others taking inspiration from them to be intrinsic to all forms of practice.

2. There is no question that some forms of heterogeneous engineering occur in relation to more established and stable networks than others. Government-sponsored bridge-building in this respect offers an interesting contrast to, for example, commercially funded software engineering. For an insightful discussion of the distinctive instabilities of the latter see Newman (1998).

3. My colleagues in this study are Jeanette Blomberg, David Levy, and Randy Trigg, co-members of the Work Practice and Technology research area at Xerox PARC.

4. Like highways, bridge projects are framed in terms of the Department of Transportation's mandate to facilitate traffic flow and the movement of goods.

5. I use "the Department" here to refer to the State Department of Transportation as an entity. The Department is divided into nine "districts," within each of which is a complex ordering of regions and projects. The "Project" in the context of this chapter refers to the particular engineering team assigned to the bridge replacement project studied.

6. The senior engineer on the project reported to us before the first such public meeting that they had been coached by the public relations firm to use certain phrases in their interactions with the public. For example, they should say in response to public expressions of anxiety "We're sensitive to your concerns" rather than (he said jokingly) "We know the Department is screwing you." This kind of ironic recognition by the engineering team of the contradictions of their own position with respect to the public was common. The irony should be read less as evidence that the local citizens were being taken advantage of than as the engineers' recognition that the project was being carried out primarily in the interest of other, nonlocal actors.

7. This account is taken from fieldnotes provided by my colleague Randy Trigg, who attended the meeting.

8. Here I rely here on fieldnotes taken by David Levy from a meeting of 6/12/97.

9. In fact, early in 1997 the Department had contracted out for design of both the cable-stayed and suspension bridge types in a West alignment. This was well in advance of the final approval of the EIS and the selection of a preferred bridge type. The consultants were told to design both bridges to 35 percent completion or until an option was chosen, whichever came first. This was considered to be the only way to keep on schedule, given the accelerated time frame.

References

Callon, M. (1991). "Techno-economic Networks and Irreversibility." In J. Law, ed., *A Sociology of Monsters? Essays on Power, Technology and Domination*, 132–161. (Sociological Review Monograph 38) London: Routledge.

Fujimura, J. (1987). "Constructing 'Do-able' Problems in Cancer Research: Articulating Alignment." *Social Studies of Science* 17: 257–293.

———. (1996). *Crafting Science: A Sociohistory of the Quest for the Genetics of Cancer.* Cambridge, MA: Harvard University Press.

Garfinkel, H. (1996). "Ethnomethodology's Program." *Social Psychology Quarterly* 59(1): 5–21.

Gherardi, S. (1998). "Competence: The Symbolic Passe-Partout to Change in a Learning Organization." *Scandinavian Journal of Management* 14(4): 373–393.

Gherardi, S.; Nicolini, D.; and Odella, F. (1998). "Toward a Social Understanding of How People Learn in Organizations." *Management Learning* 29(3): 273–297.

Lave J. (1993). "The Practice of Learning." In S. Chaiklin and J. Lave, eds., *Understanding Practice*, 3–32. New York: Cambridge University Press.

Lave, J., and Wenger, E. (1991). *Situated Learning: Legitimate Peripheral Participation*. Cambridge, UK: Cambridge University Press.

Law, J. (1987). "Technology and Heterogeneous Engineering: The Case of Portuguese Expansion." In W. Bijker, T. Hughes, and T. Pinch, eds., *The Social Construction of Technological Systems*, 111–134. Cambridge, MA: MIT Press.

———. (1994). *Organizing Modernity*. Oxford, UK, and Cambridge, MA: Blackwell.

Lynch, M. (1992). "Comment on Lynch and Fuhrman." In *Science, Technology and Human Values* 17(2) (spring 1992): 228–233.

———. (1993). *Scientific Practice and Ordinary Action*. Cambridge, UK: Cambridge University Press.

Newman, S. (1998). "Here, There, and Nowhere at All: Distribution, Negotiation, and Virtuality in Postmodern Ethnography and Engineering." In S. Gorenstein, ed., Knowledge and Society: Researches in Science and Technology, vol. 11: *Knowledge Systems*, 235–267. Stamford, CT: JAI Press.

Petroski, H. (1995). *Engineers of Dreams*. New York: Random House.

Star, S.L., ed. (1995). *Ecologies of Knowledge: Work and Politics in Science and Technology*. Albany: State University of New York Press.

Suchman, L. (1999). "Embodied Practices of Engineering." In special issue of *Mind, Culture, and Activity*, ed. C. Goodwin and N. Ueno. San Diego: University of California.

Suchman, L., and Trigg, R. (1993). "Artificial Intelligence as Craftwork.." In S. Chaiklin and J. Lave, eds., *Understanding Practice*, 144–178. New York: Cambridge University Press.

Throgmorton, J. (1996). *Planning as Persuasive Storytelling*. Chicago: University of Chicago Press.

Toulmin, S. (1990). *Cosmopolis: The Hidden Agenda of Modernity*. New York: Free Press.

Verran, H. (1998). "Re-imagining Land Ownership in Australia." *Postcolonial Studies* 1(2): 237–254.

9

To Transfer Is to Transform: The Circulation of Safety Knowledge

Silvia Gherardi and Davide Nicolini

Introduction: A Social Perspective on Knowing and Learning in Organizations

The idealist conception of knowledge, with its corollary that the production of knowledge is a disinterested and individual endeavor, originates in the numerous theories that describe knowledge as stored in various types of categorial and mental structures, and views the learning process in terms of the transmission, circulation, and appropriation of information and knowledge. In this way "knowledge" is equated to a substance that can be sent, received, circulated, transferred, accumulated, converted, and stored. From this perspective, learning is treated as the acquisition of the body of data, facts, and practical wisdom accumulated by all the generations that have preceded us, a view similar to the "brick laying" model of scientific discovery criticized by Kuhn (1970). This knowledge, whether tacit or explicit, is "out there," stored in some form of memory. By implication, the main effort of the learner is to acquire it and store it in the proper compartment of his/her mind for future use.

This rendering of the realist ontology implicit in part of the debate on organizational learning and knowledge management is necessarily a simplification due to space; yet it highlights the need for alternative approaches to making sense of, talking about, and theorizing about organizational knowing processes.

In recent years a number of versions of knowing processes have emerged to challenge the very foundation of the rationalist tradition in which many of the representationalist ideas are rooted. Based on work carried out in such diverse fields as sociology of knowledge, ethnomethodology, linguistics, social anthropology, psychology, and political science, these alternative treatments emphasize the social and constructive character of knowing and learning. Together, they have produced a "quiet revolution" in the study of learning, knowing, and the mind (Bruner and Haste 1987), and they have recently found application in organization and management studies as well (Easterby-Smith, Snell, and Gherardi 1998; Berthoin Antal et al. 2001; Easterby-Smith and Lyles 2003).

Research has begun which abandons the assumption that knowledge and learning are mainly individual and mental processes, conceiving of them instead as mainly social and cultural phenomena (Brown and Duguid 1991; Lave and Wenger 1991; Cook and Yanow 1993; Law 1994; Blackler 1995; Gherardi 1995a; Tsoukas 1996; Gherardi and Nicolini 2000). For these authors, organizational knowledge cannot be conceived as a mental substance residing in members' heads; it can instead be viewed as a form of distributed social expertise: that is, knowledge-in-practice situated in the historical, socio-material, and cultural context in which it occurs. Gergen (1991: 270) writes, "knowledge is not something that people possess in their heads, but rather, something that people do together." And Latour (1987) suggests that people interact not only with each other but also with the nonhuman that makes up the remainder of the natural world.

Although from different disciplinary backgrounds, these authors have developed a conception that portrays organizational knowledge as having the following characteristics:

- It is situated in the system of ongoing practices.
- It is relational and mediated by artifacts.
- It is always rooted in a context of interaction, and it is acquired through some form of participation in a community of practice.
- It is continually reproduced and negotiated, and hence is always dynamic and provisional.

Knowledge Is Situated in the System of Ongoing Practices

For cognitivism in its various disciplinary forms, knowledge and competence consist in the capacity to apply formal and abstract categorial contents to particular situations. The context is therefore relegated to the status of the external background that determines variations in abstract and largely universal categories. The interest of this perspective lies in its study of the patterns into which these contents of knowledge are structured.

By contrast, a socio-material constructionist approach conceives knowledge and knowing as inextricably bound up with the material and social circumstances in which it is acquired. This is an anti-generalizing and anti-abstractionist approach, which maintains that human action can only be explained in terms of the specific conditions in which it takes place (Cooper and Law 1995). Its central concern, in fact, is how people use circumstances to accomplish intelligent actions, not how they apply cognitive structures to particular situations. Unlike in the cognitivist approach, the abstraction and generalization of knowledge are considered to be phenomena which themselves require analysis in terms of their constructive and social dimensions (Nicolini and Meznar 1995).

Knowledge Is Relational and Mediated by Technological Artifacts

On this view—which stems from a variety of scholarly traditions, from activity theory to the sociology of knowledge, to the sociology of science and technology—knowledge always manifests itself as social action sustained by symbolics, technologies, and relations. The expression currently used to describe this state of affairs is that action is always "mediated." Since media are always socially constituted and sustained, it follows that action is always social action, even when it is performed individually. The essential instrument of mediation is language and the discursive practices in which action and interactions are made accountable to oneself and to others. It should be pointed out, however, that everyday action is also based on the use of discursive and material artifacts that embody not only practical knowledge and experience but also the history and social relations implicit in the mediating artifact (Ciborra and Lanzara 1990). It follows that knowledge is performed in, by, and through social relations (Law 1992) that are relatively stable and "stay in place" in their capacity to deploy a variety of heterogeneous materials in support of action.

Knowledge Is Situated in Contexts of Interaction: It Is Acquired by Means of Social Participation

The idea that knowledge is inextricably bound up with action suggests that we should discard the prejudice that, for more than two millennia, has asserted that practical knowledge is an inferior form of knowledge (Ophir and Shapin 1991). Knowledge is competence-to-act, and as such it is primarily tacit and taken for granted, as well as being deeply rooted in individual and collective identity. As suggested by authors working within the Wittgensteinian tradition, knowing and understanding are manifest in the ability to act with competence. The normalization and representation of knowledge are tied to particular circumstances—like, for example, the need to repair breakdowns in the meaning system on which action is based, or the effort to transfer such competence outside its context of origin.

Learning is no longer equated with the appropriation or acquisition of bits of knowledge; instead, it is viewed as the development of situated identities based on participation in a community of practice (Lave and Wenger 1991; Wenger 1998). Learning is not conceived as a way of knowing the world, but as a way of being in the world (Bourdieu 1990; Gherardi 1999). A key element for interpreting knowing in organizations thus becomes the process by which novices become part of professional "worlds" and master linguistic games and microdecisions in the system of social practices that regulate participation (Gherardi 1990; 1995b).

Knowledge Is Constantly Constructed and It Is Therefore Dynamic and Provisional

The overall picture, therefore, is one in which knowledge sheds its aura of universality and objectivity and is no longer conceived as a stable entity that can be located in individuals or groups. It is instead processual knowledge (knowing) in constant evolution. Knowledge is a provisional and performed set of associations among heterogeneous materials. It is therefore the outcome of a "doing" that uses as its resources for action such diverse materials as people, technologies, and textual and symbolic forms assembled within a social context characterized by the presence of multiple collective and individual actors standing in specific power relations (Latour 1986; Law 1992). Knowledge as socio-material and local crafting practice is therefore based on knowledge resources "dis-embedded" from their original context and made available through their transformation, legitimization, institutionalization, and circulation. However, these resources are then re-embedded in other contexts by a process that constantly alters both knowledge and the local context of action (Araujo 1998).

If one accepts a social constructionist view of knowledge, the customary questions of the truth value of knowledge or the manner in which it is acquired are replaced by ones which to date have been largely unexplored:

- How do the different forms of knowledge "travel" in space and time? And how is knowledge transformed by the process of its circulation?
- What form does this circulation take? And who are the agents who circulate knowledge and appropriate it?
- How are local practices shaped by the interaction between situated knowledge and formalized knowledge? And how is knowing constructed and sustained in practice?

Answering these questions will help to construct a sociological explanation of the circulation of knowledge in organizing processes.

In this chapter we shall concentrate on just one aspect of what is a complex issue: the manner in which organizational knowledge circulates with specific reference to workplace safety. We shall seek to give concrete illustrations of the theoretical assumptions just discussed, endeavoring to shed light on the circulation of organizational knowledge about safety in a field comprising organizations, local agencies, and institutions. We shall use as our empirical frame of reference the results of a recent empirical study of the building industry[1] in northern Italy carried out by the authors.

We propose to interpret the circulation of safety knowledge as a process of translation in which transportation entails transformation. The term translation is taken from the work of the philosopher Michel Serres (1974). It involves creating convergences and homologies by relating things that were previously different: it denotes more a perpetuum mobile (Brown and Capdevila 1999) than a conveyor belt. The word "translation" conveys both the original semantic meaning of the Latin word translatum in physics and mechanics, and the linguistic one of undertaking a change from one language to another in which betrayal is inextricably implicated. Both principles are at work when abstract knowledge is connected to practical knowledge, and general to situated (and vice versa).

Translating Organizational Knowledge: The Case of Safety

Workplace safety is a particular form of "organizational competence." Put otherwise, it is a form of emerging competence sustained in organizations by interactions among various collective actors (Gherardi and Nicolini 2000).

What we call "safety" is the result of a set of practices shaped by a system of symbols and meanings that orient action but consist of something more. Safety can therefore be viewed as a situated practice, an emerging property of a sociotechnical system, the final result of a collective process of construction, a "doing" that involves people, technologies and textual and symbolic forms assembled within a system of material relations. This system of relations is made up of heterogeneous components and does not display the traditional distinctions between human and nonhuman elements, cultural or natural aspects, action and constraints. Rather, all these elements are involved in a constant process of generation rooted in organizational practice and called the "engineering of heterogeneity" (Law 1992). A "safe" workplace or a "safe" organization are the outcome of the quotidian engineering of heterogeneous elements—competences, materials, relations, communications, people—integral to the work practices.

Analyzing work as culturally mediated practice means questioning the social intelligibilities of mindful practices (Engeström and Middleton 1996b;

Star 1996) and assuming a view of "expertise as ongoing collaborative and discursive construction of tasks, solutions, visions, breakdowns, and innovations" (Engeström and Middleton 1996b: 4).

Engineering heterogeneous elements involves an effort to integrate modes of action proper to several work practices in the organization and sustained by members who, in that they are engaged in different practices and in different communities of practice, deal with safety in different ways. "Safety knowledge" therefore takes the form of cultural competence able to influence the style and manner in which meaning and value are attributed to events, and to determine the use to which the resources, technologies, artifacts, and knowledge of a group or organization are put.

Safety defined as collective capacity or competence is an interesting area of inquiry relative to the circulation of knowledge in practices. We shall base our illustration on empirical examples from the construction industry. Here we conducted several research projects investigating knowing and learning at various points in time: when a novice enters a community of practices (Gherardi, Nicolini, and Odella 1998a); when different communities of practice explain why accidents happen (Gherardi, Nicolini, and Odella 1998b); when a firm recovers after a major accident; and when an institutional field deals with safety regulations.

To analyze the circulation of safety knowledge we shall use a number of concepts derived from "actor network theory" (ANT), a conceptual vocabulary that constitutes a form of "relational materialism" committed to the project of understanding the contingent, material, and processual character of the networks of the social (Law 1994). Similar to symbolic interactionism and Foucaultian poststructuralism, ANT states that agents may be treated as relational effects emerging from the endless attempts to order the sociomaterial world. Assuming no a priori distinction between the social and the technical, it tries to study empirically how patterns of social and material order emerge as a consequence of ordering efforts by the different elements in the network.

Although authors working within the ANT perspective admit that patterns of order may well be intentional but nonsubjective modes of ordering, self-reflexive strategies that resemble Foucault's discourses speak through, act, and recursively organize the full range of social material (Law 1994: 109). Their main interest is then to investigate the tactics through which heterogeneous materials are combined and made durable: that is, the tactics of "translation."

The translation model of knowledge circulation and creation challenges the received "diffusion model" of epidemiological origin usually used to interpret both the innovation process and its implementation. Comparing the two approaches, Latour (1986) points out that in the diffusion model some "object," whether a technology or a command or an idea, is transmitted by virtue of the initial impetus imparted by an authoritative source. Conversely, in the translation model a command is obeyed—if it is obeyed—because it is passed from actor to actor by translation agents that have their own reasons for performing this action. Unlike epidemiological models, ANT emphasizes that the propagation in time or space of anything whatsoever—statements, orders, artifacts, products, or goods—depends on what the concerned individual or collective actors do with it. Each of these actors may behave in a different way: they may ignore the thing, alter it, deviate its path, traduce it, supplement it or appropriate it. With each passage, the translated item acquires energy that carries it further forward, and in this chain each actor modifies and adapts the item according to its own interests and uses it for its own purposes. The process of translation, therefore, creates the network and the actors just as much as the object: actors, relational networks, and translation processes are constructed through interactions (Latour 1992).

Central to the actor network approach is the notion of intermediaries that circulate among various actors. These intermediaries include natural objects or artifacts, individuals, and groups with their competencies, texts, and inscriptions. Intermediaries both embody and perform ordering arrangements. They are both the visible result of the assembling of heterogeneous elements by a network elsewhere in time and space and the active effort of that network to produce some distant effect. The intermediaries thus represent the network—both in the sense of making it visible and in standing for it—and they translate it in time and space.

The notion of intermediary comprises a wide variety of elements of social interaction, and it relates to aspects rarely considered by other theories of knowledge. The ANT stresses this feature by asserting the fundamental heterogeneity of the networks that define the creation and circulation of knowledge.

According to Callon (1992), there are four very general types of intermediary:

- *human beings*, with the skills and knowledge that they generate and reproduce;
- *artifacts*, which include all the nonhuman entities that facilitate performance of a task;
- *texts and "inscriptions,"* which include everything that is written or recorded, as well as the channel through which they circulate;
- *money* in its manifold forms.

Because each network is defined by a specific set of intermediaries that must be identified locally, and that define the specific nature of the network and of the actors that belong to it, we shall illustrate the particular importance in the translation of safety knowledge of the following categories of intermediary:

- technological artifacts, or work equipment of varying degrees of safety;
- safety discourses and people's ability to use language in practice;
- texts, and specifically regulations as particular types of text (norms and the textual forms derived from them: interpretations of the law, circulars, inspection reports, certifications, technical standards).

In sum, the idea of translating knowledge accounts for the continuous process through which knowledge practices emerge, are sustained, become durable, and eventually disappear. A sociology of translation is a sociology of mediation, since the intermediaries represent delegations and inscriptions of actions already initiated elsewhere: they do not repeat actions but transform these in surprising and unexpected ways. A model of translation/inscription implies a model of interpretation/reading.[2]

Artifacts as Intermediaries of Safety Knowledge

According to sociologists of science and technology, every artifact can be conceived as a complex system resulting from a long and laborious political process of negotiation and conflict during which part of the practical knowledge of the most influential actors is incorporated into the artifact. The embodiment of knowledge in technological products is far from being imbued with the principles of rationality and linearity. It amounts instead to a complex form of social and technical bricolage. The artifacts that result from it somehow constitute material responses to problems and needs expressed by their users (Bijker, Hughes, and Pinch 1987; Bijker and Law 1992).

The process whereby the knowledge of a specific community is incorporated into an artifact and thus circulated is recursive. Within it one can always distinguish, although to varying extents, the following: (i) a moment of "codification" by means of which the knowledge of a specific group is synthesized into a material and symbolic system; (ii) the combination and transformation of the artifact consequent on physical, political, cultural, or economic constraints on its production; (iii) its utilization, that is, the interpretation and translation of the knowledge implicit in the artifact in the new context of use; and (iv) the modification of the conditions that gave rise to the artifact.

Because the process involves geographically and functionally very different communities and social actors (users, scholars, planners, legislators, producers, distributors), it is one of the most frequent ways in which knowledge crosses organizational and geographical boundaries to move into other areas (Czarniawska and Joerges 1998).

Figure 9.1   **Old and New Cement Mixer Wheel**

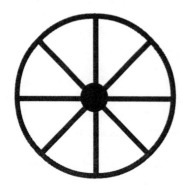 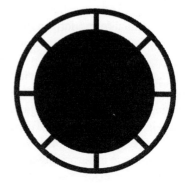

Wheel of
traditional cement
mixer

Wheel of modern,
safety-enhanced
cement mixer

The translation of knowledge through artifacts, techniques, and technologies is easy to see in the case of safety. In our research, one of our informants pointed out an apparently irrelevant difference between a relatively antiquated cement mixer and a technologically "more advanced" one. Both consisted of the familiar rotating drum, the motor, and the "handle"—that is, the steering—wheel which moves the drum into the loading or mixing position (with the mouth upward) or into the pouring position (the cylinder is tipped downwards so that the cement can be poured out of it). Whereas the antiquated cement mixer was fitted with a spoked wheel, the modern one had a solid disk instead of the spokes (see Figure 9.1).

The function of the disk is to prevent the operator's arm from getting trapped in the spokes during pouring operations, because once the drum starts tipping, its weight builds a momentum that could easily break the operator's arm. The disk itself is a simple piece of metal and certainly cannot be considered an example of high technology. And yet it conveys a concentration of knowledge onto the building site whereby the new design incorporates the experience gained from a number of accidents and injuries, the search for a solution, and its inscription into an artifact.

The spoked wheel is an intermediary in the translation process and like every technology it enables practical activity but at the same time conditions it. It attempts to introduce into the situation the designer's point of view on a safer practice. For the translation to be successful for the designer, the script implicitly carried by the artifact must be taken up by the user. However, the attempt to exert distant control on the action of its users via the artifact may well be counteracted by the tendency of the latter to persevere with established practice, for example, by users trying to reinterpret the artifact in terms of their normal routines: some users may decide to take the disk off and keep on rotating the mixer "as usual." Authors call this the "interpretative flexibility of technology" (Giddens 1979; Barley 1986; Orlikowski 1992), an expression that emphasizes the fact every artifact and technology can be modified when it is first adopted and as it is used, although this reinvention or modification is not infinitely possible, because it is restricted by physical and institutional constraints. However, the notion suggest that, paradoxically, the capacity of artifacts and technologies to convey knowledge is at times a function of their inflexibility: the less modifiable and disposable the artifact, the more it is able to produce effects in the user's practice. This, for that matter, is a problem of which the designers and manufacturers of safety devices are well aware, and they endeavor to design devices that are "human-proof."

As an expert in safety artifacts put it:

> It's practically impossible to erect normal scaffolding safely. . . . H-shaped scaffolding, though, has an in-built rigidity which prevents you from erecting and using it insanely . . . the only way for scaffolding to give this guarantee is if it's made so that even if you want to, it's difficult to erect it insanely.

In sum, if one conceives the introduction of innovations—either material, behavioral, or conceptual—as a deliberate attempt at control from a distance, it appears that the success of such translation efforts depend on the effectiveness of the tactics used by the intermediaries to discourage alternative interpretation.

Competing Discourses on Safety as Intermediaries of Knowledge

The example provided in the previous section has illustrated the idea that the translation of safety knowing is the result of complex and intricate work by the various actors-translators-intermediaries constituting an action net (Czarniawska and Joerges 1996). The cement-mixer wheel is therefore an intermediary that has the power to exert control at a distance. Its capacity to alter ongoing practices, and therefore import or generate knowledge, depends, however, on the process of its translation in the collective "doing" of safety and on the diverse strategies of translation and "discourses" on safety sustained by specialized action nets.

The term "discourse" is used to denote a set of texts able to give a (relatively) stable form to an object or set of objects, together with the structures and practices involved in their production and circulation. Discourses are forms of strategic arranging that are intentional but do not necessarily have a subject (Law 1994: 21; Foucault 1981: 95). Discourses are therefore themselves relational effects and, as such, they are necessarily contingent, no matter how durable and established they may appear or be made to appear. To every discourse there corresponds an entrenched action-net of alliances that facilitate translation and mobilization of knowledge and modes of knowing. In the case of safety, competing discourses face each other: a technological, a normative, an educational, an economic, and a managerial.

The technological discourse of safety is matched by a network of institutional actors that comprises, among others, engineers, physicists, planners, legislators, producers, and distributors of organizational learning practices and products. Though formally independent, these actors operate in close contact with each other, both because they have well-established channels of communication and because they sustain common and complementary practices of organizational learning that do not halt at the formal organizational boundaries. All together, they sustain the technological discourse of safety well expressed by the designer of safety devices who said, "You can build safety into the equipment, the work, and the machinery." This safety discourse reveals a specific understanding of the issue and a specific manner of interpreting and explaining events and actions, and working to encourage them or prevent them.

In our study, we found that the capacity of the artifact to exert its control at a distance depends on a well-established alliance between the discourse of safety—as in the use of "safe" artifacts—and the bureaucratic and repressive discourse of safety.

The latter discourse is asserted mainly by governmental or paragovernmental agencies of control and prevention, and by the judiciary. Though formally independent, these agencies operate in close contact with each other: together they constitute a crucial node in the circulation of safety knowing in the construction industry. They derive part of their importance from the fact that they occupy a central position in the perpetuation of the dominant bureaucratic discourse on safety. The conception of safety asserted by the control agencies is based on the idea that safety results from the correct application of rules and from obedience to regulations. These agencies impose a discourse of safety where, as one of their members put it, "every accident is always due to a lack [of respect for the law]," so that control "is the precondition for any reduction in the number of accidents and injuries."

For these agencies, the promotion of safety hinges on control and on information about the rules. The alliance between the technological and the normative discourses on safety is made manifest in the support that the control and prevention agencies provide for the artifact, in order to reinforce its capacity to exert control at a distance and to alter ongoing practices, and thereby generate "safety." The interpretative flexibility of technology thus becomes an arena of conflict in which the premises of action imposed by the artifact and the action net that sustains it are rejected.

A typical first refusal strategy is an attempt—often successful—to adapt the artifact to the routine practices, thereby thwarting (and traducing) the intentions of its designers. To forestall such maneuvers of translation by users, the technology, and with it the entire action net that has brought it into existence, must ally itself with the control and prevention agencies in order to discourage "interpretation" by alteration. Through the work of inspectors and controllers, the technology "mobilizes" all the coercive power imparted by the institution of control and prevention, as well as that of the judicial system, to discourage the "decomposition" of the device and its material reinterpretation in everyday practices. The alliance is institutionalized in industrial standards of shape and use, giving rise to specific intermediaries in the form of statutory rules, inspections, testing processes, and certificates showing that an item meets legal standards.

Another way in which the vigilance and prevention agencies back up an artifact's ability to exert control at a distance consists in their endeavor to neutralize a further very elementary but extremely effective strategy of resistance: simply ignoring the artifact or the intermediary (for example, by not carrying out one of the tests prescribed). This disregard may be deliberate—claiming economic reasons for not purchasing new technologies "meeting the legal standard"—or nondeliberate and due to simple ignorance. In both cases the shared goal of "technology safety experts" and the control agencies is to enforce the use of items which in their turn produce a control effect.

The former ignoring strategy is usually dealt with by inspections and controls. Such enforcement strategy, however, prefigures new alliances and new maneuvers in the action net. The representatives of the machinery's users may form an alliance and employ lobbyists who argue that adopting the technology is economically damaging to companies, so that the law must be watered down or postponed. Enforcement is therefore often backed up by other motivation discourses, such as "progress" or "workforce well-being." The maneuver is an effort to involve other actors in the dispute who will use the issue for their own purposes: the unions to reaffirm their role as defenders of the rights of workers, entrepreneurs to gain legitimacy as "modern and progressive," and so on.

Also in this case, there are further actors mobilized to enforce the safe use of equipment. For example, the companies manufacturing the technology are pressed into service. It is obviously in their interest to argue that safety levels should be improved, since this provides them with opportunities to sell a new generation of products, thereby increasing profits. Their commercial representatives thus become the brokers of the normative discourse, which they assert in order to make sales. Simultaneously, however, they also act unknowingly as the intermediaries of the knowledge and culture embodied in the artifact.

At the same time, the institutionalizing effect of the control agencies and their system of mobilizations and alliances frequently leads to the involvement of agencies that sustain the discourse of safety as education and training. Information about the importance of the correct use of the artifact is conveyed by training and retraining courses and is included in manuals and information material.

Inclusion of innovation in manuals signals the success of previous maneuvers, but it also exerts a powerful influence on its own. It affects, in fact, a further important actor, namely the novices who, preconditioned during their training, perform processes of microtranslation in the workplace. When novices are asked to use substandard equipment, they may refuse, enlisting the use of innovation in their effort to construct a work identity that differentiates them from the "old workers." To highlight their difference they may therefore flaunt the use of innovation ("a good and up-to-date building worker always uses a cement-mixer up to standard"), thereby acting as a further link in a chain of alliances and mobilizations without being aware of it.

Therefore, safety can be conceived as the effect of an action net in which competing discourses coexist: the technological discourse with other discourses, like those of safety as rules and punishment, of safety as education and training, of safety as profit or loss, and of safety as management and planning. Our argument is that discourses among specific practices are not directly aimed at reaching understanding and/or the production of collective action, but rather at knowing mediated by comparison among the perspectives of all the co-participants in a practice. Comparing among different perspectives does not necessarily involve the merging of diversity into some sort of synthesis—harmonizing individual voices and instruments into a symphony (or a canon)—but rather the contemplation of harmonies and dissonances may coexist within the same performance (Gherardi and Nicolini 2002).

Translation as the Effect of the Circulation of Knowledge in the Action Net

Consider, for example, the *inspection*, which is one of the principal practices around which the previously mentioned bureaucratic discourse of safety as respect for the rules is organized. Inspections are the main way in which the vigilance and control agencies participate in the social construction of safety, and one of the chief mechanisms by which they construct their identity and contribute to the process of organizing.

Inspections in Italy are carried out by one or more inspectors who conduct spot checks on building sites in specific geographical areas. Since there are more building sites than officials—who pass more than half their time doing paperwork back in the office—checks are not carried out on all sites but on a sample of them. The criteria by which those to be inspected are selected are formally random, although at closer scrutiny it is only apparently so. As an inspector explained: "[I]f [from outside] the site seems in order, then we don't stop. If instead, something strikes us as irregular, then we stop and inspect the site. From the outside it is possible to see if there are electricity lines and scaffolding, and what this scaffolding is like."

The inspection continues on-site. The inspector enters and checks whether it complies with safety standards: Is there protection against accidental falls? Are the electrical installations safe? Does the equipment meet standards? Is it used properly? In short, does the building site comply with safety standards?

At the end the inspector writes a *report*, which always imposes a fine and prescribes corrective action to be taken by a certain date. On the established date, the inspector returns. If the changes have been made, the firm pays the fine and the offense is extinguished. Otherwise, in the case of noncompliance or nonpayment of the fine, the matter becomes a criminal one and is referred to the judicial authorities.

The inspection is the means by which the control authorities transfer and impose their decision premises on the construction of safety and "translates" the knowledge implicit in the rule. Consider, for example, the criteria with which the inspectors select the building site to visit. These constitute rules of attention which, once learned by the community of practice, influence work practices and the construction of safety. Thus, a major safety skill on building sites is the ability to "make the site look in order" so that the inspector is not "attracted." That this is a skill tied directly to inspections is highlighted by the fact that the more visible sites—those located in the city center where the inspectors live and work—are in better order than outlying ones, and that it sometimes happens that scaffolding "up to standard" is only erected on the part of the building facing the road.

A similar mechanism operates on building sites during inspections. In this case the attention rules are manifest in what the inspectors observe or otherwise, and what they include or decide to overlook in their reports. The inspection therefore tacitly influences work practices relative to building-site safety. Events during inspections more closely resemble negotiation than the simple imposition of a point of view. During the spot check, the site foreman accompanies the inspector, seeking to negotiate the meaning of what the latter sees:

> *Inspector:* "This parapet is out of order."
> *Site foreman:* "You must be joking, it's standard workmanship."
> *Inspector:* "No, no, it's too low."
> *Site foreman:* "Aw, come on, it's five centimeters."
> *Inspector:* "No, I must be strict about this."

The site foreman trying here to negotiate the meaning of the rule is also learning the attention rules of the inspector and his colleagues, so that this knowledge can be implemented when the next inspection is made. On the other hand, the inspector constructs both the rule and the safety practice, since it is probable that on the next occasion the site foreman will point out that the parapet is of regulation height. Within the site, the competence deriving from this type of interaction with the control authority is described as "learning to get ready for an inspection." This involves the ability of the site foreman to identify the aspects on which the inspector will focus and which should therefore comply with the regulations. Interestingly, "getting ready for the inspection" includes a deliberate decision to neglect certain details so that the inspector can write a "minimum" report. All inspections, in fact, must conclude with a fine. Consequently, the site foreman helps the inspector in his work so that he is dissuaded from producing new attention criteria. Once acquired, this competence is transmitted within the community of practice together with implicit fragments of "practical wisdom" on how to construct a safe building site.

The inspection as practice is the fulcrum of the daily activities of the control and prevention agencies, as well as being the principal way in which they participate in the local safety culture. Through inspection these agencies exert their influence on the practices of safety and circulate competence and knowledge. At the same time, however, inspection is also one of the chief mechanisms by which they construct their own identity and a routine part of the everyday practice of managing a construction site which contributes to the process of organizing of the controlled firm.

First, the inspection practice is the main way in which the agency "constructs" the rule, determining its effective meaning at the moment of its application. Second, the inspection is a prime locus of conversation between the viewpoint and premises of the control agencies and those of other institutional actors. At the same time, the inspection report is a text that acts as intermediary between the agency and firms, between the agency and the judiciary, and between the agency and other institutions. In a very concrete sense, therefore, the implicit rules followed during inspections, and the content of the inspection reports, give precise indications on how to set up "good safety practice" in the geographical area under the agency's jurisdiction. The report's function of intermediary with other agencies is matched by that of notifications: documents used by other control agencies to start an inspection. Like reports, notifications set out the validity criteria used by the community, providing those who issue them with an opportunity to confirm the criteria with which "safety" is evaluated in the community.

Third, the inspection is one of the ways in which other actors in the community of practice, such as the construction companies and professionals, influence the premises and activity of the control agency. Thus, even without having to establish formal relations with other agencies and other actors, the inspectors develop their practical knowledge in relation to other discourses and approaches by participating in the "conversation" among organizations that determines local safety practices—and that distinguishes them from those of other communities of practice.

On the one hand, inspection involves the reflexive construction of the identity of the control agency as the "custodian" of the rules, and it reinforces the notion of safety as compliance with the regulations (what we have called the bureaucratic vision of safety). The inspector never explicitly asks whether the building site is safe, but always whether it complies with the rules—accepting and confirming the equation between the two terms. Moreover, the fact that every inspection concludes with a report and a fine sanctions the idea of safety as an unachievable bureaucratic ideal and confirms the principle that accidents are due to failure to apply the law, which gives further legitimacy to the agency. On the other hand, inspection contributes to the organizing process of the controlled firm: by means of identifying the responsible person on site, completing reports and notifications, and prescribing actions, the inspector enacts a distinction between the "firm and its environment," establishes hierarchical distinctions between members, and generates courses of action and a division of labor, thus contributing to the process through which the organization as a social, legal, economic "object" is recursively constituted.

The transformation of practice and experiential knowledge into prescriptive texts (norms, manuals, standards) transfers reflection on knowledge, and its conversion into formalized knowledge, outside the domain in which it is generated and sustained. When the outcome of the long process of translation is once again made available to the actors engaged in the local construction of knowledge, it is unrecognizable because it has acquired a general and universal form. This generalized and universalized form of discourse is both the hallmark of the action net that has generated it and the main strategy whereby the intermediary seeks to deploy its effect of exerting control at a distance.

Concluding Remarks: Knowledge, Power, and Translation in Organizing

In previous sections we have shown how a concrete form of knowledge (practical and theoretical) circulates within an action net. With the help of ANT we have described the circulation and constitution of organizational knowledge as the process and product of the translation made by an action net comprising individuals and communities, organizations and institutions, and their intermediaries, the latter being human and nonhuman actors like technologies, discourses, texts traveling and carrying situated knowledge. Under this approach, the constitution, circulation, and institutionalization of organizational and interorganizational knowledge take the form of a process of translation that connects the local to the global, the practice to the theory and vice versa.

We chose the issue of safety in a local building industry as an example of a body of knowledge to which many organizations and institutions contribute either in its abstract and disembodied form (i.e., universities, schools, or research institutes) or in its mediated one in artifacts like technologies or manuals, regulations, conferences. This body of knowledge, however, does not produce safety by itself, but only when it is put to work by situated actors in situated work practices and in local interpretations of its meaning and constraints. In this sense we conceive safety as a social competence enacted by an action net that recreates its context by means of institutional reflexivity (Beck, Giddens, and Lash 1994). In fact, the societal idea of what is safe and what is dangerous, which institutions should be responsible for social safety, and which regulatory instruments should oversee this on the one hand grounded is in situated practices of safety, and on the other hand, envisages better practices.

The notion of translation furnishes a social constructivist explanation of the constitution, acquisition and circulation of organizational knowledge without resorting to metaphors and models rooted in individual psychology or assuming the existence of a learning subject. To describe the circulation of knowledge as a process of translation within social systems shaped by power relations, by competing discourses, and by the engineering of heterogeneous materials entails description of a transformative process in which knowledge is at the same time displaced and interpreted.

A social constructionist approach to knowledge restores to the agenda an issue absent from debate on organizational learning: namely the question of power. In the tradition of Foucault and poststructuralism, in the present context power is used with its twofold meaning as enabling and constraining (Foucault 1977; Townley 1993). Power is conceived as a recursive, ubiquitous, and contingent relational effect. As defined here, knowledge and power are therefore difficult to distinguish, in that they are aspects of the same phenomenon, inextricable dimensions of the action net. This, therefore, is power/knowledge (Foucault 1980) that is relational and positional, and thus differs from the idea of power as capacity or as the possession and control of resources that largely prevails in the organizational literature. Hence the issues of organizational boundaries or of levels of learning dissolve, and knowledge can be viewed as traveling in time and space by virtue of global and local carriers, assuming local shapes in accordance with the characters of a situated web of power/knowledge.

Translation maneuvers are one aspect of the social process of organizing, and they are part of the constitution of the object "organization." The ANT approach, however, suggests that in order to understand the dynamics of organizational knowledge, one has to include broader phenomena such as the rise and fall of modes of organizing and organizational discourses. The approach therefore indicates that a full explanation may require the reflexive inclusion of the academic community (i.e., the observer) in the processes that they seek to understand. An intriguing question is, for example, why has the idea of knowledge management met with such success among managers? At the same time, one might ask who is involved in the discourse of transfer of commodified knowledge, whose interests are served by the idea, whether it sustains the managerial discourse of control and how, and what role is played by academics and consultants in this dynamic.

Notes

1. We refer to a research project into organizational learning, part of a project for the Kolleg Organizational Learning in Various Environmental Conditions study, financed by the Daimler-Benz Foundation.

2. We acknowledge Jay Zimmerman's help in forcing us to be more explicit on the hermeneutical element implied by our reasoning.

References

Araujo, Luis. (1998). "Knowing and Learning as Networking." *Management Learning* 29(3): 317–336.

Barley, Stephen. (1986). "Technology as an Occasion for Structuring: Evidence form the Observation of CT Scanners and the Social Order of Radiology Departments." *Administrative Science Quarterly* 31: 78–108.

Beck, Ulrich; Giddens, Antony; and Lash, Scott. (1994). *Reflexive Modernization.* Cambridge: Polity Press.

Berthoin Antal, Ariane; Dierkes, Meinolf; Child, John; and Nonaka, Ikujiro (2001). "Introduction: Finding Paths through the Handbook of Organizational Learning and Knowledge." In M. Dierkes, A. Berthoin Antal, J. Child, and I. Nonaka, eds., *Handbook of Organizational Learning and Knowledge,* 1–7. Oxford: Oxford University Press.

Bijker, W., and Law, John. (1992). *Shaping Technology-Building Society: Studies in Sociotechnical Change.* Cambridge, MA: MIT Press.

Bijker, W.; Hughes, T.P.; and Pinch, T.J., eds. (1987). *The Social Construction of Technical Systems: New Direction in the Sociology and History of Technology.* Cambridge, MA: MIT Press.

Blackler, Frank. (1995). "Knowledge, Knowledge Work and Organisations: An Overview and Interpretation." *Organisation Studies* 16(6): 1021–1046.

Bourdieu, Pierre. (1990). *The Logic of Practice.* Cambridge: Polity Press.

Brown, John S., and Duguid, Paul. (1991). "Organisational Learning and Communities of Practice: Toward a Unified View of Working, Learning and Innovation." *Organisation Science* 2(1): 40–57.

Brown, Steven, and Capdevila, Rose. (1999). "Perpetuum Mobile: Substance, Force and the Sociology of Translation." In J. Law and J. Hassard, eds., *Actor Network Theory and After,* 26–50. Oxford: Blackwell.

Bruner, J.S., and Haste, H. (1987). *Making Sense.* London: Methuen.

Callon, Michael. (1986). "Some Elements of a Sociology of Translation: Domestication of the Scallops and the Fishermen of St. Brieuc Bay." In J. Law, ed., *Power, Action and Belief: A New Sociology of Knowledge?,* 196–233. London: Routledge and Kegan Paul.

———. (1992). "The Dynamics of Techno-Economic Networks." In R. Combs, P. Saviotti, and V. Walsh, eds., *Technological Change and Company Strategies. Economic and Social Perspectives.* London: Academic Press.

Ciborra, Claudio, and Lanzara, GianFrancesco. (1990). "Designing Dynamic Artifacts: Computer Systems as Formative Context." In P. Gagliardi, ed., *Symbols and Artifacts,* 147–165. Berlin: de Gruyter.

Cook, Scott, and Yanow, Dvora. (1993). "Culture and Organisational Learning." *Journal of Management Inquiry* 2: 373–390.

Cooper, Robert, and Law, John. (1995). "Organisation: Distal and Proximal Views." In S. Bacharach, P. Gagliardi, and B. Mundell B., eds., *Studies of Organisations in the European Tradition.* Greenwich, CT: JAI Press.

Czarniawska, Barbara, and Joerges, Bernward. (1996). "Travels of Ideas." In B. Czarniawska, and G. Sevón, eds., *Translating Organisational Change,* 13–48. Berlin: de Gruyter.

———. (1998). "The Question of Technology, or How Organizations Inscribe the World." *Organization Studies* 19(3): 363–386.

Easterby-Smith, Mark, and Lyles, Marjorie. (2003). "Introduction." In M. Easterby-Smith and M. Lyles, eds., *Blackwell Handbook of Organizational Learning and Knowledge Management.* Oxford: Blackwell.

Easterby-Smith, Mark; Snell, Robin; and Gherardi, Silvia. (1998). "Organizational Learning and Learning Organization: Diverging Communities of Practice?" *Management Learning* 29(3): 259–272.

Engeström, Yrjö, and Middleton, David. (1996a). *Cognition and Communication at Work.* Cambridge: Cambridge University Press.

———. (1996b). "Introduction: Studying Work as Mindful Practice." In Y. Engeström and D. Middleton, eds. *Cognition and Communication at Work,* 1–14. Cambridge University Press, Cambridge.

Foucault, Michel. (1977). *Discipline and Punish: The Birth of the Prison.* Harmondsworth: Penguin.

———. (1980). *Power/Knowledge.* New York: Pantheon.

———. (1981). *The History of Sexuality: Volume 1, An Introduction.* Harmondsworth: Penguin.

Gergen, Keneth, J. (1991). *The Saturated Self: Dilemmas of Identity in Contemporary Life.* New York: Basic Books.

Gherardi, Silvia. (1990). *Le micro-decisioni nelle organizzazioni* [Micro-decisions in organizations]. Bologna: Il Mulino.

———. (1995a). "Organisational Learning." In M. Warner, ed., *International Encyclopaedia of Business and Management,* 3934–3942. London: Routledge.

———. (1995b). "When Will He Say: 'Today the Plates Are Soft'? Management of Ambiguity and Situated Decision-Making." *Studies in Cultures, Organizations and Societies* 1: 9–27.

———. (1999). "Learning as Problem-driven or Learning in the Face of Mystery?" *Organization Studies* 20(1): 101–24.

Gherardi, Silvia, and Nicolini, Davide. (2000). "The Organizational Learning of Safety in Communities of Practice." *Journal of Management Inquiry* 9(1): 7–11.

———. (2001). "The Sociological Foundation of Organizational Learning." In M. Dierkes, A. Berthoin Antal, J. Child, and I. Nonaka I., eds., *Handbook of Organizational Learning,* 35–53. Oxford: Oxford University Press.

———. (2002). "Learning in a Costellation of Interconnected Practices: Canon or Dissonance?" *Journal of Management Studies* 35(4): 419–438.

Gherardi, Silvia; Nicolini, Davide; and Odella Francesca (1998a) "Toward A Social Understanding of How People Learn in Organisations: The Notion Of Situated Curriculum." *Management Learning* 29(3): 273–298.

———. (1998b). "What Do You Mean By Safety? Conflicting Perspectives on Accident Causation and Safety Management Inside a Construction Firm." *Journal of Contingencies and Crisis Management* 7(4): 202–213.

Giddens, Antony. (1979). *Central Problems in Social Theory.* London: MacMillan.

Kuhn, Thomas. (1970). *The Structure of Scientific Revolutions.* 2d ed. Chicago: University of Chicago Press.

Latour, Bruno. (1986). "The Power of Association." In J. Law, ed., *Power, Action and Belief: A New Sociology of Knowledge?,* 264–280. London: Routledge and Kegan Paul.

———. (1987). *Science in Action.* Cambridge, MA: Harvard University Press.

———. (1992). "Where Are the Missing Masses? The Sociology of a Few Mundane Artifacts." In W.E. Bijker and J. Law, eds., *Shaping Technology/Building Society: Studies in Sociotechnical Change,* 225–258. Cambridge, MA: MIT Press.

Lave, Jean, and Wenger, Etienne. (1991). *Situated Learning. Legitimate Peripheral Participation.* Cambridge, MA: Harvard University Press.

Law, John. (1992). "Notes on the Theory of the Actor-Network: Ordering, Strategy, and Heterogeneity." *System Practice* 5(4): 379–393.

———. (1994). *Organising Modernity.* Oxford: Blackwell.

Law, John, and Callon, Michel. (1989). "On the Construction of Sociotechnical Networks: Content and Context Revisited." *Knowledge and Society* 9: 57–83.

Nicolini, Davide, and Meznar, Martin. (1995). "The Social Construction of Organizational Learning." *Human Relations* 48(7): 727–746.

Ophir, A., and Shapin, S. (1991). "The Place of Knowledge. A Methodological Survey." *Science in Context* 4(1): 3–21.

Orlikowski, Wanda. (1992). "The Duality of Technology: Rethinking the Concept of Technology in Organisations." *Organisational Science* 3(3): 398–427.

Serres, Michel. (1974). *La Traduction, Hermes III.* Paris: Les Editions de Minuit.

Star, Susan Leigh. (1996). "Working Together: Symbolic Interactionism, Activity Theory, and Information Systems." In Y. Engeström and D. Middleton, eds., *Cognition and Communication at Work*, 296–318. Cambridge: Cambridge University Press.

Townley, Barbara. (1993). "Foucault, Power/Knowledge, and its Relevance for Human Resource Management." *Academy of Management Review* 18: 518–545.

Tsoukas, Haridimos. (1996). "The Firm as a Distributed Knowledge System: A Constructionist Approach." *Strategic Management Journal* 17: 11–25.

Wenger, Etienne. (1998). *Communities of Practice.* Cambridge: Cambridge University Press.

10

Allegory and Its Others

John Law and Vicky Singleton

Hospital

Imagine a patient who presents with jaundice. This patient might be referred from the GP [family, or community, doctor], or from the Accident and Emergency Unit. He might go to the hospital ward, or perhaps to the outpatient clinic. This would depend on how ill he was. They would do a blood test in order to exclude other causes of jaundice. They would probably do a liver scan, and maybe a liver biopsy. The patient would be told to abstain from alcohol, and if the patient was in the ward then he could usually be kept abstinent, though even this is not completely certain because relatives have been known to bring in alcohol disguised as lemonade. If the patient was very ill he would stay in the ward, perhaps for a week or two. Then he would be discharged and asked to attend the clinic. Some patients do not accept this, and do not attend the clinic, but then you are onto a loser. They would attend the clinic for six months to a year, and if they have established cirrhosis they would never be discharged. In the normal course of events, a patient would be asked to come back to the clinic six weeks after being discharged from the ward, and if they were better they would be asked to attend again in three months, and then perhaps six months.[1]

This is one of the three senior doctors specializing in gastroenterology at Sandside District General Hospital.[2] He is talking to us, Vicky Singleton and John Law. And he is responding to a question that we have put to him about the "trajectory of the typical patient." The typical patient, that is, with alcoholic liver disease. Of course there is no such thing as a "typical patient." That is why he has imagined a patient presenting with jaundice.

Mapping Trajectories[3]

So what is going on here? Part of the answer lies in the way we have set up this study. Here is an excerpt from the description of the project that we sent to the people we wanted to interview:

Pilot stage: in the pilot stage of the research we are hoping to map how patients diagnosed with alcoholic liver disease move through the system of the hospital, and where the key decisions about care are made.[4]

And here we are again in a somewhat longer version of the same sentiment sent to another of the senior gastroenterology specialists—the one who made the initial approach to us and acted as gatekeeper:

> In the first stage of the research we will seek to map out the processes involved in diagnosing and treating a "typical" patient with alcoholic liver disease—so to speak, the typical "trajectory" of a patient within the organisation of medical care.[5]

Look at the key phrases here: "to map out"; to "move through the system"; the idea of a "trajectory"; the "organization" of medical care, and the notion of "key decisions." What is the significance of these?[6]

Notes on Mapping

A partial answer is that if we talk in this way we are living in and helping to produce a particular version of the world, one that is cartographic, indeed cartographic in a particular way. We are imagining and trying to operationalize the health-care equivalent of the AAA route map. How to get from Carlisle to Bristol. Or, in the case of the hospital-based treatment of alcoholic liver disease, how to get from admission through diagnosis to treatment, discharge, and continued care as an outpatient. We are interested in charting the traffic flows and the most frequently used route. And (since we also talk about "key decisions") as a part of this we are also interested in depicting the junctions or the options in the network of roads, trajectories, passages.[7] The nodes. We would like, in short, to be able to draw the "system of health care" for alcoholic liver disease in Sandside District General Hospital[8] as a network of nodes, links, and flows, perhaps something like Figure 10.1.

And there is more to say about our experience of mapping. When we began our work, we wanted to get a "proper overview" of the "main features" of the network, the system, and the trajectories in question, like the route planner map so kindly provided at the front of many road atlases. We wanted (as they say) to "make a context," get a sense of the overall character of the trajectories of those suffering from alcoholic liver disease in the health authority area in question. We will return to some of the difficulties about this in due course.

Conversely, we frequently learned more detail about specific parts of the trajectory, specific locations and arrangements that lie within the larger context. Here is an empirical example:

Figure 10.1 **A Possible Network of Care for Patients with Alcoholic Liver Disease**

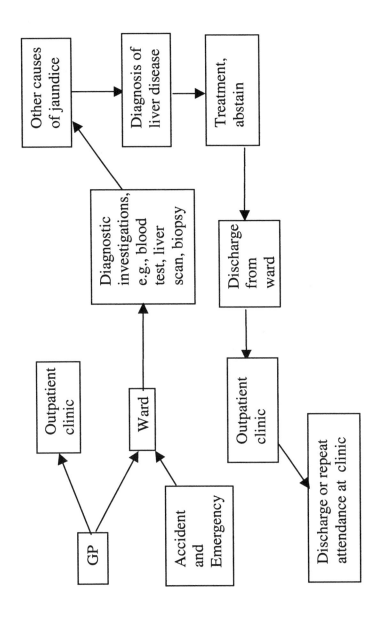

Vicky: Could I ask you about diagnosis? Is this done on the basis of blood tests?

Specialist: The answer again is that diagnosis is quite varied and complex. It may be as the result of blood tests or an abnormal liver test, but this is combined with a history, with other tests, and what the patient and the relatives say. For instance, there may be weight loss, suspicion of liver disease, a history in which a woman says that she does not drink much—perhaps two to three glasses of wine a day. Then somebody from her family phones in, and says that she is drinking a bottle of whisky a day.[9]

In this case, what took form as a small part of Figure 10.1,

> Diagnostic
> investigations,
> e.g., blood test,
> liver scan,
> biopsy

became something more elaborate, perhaps like Figure 10.2 (there are differences too, but perhaps we can ignore them for the moment).

So specificity or detail is added, like the city center route maps that appear at the back of many road atlases. We are now being shown the more important roads in the city. But the process can continue, for alongside the main roads there are maps of side streets showing the way they join onto the main roads: that is, maps of the "same places" scaled up yet again. Look at this:

Blood tests: The specialist talks about AST and ALT. "A ratio of 2 to 1 is suggestive of alcoholic liver disease. The Americans say that the ratio of 3 to 1 is diagnostic." "When I came here seven years ago they didn't do ALT."[10]

More detail—and, though we do not want to go into it further here, even now the process of magnification is far from complete.[11] And what can be done for blood tests can also be done for any part of the smaller-scale map. For instance:

"The *ultrasound scan* . . . may not affect management of alcoholic liver disease. It may not be used. . . ." Alcoholic cirrhosis is histological. An ultrasound scan cannot diagnose it. "We use them to look at blood flow patterns to the liver."[12]

So, what is going on in the process of mapping?

Figure 10.2 Detail in a Possible Network of Care for Patients with Alcoholic Liver Disease

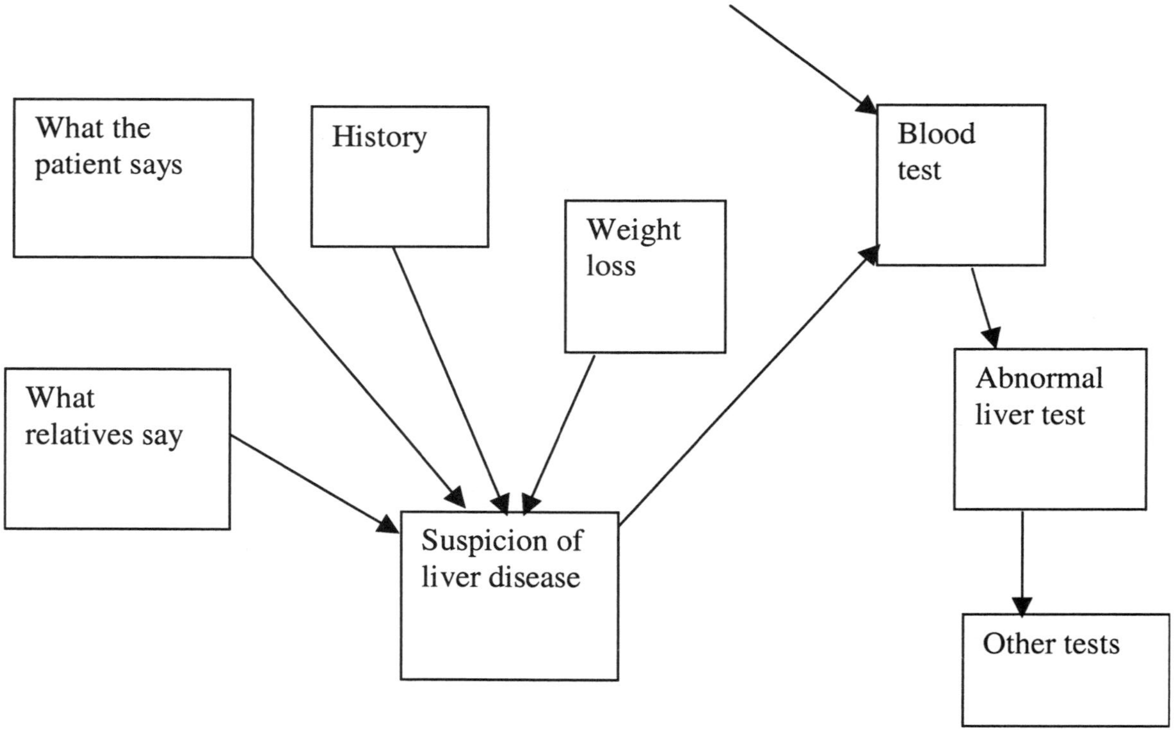

Mapping and Its Assumptions

A study to map the "trajectory of the typical patient" is a study that aims to *represent* a health-care reality.[13] Fine. But representation, as we know, is not a neutral tool. It makes assumptions about what can be known (also known as "epistemology") and about what it is that can be known about (also known as "ontology"). That is, mapping, as the particular version of representation that we are interested in here, carries a series of assumptions.

We have hinted at one of these ontological and epistemological assumptions above—that scale, size, is given in the order of things. We wanted to map the typical trajectory of a patient with alcoholic liver disease—we wanted to scale down, to get the overview, the "big" picture. We can also write about the detail, the specificity of various nodes in the trajectory as we scale up and these nodes are magnified.

A second assumption presupposed in the talk of mapping, and particularly audible in the talk of scaling, is *realism*. In other words, it is being assumed that these maps might represent something real. A real set of processes that are (to belabor the point) actually there, which is a way of saying at least three things:

First, whatever is being mapped is indeed there. It exists prior to the mapping, as independent of and outside of the mapping. Call this the ontological assumption of *out-thereness*.

Second, whatever is being mapped has a definite form. It has attributes, relatively stable attributes, that may be represented in the map. Think of this, then, as the assumption of *singularity*. That we are in the process of creating, whether adequately or not, a map that depicts "the" real world—which means that there is indeed a single, real world available to be depicted. Again, then, we are in the realm of ontology.

And third? This is the possibility of error that removes us from ontology into the classic domain of epistemology. The issue is easily stated: We might simply be getting our representation of the "typical trajectory of the patient" wrong. Perhaps we are being told lies. Perhaps we are asking prejudiced questions. Perhaps we are asking the wrong people. Perhaps the people we are asking have a particular interest in depicting reality one way rather than another. Perhaps they have forgotten "the detail." Perhaps they do not think that we will be "interested" in certain phenomena. The possibilities are endless—and indeed fill libraries of books on the philosophy, history, and sociology of science. This third point, then, we might think of as the assumption of *possible error*.

There are a lot of complexities here. Scale, singularity, out-thereness, and the possibility of error, all these taken together tend to produce a more or less stable self-bracing representation-and-the-reality-it-represents. To take one example: contradictory stories or maps do not raise doubts about singularity because their differences may be attributed to error, or perhaps to different perspectives. Like the a route map of the UK, which is a great tool if you want to drive from one place to another across the country but not nearly so good—close to useless in fact—if you want to study geomorphology, or go for a walk in hill country. Error in its various forms and differences in (pragmatic) perspective—these are epistemological tools that work to protect ontological singularity.[14]

Which brings us back, to be sure, to the reason we were asking the questions in the first place. Why the attempt to map at all?

Spaces—Compartments

Here is the formal response:

> *Aims:* the project is a study of multidisciplinary judgments of medical effectiveness in the context of complex decisions about diagnosis, care, and treatment. Our concern is thus with how complex medical judgments are made. It will focus on aspects of alcoholic liver disease.[15]

So in this work we were concerned with complexity, and in particular with complex "multidisciplinary judgments." We were interested in how such judgments are achieved as a part of creating the patient trajectory. Here is Specialist Doctor B:

> [I'm concerned with] the multidisciplinary aspects of managing complex medical conditions. The communication aspects, how people communicate, how teams work together, how they determine the treatment for patients.[16]

Perhaps unsurprisingly, the way in which he talks is similar to our own. This is unsurprising because he was our gatekeeper, the person who asked us to carry out this study and with whom we established its terms of reference.[17] More thoughts from Specialist Doctor B:

> There are differences in training between different doctors and different groups. So one of the questions is, how far do members of the team other than doctors understand the *essentials* of what we are trying to achieve.[18]

> And another problem has to do with the differences between specialists and generalists. . . . At the medical level, it is clear enough that X is treated

Figure 10.3   **A Map of Compartments in Health Care**

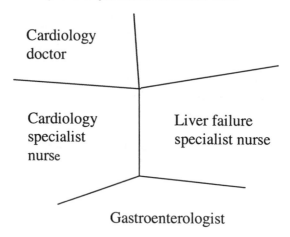

Cardiology
doctor

Cardiology
specialist
nurse

Liver failure
specialist nurse

Gastroenterologist

by X-ologists, but who decides what is X and what is Y? . . . . And then, in addition, nurses are becoming specialists—there are cardiology nurse specialists and so on . . . those who work on liver failure generally know more about that . . . which is okay, but the work of nursing is not rigidly compartmentalized in this way.[19]

A lot is going on here. But we have chosen these citations because we are interested in the repetition of certain forms of imagery: the persistence of different *groups;* different *disciplines; specialists;* the idea of the specialist "X-ologist"; and then (for us the give-away) "nursing *is not rigidly compartmentalized* in that way." Put on one side the fact that we have a doctor talking about nurses (which clearly raises its own problems). Attend instead to the spatiality of the imagery. Our contention is that we are dealing here with a *language of compartments*—and the communication between different compartments. All of which can also be understood as a further form of cartographic representation: the map of an area with its boundaries (see Figure 10.3).

This is a language, a set of preoccupations, and a representational style that is going to recur:

John: Where do patients with alcoholic liver disease go in the hospital?
Nurse C: They do not necessarily come to ward X (or ward Y if they are men). Ideally, they would do so. But the beds may be full, in which case they will go to another ward, and be under another specialist doctor. It turns out that, at least in principle, the same patient may have 12 different specialist doctors on 12 different visits to the hospital. If a serious problem arises on another ward the senior doctor there may seek advice of one of

Figure 10.4 **A Map of Organizational Compartments in Health Care**

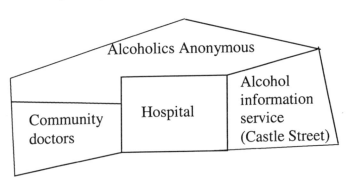

the gastroenterology specialist doctors. She mentions that patients with alcoholic liver disease may end up on the medical wards, numbers A, B, C, and D. On occasions they may end up in E, F, and G, as well as X or Y. Indeed, if there is no space on medical wards, they might end up on surgical wards too![20]

Nurse C is telling us about trajectories—but at the same time organizational and architectural divisions (and the communications between them). It is like a map of a country that highlights the regions and their boundaries, in addition to the roads, which as a result suddenly become less prominent, even though they may still be there. So it is taking us into and highlighting the hospital. And then a list of different wards as long as your arm. As well as the trajectories.

And we can fly with our respondents up and out of the hospital and look down to discover other seemingly larger areas, different distinctive compartments.[21] Here is Nurse C again:

> [W]e have a social worker who may offer financial advice. Not very many patients get to see the psychiatrist. But we give them information about Alcoholics Anonymous, and also about the Alcoholic Information Service, which offers counseling and support one-to-one. Many patients prefer that to the group sessions of Alcoholics Anonymous.[22]

Reading this, then, as compartments rather than pathways, we discover new organizational areas. We might depict them in this way as in Figure 10.4 (adding in at the same time the local community doctors who will appear in a citation below).

And again:

There is talk about the differences between the Community Trust and the Sandside Acute Hospital Trust. It appears that the Community Trust is much more decentered in the way in which it has made decisions, and implemented guidelines. In the Acute Trust, decisions "fly down from London."[23]

The Community Trust that this doctor refers to includes, for example, localized health-care services such as community doctors (general practitioners), while the Acute Trust includes Sandside Hospital.[24]

Acute Hospital Trust	Community Trust

By now we are far "above" the hospital wards (or for that matter the pathways between the wards). The hospital, which (presumably) "contains" the wards, is itself (presumably) contained within the Acute Hospital Trust. We have moved to the compartmentalization of "large-scale" health-care structures, and then, at the same time, into what we might think of as "cultures": one culture in the community and another in the acute trust. Or (to revisit Specialist Doctor B above) one among X-ologists and (presumably) another among Y-ologists.

Interferences

So the official purpose of the research is to study multidisciplinary judgments of effectiveness. But this language, and a great deal of the talk about the organization of health care for those with alcoholic liver disease in Sandside, turns out to reflect not only a model of representation that depicts trajectories and pathways, the nodes and the lines of a network, but a complementary model of depiction having to do with compartments—that is, having to do with regions and with boundaries between the regions. So we have two cartographic visions, but the quotes below suggest that *the two are interfering with one another.*[25] They come from two workers at Castle Street, a community-based alcohol information center.

What happens in Sandside is that sometimes patients are referred from the hospital to Castle Street. Then they may be given wrong expectations about what can be achieved, and they get lost to the system. In the hospital it depends on who they see. The psychiatric liaison nurses . . . are very experienced, but junior consultants [specialist doctors] do not have that experience. Wrong expectations are built up, when patients think they can come straight to Castle Street, and do not realize that it is by appointment only.

We have meetings between General Practitioners, staff working on accident and emergency, and psychiatrists at Sandside, and ourselves, to discuss what to do with people. It is important for the hospital to understand that Castle Street has no crisis facilities. In any case, an assessment demands that the client be relatively sober. Links with GPs are a bit variable. Some do not refer to Castle Street at all.[26]

Here, then, the compartments—Sandside Hospital, Castle Street Information Centre, community doctors—are interfering with the trajectories.[27] The generally agreed result is that the passages—the parts of the trajectories that move across the boundaries—often do not work as well as they might. Like the roads that petered out in the minefields along the old Iron Curtain, there are trajectories that lead nowhere. Or they lead back into "the community" where, for instance, those who have been dried out in the wards tend to take up drinking again. All of this—the difficulty in moving down passages from one compartment in the health-care system to the next—was something we endlessly encountered. Here is a community doctor speaking:

These patients cannot be referred to the psychiatric services at the hospital because the hospital will not treat patients with drug or alcohol related problems. They have a strict exclusion policy and alcohol problems will not be admitted. Patients are referred to Castle Street but are firstly assessed by a psychiatric nurse at the surgery.

Patients may go on to detox or may be seen by the alcohol counselor who is related to Castle Street and comes to the surgery. The counselor offers support while drinking and encourages patients to rethink whether they may be able to stop drinking.

Vicky adds in her notes: This all seems to be rather problematic. The psychiatric unit will not take patients, Castle Street will only see patients when they are not drinking and drunk and only during office hours. Where are patients to go?[28]

Some of the passages between the compartments, and hence some of the trajectories, "kinda work."[29] There is *some* traffic across the boundaries. There are, indeed, sets of partial connections—and these vary in quality and character.[30] But the passages do not necessarily work—which returns us to the concerns of the specialist gastroenterology doctor who led us into the study[31]

Here are some of the presenting symptoms of the interference between compartments and trajectories:

- Some border crossing points—passages—*did not seem to be open.*
- Some *narrowed themselves down* and choked off what was taken to be inappropriate traffic from at least one of the compartments. (More data: for reasons that made perfect sense in terms of the priorities of that service it was, for instance, pretty difficult to get help from the psychiatric service.)[32]
- There was what the participants called *miscommunication* between different compartments about the nature of trajectories—different understandings or interpretations of appropriate traffic.
- There was what one might (misleadingly) think of as *simple ignorance* of events in, and passages to, other compartments.

All of this made the lives of patients complex, difficult. And it also made the job of cartography as route map frustrating too. For instance, starting as we did with our happy notion of trajectories in the Sandside District General Hospital, it was only after quite a number of interviews that we even became aware of the existence of Castle Street Alcohol Information Centre.

What to make of all this?

First, we cannot say we were not warned. We were endlessly told that there *is* no typical patient. And, indeed, we were warned about the difficulties of mapping itself. Here are John's notes about one of the first interviews of the study, an interview with Specialist Doctor D and NHS Researcher E:

> [They are telling us that] our metaphor of mapping is too simple. I feel we should have seen this. We will need multiple maps, with multiple points of entry. Then we will have the job of seeing how these multiple maps partially connect with one another. Perhaps the metaphor of a map is a bad one?[33]

Multiple maps with multiple points of entry.

Second, we have a decision to make about the consequences of the interferences between trajectories and compartments. And that decision has ontological as well as epistemological implications.

- First, it can be treated as a cartographic or *epistemological problem.* This suggests that there *is* the possibility of an overall map. We just need to sort out our perspective—and try a little harder.
- Second, it can be treated as a *managerial problem.* This suggests that a route map should be possible. It is a matter of coordinating realities across compartments. This possibility is closely related to the first.
- Third, the interference can be treated as producing—or being indexed

by this *displacement and slippage*—seemingly purposeless ebb and flow. Which suggests that the latter becomes a phenomenon worth thinking about—and representing—in its own right, even if this means it does not conform to the cartographic conventions.

- Or fourth, it can be imagined as a set of elements, structures, arrangements that *could never fit together as a whole, and that could never be mapped together as a whole*. In which case we are left with Lenin's question: What is to be done?

We will review each of these in turn, combining the first two.

Managing Epistemology

It is, to say it quickly, possible to treat the whole difficulty as a technical problem: that things might be pulled together into some kind of coherence whether cartographically (Vicky and John, or those who run the system need to try harder) or managerially (those who run the system need to impose a kind of uniformity). Perhaps the two run together in this citation, where the specialist doctor–gatekeeper is talking about information, in part with a senior nursing officer:

> Information should, says the specialist doctor, be easily available in the hospital. But in practice, despite the new manager of information systems . . . information is difficult to get. In principle it should be possible to get information about, say, the proportion of people discharged in which alcohol is mentioned on the discharge summary. Because the information on the discharge summary is coded up. But in practice this is not easy. Access is difficult. . . . As a senior specialist doctor I should be able to get information, they should give me information if I ask for it. But, well, they are constantly being pushed by tighter "management" squeezes, and there are not enough staff or time. . . . And then they talk about the practical difficulties of getting data, because there are difficulties with getting the coding right, with date sequencing, and the codes themselves are opaque.[34]

This reveals an ontological commitment to singularity and the realism of "out-thereness," combined with the epistemological frustration that comes from perceived representational failure. If only we could get the instruments right we could see reality. And (hovering not very far in the background), if only we could get the management right we could make a decent set of trajectories for patients—a sentiment from which it is obviously difficult to dissent. But what happens if we shift from this understanding of trajectory? What happens if we attend, instead, to displacement and slippage?

Slippage, Ebb, Flow

John asks Nursing Officer G if they have success stories. "Yes," she says, "sometimes." Then she talks about the symptoms which are very diverse: confusion, hematosis, malnutrition, DTs. These are people who may be homeless because they have been spending all their money on alcohol. Their families may also be aggressive. Indeed members of the family may be worse than the patient. The patients are socially diverse, including businessmen and middle-class women left at home. People with alcoholic liver disease are all ages and from all social classes. The treatment depends on the stage they are at, and also their attitude to alcohol. They *have* to come off the booze, and this is impossible if they deny that they have a problem.[35]

This describes what one might think of as the *diffuse* character of alcoholic liver disease and its correlates. Presenting symptoms, patient backgrounds, patient attitudes, families, and outcomes—all are variable. Here is a specialist doctor:

Patients present with a range of different symptoms including liver disease, jaundice, other liver complications, bleeding from the stomach, diarrhea (which may be the result of drinking fifteen pints a day, even though they do not realize this), pancreatic disease, fits, and epilepsy. In addition to these physical problems, there are also socioeconomic problems which include lost jobs, overdoses, and family conflicts.[36]

Note that: physical *and* socioeconomic problems. And, if they are different, what one might think of as personal problems too:

When we are managing patients with alcoholic liver disease, we address the initial problem. But we also look for precipitating factors. We look for anything that is treatable. For instance, many alcoholics start drinking because of depression. If we think they are depressed, we will send them to the psychiatrist. So we try to look at their mood after withdrawal.[37]

In practice, the patient diagnosed with alcoholic liver disease is slippery, variable, elusive, and difficult. Almost everyone involved says things about such patients that can be interpreted in this way. We know that there is no such thing as the *typical* patient trajectory—but *individual* patients too are difficult and elusive. Nursing Officer G says:

Proper counseling is needed, but in fact there is not much psychiatric treatment available, so there is a waiting list, and while they are waiting they are more likely to go on a binge, and be readmitted. . . . The nurses also get to know many of the patients quite well because they keep on coming back. But the kind of attachments which grow up between nurses and patients with some other diseases don't happen . . . so much, and this is because the patients are difficult, self abusive, and need to (but often don't) recognize that they have a problem. Indeed . . . the majority are difficult, aggressive because they are withdrawing from alcohol on the ward; which means that they can be very disruptive of ward routine.[38]

Not everyone agrees that staff never get attached to patients—as we will see from a citation below. But the basic point, that many of the patients slip through the net, recurs. "Slip" through the net.

Tidal Objects and Subjects

So patients, symptoms, causes, and results are all diffuse. As, too, or so we found, is the *disease itself.* It is not only that definitions of the disease tend to vary from one location to another, though they do.[39] In addition, it turned out that alcoholic liver disease was a category that only made sense in particular locations, and not in all. Yes, it was relevant as a possible cause of hepatitis. Yes, it was potentially relevant to the process of drying out. But in other aspects of nursing the origins of that hepatitis were not relevant. And in most locations in community health care, alcoholic liver disease was only one aspect—not indeed a necessary aspect—of alcohol dependence whose correlates extended, as the above citations suggest, into family, lifestyle, occupation, life events, and depression. So the compartment of alcoholic liver disease was variable, and *it went on varying* as we talked to the professionals involved. So that we were just as likely to find ourselves speaking of alcohol dependence, alcoholism, or indeed alcohol abuse as we were of alcoholic liver disease itself:

- At least 20 percent of acute medical admissions are in some way related to alcohol.[40]
- 75 percent of night admissions are alcohol-related in diverse ways. This is an approximation.[41]

Two senior hospital doctors are speaking, one in Gastroenterology and the second in Accident and Emergency. And the "object" is no longer alcoholic liver disease.

Perhaps we were guilty of poor scholarship, of poor map-making. Perhaps we simply had difficulty in mapping the walls of the compartment, the boundaries of an object that is in reality relatively stable. But perhaps there is simply something diffuse about the object itself, the compartment of alcoholic liver disease, alcoholism, alcohol abuse. Perhaps it simply slips, slides, and displaces itself. Perhaps its boundaries move about from one location to another, and do not stay still. Perhaps they ebb and flow. But if this is the case, then something similar goes on, too, for the patients, clients, citizens who experience this condition (or set of conditions). Consider this:

> John asks whether they fear that patients whom they've discharged will come back in again. Does it affect their attitude to the patient? Nurse H says that a lot of patients do come back in, but that the girls [the nursing and ancillary staff] build up relations with them, and often this is good. They will know how a patient is going to be, how he is. People are not as judgmental as you hear they are. If patients treat staff well, then you get along OK.[42]

Here the Nurse is talking about one part of a well-recognized cycle that many health professionals refer to as the "revolving door." And many are not as forgiving as Ward Nurse H about that cycle. Here is Specialist Doctor F:

> We spend weeks getting them right, and we discharge them, and they go out and start drinking again, and it is back to square one. It is soul-destroying to get them back again.[43]

So the story is that patients are dried out on the ward, discharged, told to report to the out patient clinic, either do or do not, but in any case, in the majority of cases take up drinking again—and in due course return with acute symptoms and are re-admitted, only to be dried out again. Which suggests that here we have discovered (it was not difficult) another trajectory—though patients might leak out of this trajectory too.[44] But also we have learned that there is something wrong with that trajectory. It is not the kind of trajectory that Specialist Doctor B (or indeed any of the other professionals) were happy about. It is a trajectory that causes trouble. But *why* exactly does it cause trouble?

The quick answer is that it is frustrating since there is no sense of progress. This also means that it is expensive for the health-care system since beds are occupied again and again by the same people: this is also implied in several of the above citations. At the same time it also implies a gradual deterioration in the condition of the patient. As time passes patients do not get better. Instead they get worse.

[The ward nurse] . . . talks about the way in which they come back in, and the way in which they are worse than they were before. "We think, she's not going to get out this time."[45]

All of this makes sense so far as it goes. But there is something about the *shape* of these frustrations that is important too. It is that, like the disease category, within this loop *the patient is also so variable.* He or she is drinking or not. Back and forth. He or she is responsible, or not. Back and forth. And he or she is properly supported—or not. Again, back and forth. For us this implies that the metaphor of trajectory or loop, though it is not exactly wrong, does not quite catch the logic of what is going on. We have offered a clue to the metaphor we want to use above. Our suggestion is that we are dealing with something more like the *tide.* Back and forth, patients, alcohol-related conditions come and go, changing shape and changing character. There is an endless flow, ebb, and wash instead of the more purposive displacement of trajectory implied in a "proper cartography." Though, to be sure, it depends on the way you look at it.

Failed Trajectories/Failed Representation

Most of the professionals see slippage, frustration, deterioration, an endless downward spiral. This is a slippage that can sometimes be fixed in place in a way that breaks the spiral and turns it into a more progressive trajectory. Our data suggest that fixing comes in two great forms: on the one hand, there is fixing from *within* the patient. Gastroenterologist A:

> It is crucial to get patients to abstain from drinking. But the results aren't brilliant. About 40 percent will abstain, but one in two of those will relapse within a year. If someone with cirrhosis says can he have an occasional pint, then I say no. It is essential to get the patient to take responsibility, and I need to be quite firm about it. If they don't take responsibility, then you won't get anywhere.[46]

The other is fixing from *outside:*

> John asks if there is anything she [the Nurse] would like to see changed, improved. "I would like to see more support for alcoholics. The fact that there is no psychiatric support makes me mad. Social work support is limited. If they can't re-house them, can't move them, then they are likely to be going back to the situation which made them drink in the first place. That's distressing. If they want to get out it would be much easier it if they could have proper support."[47]

But if many professionals see a deteriorating loop, a repetitive downward trajectory in which patients oscillate between abstinence and drinking, it is not clear that the world is experienced that way by those who have been diagnosed with alcoholic liver disease.[48] Data from the Castle Street center cited below reveal one version of this: the cycle is necessary before clients will take responsibility: come to the necessary "internal" fix. But here is another, as told by a community doctor in a poor housing project far from the center of Sandside town:

> [It] is not an issue to [talk with patients] about the physical consequences of alcohol. I cannot talk about such things to many of the clients—this might provoke a violent response. It just is not relevant to them. Long-term issues are not considered. Many people have accepted that they will never work again and do not aspire to a fancy car and different housing.[49]

She also described how a warning issued by one of the specialist doctors at the hospital—"You will be dead very soon unless you give up drinking," which was intended to shock the patient into abstinence—instead led to the inquiry: "So how many months have I got left, Doctor?"

What are we saying here? The answer is we are suggesting that there are certain realities—indeed certain categories—that escape the techniques of cartography both as a network of trajectories and as a set of compartments. These realities are either misrepresented by those techniques or more or less invisible to them. In particular, we are suggesting that the fluidities of displacement and slippage are not well modeled as failing trajectories—either representationally or managerially.[50] Instead, they would be better imagined as flows, tidal ebbs and flows, which come and go, though perhaps without the regularities implied in the tidal tables. But if this is right, then this has ontological as well as epistemological consequences. For it is not simply that we might think of mapping differently, though this is certainly a possibility. It is also that within the existing conventions of representation these subjects and objects—patients, disease conditions—look as if they are changing in character. They do not look as if they are the same at different times. They look and feel slippery. Or fragmented.

But the ontological hypothesis that follows if we take fluidity seriously is that these slippery, multiple, undefined subjects and objects—patients, diseases—are, in fact, *perfectly definite*. That is, sometimes, in certain realities, "things" such as alcoholic liver disease which lack any definite structure or stability, do have perfectly definite boundaries and perfectly definite structures. "Things" are stable and well shaped. "Things" are coherent and constant.[51]

If this is right, then it implies that the elusiveness of subjects and objects, such as a patient and alcoholic liver disease, is not produced by them. It is produced, instead, in the way in which the patient or the alcoholic liver disease interfere with the epistemologies and ontologies that constitute the notions of trajectory and compartment. It is, in short, a representational failure (which is at the same time the imposition of an inappropriate ontological presupposition) that makes them so fuzzy. So difficult. So elusive. So inconstant.[52] Tidal objects can be well formed. But they just do not fit the predominant methods of cartography.

Imagining

And then again, perhaps there are other possibilities, other ways of treating this lack of fit.

If the ontologies and the epistemologies of trajectory and compartment— if the representational technologies and their presuppositions—produce the *fuzziness* of tidal objects by failing to know and treat them as definite, then perhaps there are other ways of knowing, and not knowing too. Other epistemologies and ontologies. We stumble toward one of these. Indeed, it is implicit in the metaphor of interference, interference between versions of what can be known and the corresponding versions of what there is. Let us say it in as many words, before we go any further. *Imagine that the real is a set of elements, structures, arrangements, which does not fit together and cannot be mapped as a whole. But imagine that it is all there anyway.*[53]

There are theoretical and empirical studies that explore this possibility.[54] But let us take it empirically by returning to our materials.

Here are some of those elements. Some of the compartments: the Sandside Acute Hospital Trust; the Sandside Community Health Trust; the Portway Community Health Trust (which runs the community alcohol and drug abuse service in Sandside even though Portway is more than twenty miles from Sandside); the District Health Authority; and the Castle Street Centre for alcohol information.[55]

Since that is where we are going to end up, let us focus on some of the things told us by the staff at the Castle Street Centre:

> Fresh Start at Beach Road . . . offers counseling and day facilities. It helps people to settle into the community, finds work for clients, and provides advocacy. . . . [T]here are very good centers in Edinburgh, Leicester, and Leeds. There is the Lighthouse Centre in Castle Hill, which dries people out. And then there is Prospect House in Sandside.[56]

This starts the list of the other compartments with which they are in touch. Then they talk too about:

> the Salvation Army, with its homeless project. Working Together, which is a center for young people. And Linkup, which offers counseling for young people.[57]

A long list—and there are others too. But the world of compartmentalization stretches off in other directions too. For instance, Castle Street itself—how is it financed? The answer is:

> from a variety of sources: Sandside Borough Council; Sandside District Council [both local government administrative units]; the AH [a charity based in Nottingham]; the Portway Community Health Trust; the District Health Authority.[58]

This means, the Castle Street staff also note, that the community psychiatric nurses are financed by (and responsible to) one authority and the counselors to another—one result being that their terms of service are different, and indeed, their contracts run out at quite different times. Thus, there are compartments *within* Castle Street.

These, then, are accounts that are all about *compartments*—though they also have something to do with trajectories. But the staff are full of stories that tell more explicitly about trajectories. We have already cited this:

> What happens in Sandside is that sometimes patients are referred from the hospital to Castle Street. Then they may be given wrong expectations about what can be achieved, and they get lost to the system.[59]

And this too:

> Links with community doctors are a bit variable. Some don't refer to Castle Street at all. Counselors will only see people whose refer themselves.[60]

But here is a new trajectory story:

> [S]ixty percent of the clients are self-referrals, and the majority of the rest come from community doctors. A few are referred by the hospital, or from the probation service.[61]

And another:

Certain clients end up in the center by mistake. Those with anorexia bulimia for instance. These are referred elsewhere.[62]

And there is another trajectory to do with the area that is covered, which is:

> . . . very wide. This can be difficult and costly, but (spending money on bus fares) is also . . . an expression of motivation [on the part of the client].[63]

And another that this time points to the paucity of resources:

> There is a three-week waiting list to see the community psychiatric nurse. And a five-week waiting list to see the counselor.[64]

And yet another trajectory, which is also about resources:

> If we had better premises we could have groups on the ground floor, and give each of the eight counselors their own room. We would have room for more volunteers to work and run groups, and it might be possible to have a drop-in center.[65]

That is enough. But it makes the point that we could tell stories—these little excerpts would be some of the elements—that would map the world from the point of view of Castle Street: treat it as a set of compartments interfering with a set of trajectories, or indeed vice versa (because, for instance, the compartmentalized approach to finance inhibits some of the possible trajectories, appears to choke them off). In addition, though we will not do it here, we could perhaps rework our data quite differently, in order to make Castle Street ebb and flow—for it does seem remarkably variable in the stories of others if not its own. But let us try something very different instead.

In-Direction

Think about the story that follows. No. Do not so much think as *feel* the story. Try to *visualize* it. Try to *smell* it. Try to *be* there. Suspend your disbelief and read between the lines. Try to see what is *not* being said in addition to what is.

> *Finding the door is difficult enough. In a terrace, between two cheap storefronts in a rundown part of Sandside. The kind of street only three blocks from the big store that does not make it. That does not make it at all. That smells of poverty. That speaks of hopelessness.*

It is a nondescript door. Unwelcoming. A tiny spy glass. An inconspicuous notice. Nothing very obvious. Nothing very appealing. We are ringing the doorbell. Is anyone listening? Has anyone heard? Dimly we hear the sound of footsteps. We sense that we are being looked at through the spy glass. Checking us out. And then the door opens. And we are being welcomed through the door by a middle-aged women. To find that there is not a proper lobby. Instead, we are facing a flight of stairs. Carpeted, cheaply. Yes, shoddily.

So we've been admitted. We are, yes, Vicky Singleton and John Law from Lancaster University. And now, we are being led up a flight of stairs. And the building is starting to make an impression. An impression of make-do. Of scarce resources. Of inadequacy. For we are being told people have to come up all those flights of stairs. Some of them can hardly walk through drink. And some can hardly walk, full stop. Up this long flight of stairs. For we're in the kind of Victorian building where the rooms on the ground floor are twelve feet high. Big fancy three-story houses. Built at a time of optimism. At a time of some kind of prosperity. Which, however, has now drained away.

So the clients need to negotiate these stairs, turn around the half landing, up a further short flight, and then they are on the first floor. Next to the room that is the general office, library, meeting room, leaflet dispensary, the place with the filing cabinets, the tables, the chairs. People are milling about. At the moment no clients, but a researcher who is smoking. Several social workers, the manager, community psychiatric nurses coming and going.

The leaflets and the papers are spilling over everything. Brown cardboard boxes. Half-drunk mugs of coffee. New mugs of coffee for us. Clearing a bit of space. Not too much. There is not too much space. Files and pamphlets are pushed to one side. Two more chairs. And the numbers in the room keep on changing as clients arrive, or people go out on call, or the phone rings. One client has not turned up. Relief at this. The pressure is so great. And then there is another with alcohol on his breath. A bad sign.

The staff are so keen to talk. Keen to tell us about their work. Keen to talk about its frustrations and its complexities.

How to *tell* this?

Appreciating

The fact is, it cannot be *told.* Or if it is told then it loses something. Or, no, the telling of it is the telling of something else. *Which is the stuff of allegory.*

Imagine it, then, this way. There is a building—or a story about a building—which is an allegory. An allegory for? An allegory for *that which cannot be told*. That which cannot be held together. That which cannot be represented within any of the traditions of cartography, compartmental, trajectorial, or for that matter tidal. It is that which evades the epistemologies which tell that it can all be drawn together and placed on a surface, seen by a single eye, represented by traces on a sheet of paper. That which resists the ontological assumptions that sustain, and are sustained by, those representational traditions. The notion that there is indeed an out-thereness that is singular. The idea that this out-thereness has an intrinsic size. The idea that whatever is out there is homogeneous—or that it occupies a homogeneous sort of out-thereness that is reducible, perspectively or otherwise, to a representation at some scale or another, that is able to handle it satisfactorily at least in principle. That can picture it. For, by contrast, allegory is about what cannot—or has not—been told. Or drawn. Or mapped. It is about excess. It is about *figure* as opposed to *discourse*. It is about alterity. It is about motility. It is about the presence of absence, or the absence of presence.[66]

Now this. The Castle Street building tells a story. No. It does not *tell* a story. Or it tells a story about something else. *But the story, one of the stories, that it does not tell is about interferences.* It reports about, witnesses, resonates with (we lack the metaphors), the interferences between different compartments—which interferences will resist the attentions of the cartographer. It evokes, too, the interferences between different trajectories—which exert similar intractabilities from the point of view of the mapmaker. And then, yes, it calls forth the interferences between the compartments and the trajectories of the kind we have discussed above—interferences that always pose the trickiest problems of representation. And have led to the fuzziness and seeming indeterminacy of the fluid, of the tidal, the sense that things go in and out of focus, ebb and flow, that they are not under control. That they cannot be pinned down.

So the Castle Street building does not *tell* a story about ontological heterogeneity. Instead it *appreciates,* it *witnesses,* it *enacts,* it *evokes,* and it *condenses* the lumpiness of a non-homogeneous reality: not so much the interagency squabbles (though those can be read there too); not so much the fact that different locations have different versions of trajectory (for this can be understood perspectivally). Instead it summons up the irreducibility of different and only partially connected realities. And it witnesses these allegorically, in the enactments of its materials. In the chaos of leaflets, chairs, contracts, rooms, clients, agendas, files, doors, and stairs. In the different speeches. In the realities that these index: realities that cannot be brought to presence. In the conjoining of that which is present and that which is other.

In the juxtaposition of realities that are necessarily Other to each other. It witnesses these Othernesses, these presences that are also absences, in the condensation of elements—the incredible but *working* condensation of elements that makes it up. It witnesses the irreducible as allegory, as absent presence, if we can but learn to sense it.[67]

Now, for the first time, we sense the blindness of the all-seeing eye. For the lust to map *creates* its blindness. That which it cannot see—it simply cannot see it. Which leads us to want to say that for a long time, for too long, we have been caught in one or another of the limited regimes of cartography. And that, as a result, we have lost the art of detecting that which is not told in that which is. And we have prided ourselves too much in telling it as it is. But for us this exercise in cartography, which started so grandly, ended in ontological humiliation. We could not see. We could not trace the trajectories. We could not even draw the boundaries. Was it simply that we were not up to the job? Or was it, as we now believe, that the very forms of the world, its heterogeneities, rendered much unseeable and unsayable? In which case knowing is as much about feeling and sensing and smelling difference, as it is about telling or drawing. It is as much about appreciating the textures of performance, or performing, of reading between the lines, as it is about the lines themselves. It as much about evoking as it is about describing. *The art of evoking.*

Leibniz wrote:

> In a confused way [monads] all go towards the infinite, towards the whole; but they are limited and distinguished from one another by the degrees of their distinct perceptions.[68]

If we use Leibniz's terminology, then we can say of Castle Street that it is a monad. It evokes *everything* in the world: some things directly and distinctly, and others allegorically or (as the translation puts it) "in a confused way." It is a monad that (as monads do) defies the understandings of scale built into cartography. Which turns those understandings inside out by including that which is "big" within that which is "small" or local. But let us not forget: in Leibniz's monadology *every* location of consciousness is a monad. Here that means that all the other places that we have visited are monads too: the hospital ward; the community doctors; the community clinic; the office of the specialist doctor. It is not, then, that Castle Street is *specially allegorical.* Indeed, if there is anything special about it at all, then perhaps it is something to do with humility. In a place where it is difficult to see well, to command boundaries or trajectories into being, in a place, in other words, far removed from the privileges and the hubris of the cartographies of power—there it is perhaps easier to feel, to smell, to taste, and to read between the lines, to know the ontological heterogeneity of the world by indirect means. There it is perhaps easier to practice the evocation needed in a *sensibility to allegory.*

Notes

Many friends and colleagues have helped us to think about representation, interference, silence, complexity, fluidity, and allegory. Important among these have been Kevin Hetherington, Annemarie Mol, Ingunn Moser, Tiago Moreira, Mimi Sheller, Bron Szerszynski, John Urry, and Helen Verran. We are also most grateful to the anonymous medical and administrative staff who gave up their time to respond to our questions, and to the senior doctor who asked us to undertake the study and facilitated it at every stage.

1. Reconstructed from interview notes with hospital senior doctor specializing in gastroenterology—Specialist A, February 8, 1999, p. 10/2.

2. All names (other than a passing reference to the international Christian charity, the Salvation Army) and some details are changed in this chapter in order to preserve anonymity. Please also see note 8.

3. There is interesting and important work exploring the notion of trajectory in medicine that it would be inappropriate to expand upon here. Perhaps most notable is that of Anselm Strauss (1993), which seeks to highlight the ongoing, practice-based, and thereby processual, nature of ordering/trajectory. See also Michel Callon and Vololona Rabeharisoa (1998), which reconfigures the notion of trajectory through consideration of the patient as a collective. Tiago Moreira (2000) furthers this work through his fascinating ethnographic study of neurosurgery. The current chapter differs from this work in that its main purpose is to explore an alternative to the notion of trajectory, rather than to develop it.

4. Excerpt taken from letter sent to hospital gastroenterology specialist B on December 24, 1998.

5. Excerpt taken from letter sent to hospital Specialist Doctor B on October 7, 1998. It may seem that one assumption built into mapping the trajectory of patients with ALD is that the patient will pass from illness to wellness. However, we would argue that this is not the case. Rather, the assumption is that patients with ALD rarely achieve wellness and will probably return to hospital with the same symptoms in the near future—what the medical practitioners refer to as "the revolving door" (please see note 31). Mapping the trajectory of the ALD patients is about tracking their movement through the hospital systems—from acute illness to a state of relative wellness that allows discharge from the hospital.

6. As will become clear later in this chapter, these are "key" phrases because those were the phrases that were used by the senior doctor specializing in gastroenterology (Specialist Doctor B) when he approached us to carry out the study. In this way the phrases and the assumptions embedded within them framed this study. However, it became clear as we carried out the research that these phrases are used by the medical staff with a pinch of irony. We describe this in some detail later in the chapter and also in Law and Singleton (2000).

7. The term *passages* is explored in Ingunn Moser and John Law (1999).

8. This is the central and largest acute general hospital in the geographical area of the study. In the United Kingdom, the term District General Hospital has been replaced by the term Hospital National Health Service Trust. This change, in large part, reflects national changes in health-service funding policy and management. There has been a move to localized funding with geographical areas being fund holders and managing their own health-care budgets in their own ways. In the area of this study there are continuing organizational changes so that currently coming into being is a large Primary Care Trust, one aspect of which is Sandside Hospitals National Health Service Trust representing a collection of nine hospitals (providing both acute care and chronic day care). We also have the community care provided outside the hospitals, including the extremely localized community clinics staffed by, for example, doctors (general practitioners), child-care practitioners, and community nurses.

9. Reconstructed from interview notes with Specialist Doctor A, February 8, 1999, p. 9.

10. From interview notes with hospital Specialist Doctor F, March 10, 1999, p. 22.

11. See, for instance, pp. 19 and 32 to 34 in Sherlock (1989).

12. From interview notes with hospital Specialist Doctor F, March 10, 1999, p. 22.

13. We are aware that there is an important issue here about whose version of health-care reality is represented in such a study. For the record, we spoke to a variety of health-care practitioners in the course of the study. The crucial point is that the focus of the current chapter is to trouble the notion of mapping rather than to explore and interrogate the production of different health-care realities.

14. And in terms of which it is possible to understand much of the history, philosophy and sociology of science. The issue is explored at great length in Law (under consideration).

15. Further excerpt from the letter sent to Specialist Doctor B on December 12, 1998.

16. Reconstructed from interview notes with Specialist Doctor B, December 10, 1998, p. 5.

17. Please see note 6.

18. Reconstructed from interview notes with Specialist Doctor B, December 10, 1998, p. 5.

19. Ibid., pp. 5–6.

20. Reconstructed from interview notes with Nurse C, March 10, 1999, p. 17.

21. Like the flows and links of trajectories, mapping compartments also involves judgments—and presuppositions—about scale. Here we are concerned with the imagery rather than with the performance of scale.

22. Reconstructed from interview notes with Nurse C, March 10, 1999, p. 16.

23. Reconstructed from interview notes with Specialist Doctor D and NHS Researcher E, February 5, 1999, p. 8.

24. Since the time of the study there have been national and local changes in the funding and organization of health-care services. These are currently continuing in the area covered by this study. Please see note 8.

25. The term *interference* is used by Donna Haraway (1992). See also Haraway (1997) and Law (2000).

26. From interview notes with the staff at Castle Street Centre, Sandside, June 10, 1999, p. 39/7E.

27. In the present study we came across fewer complaints about trajectories interfering with compartments. Though this happens often enough, sometimes in the form

of complaints about the movements of money (fraud or money-laundering), and sometimes as worries about following proper administrative procedures. For discussion of the latter, posed in an alternative idiom, see John Law (1994).

28. From interview notes with Community Doctor F, June 11, 1999, p. 54/2.

29. The reference is to (and from) a paper by Ed Constant (1999).

30. The term partial connection is drawn from Donna Haraway, and developed by Marilyn Strathern (1991).

31. For he and most of the other people involved knew that the passages and the trajectories did not really work, if only because they were frustrated at the way in which patients who had been dried out in the Sandside District General Hospital reappeared in Accident and Emergency within a few weeks or months (some trajectories, like this "revolving door," seemed to circulate freely, a point to which we will return below). And also the ontological and epistemological problems of representing the treatment of alcoholic liver disease within the Sandside area.

32. This should not be taken as a complaint about the psychiatry department, which had been directed, in conformity with national policy, to focus its resources on patients with serious psychiatric problems.

33. Reconstructed from interview notes with Specialist Doctor D and NHS Researcher E, February 5, 1999, p. 8/1.

34. Reconstructed from interview notes with Specialist Doctor B and Nursing Officer G, December 10, 1998, p. 6/3.

35. Reconstructed from interview notes with Nursing Officer G, December 10, 1998, p. 2/2.

36. Reconstructed from interview notes with Specialist Doctor A, February 8, 1999, p. 9/1.

37. Reconstructed from interview notes with Community Specialist Doctor I, March 19, 1999, p. 28/1.

38. Reconstructed from interview notes with Nursing Officer G, December 10, 1998, p. 2/2.

39. We have discussed this in Law and Singleton (2000).

40. Reconstructed from interview notes with Specialist Doctor A, February 8, 1999, p. 9/1.

41. Reconstructed from interview notes with Specialist Doctor J, June 11, 1999, p. 49/3.

42. Reconstructed from interview notes with Nurse H, March 3, 1999, p. 13/1.

43. From interview notes with Specialist Doctor F, March 10, 1999, p. 22.

44. "If patients are mistreated, then they become difficult to manage. They come to Accident and Emergency, but then if they get difficult there they are likely to end up in police cells, and fall through the net." From interview notes with Nurse K, March 19, 1999, p. 26/2.

45. Reconstructed from interview notes with Nurse L, March 3, 1999, p. 19/4

46. Reconstructed from interview notes with Specialist Doctor A, February 8, 1999, p. 9/1.

47. Reconstructed from interview notes with Nurse H, March 3, 1999, p. 14/2.

48. Our data suggest the importance of a future study about the experiences of those diagnosed with alcoholic liver disease in Sandside. Such a study was not possible within the remit of the current research.

49. From interview notes with Community Doctor F, June 11, 1999, p. 55/3.

50. Or even as alternative trajectories. As previously stated the purpose of this chapter is to imagine alternatives to the notion of trajectory rather than discovering alternative trajectories.

51. Here, then, we work in the opposite direction to an argument we made, using the same empirical case in an earlier paper (see Law and Singleton [2000]). There we wanted to say that alcoholic liver disease is not an object because it is enacted in different ways in different locations—and because it displaced itself, in the way we have noted here, into different objects such as alcohol abuse. We do not necessarily recant the earlier argument: but the fluidity, the process of ebb and flow, that we have developed here, makes it possible to say that in certain realities "it" is indeed an object after all.

52. This is very difficult to say in the standard representational languages available to us, because the temptation, all the time, is to talk in terms of change, displacement, fuzziness, slipperiness, or other similar terms. Fluids become, then, some kind of other to compartments or to well-ordered trajectories, exceeding them. This issue, and the general character of fluidity as a spatial form, is discussed in Annemarie Mol and John Law (1994), Marianne de Laet and Annemarie Mol (2000), and John Law and Annemarie Mol (2001). Vicky Singleton has tackled similar issues using the related vocabulary of ambivalence. See Singleton and Michael (1993) and Singleton (1996; 1998).

53. In contrast to the consultant that we quoted right at the beginning of this chapter, perhaps here we are talking of the atypical—or perhaps, and more likely, what we are describing escapes the space between typicality and atypicality.

54. See in particular the important line of work on medical materials by empirical philosopher Annemarie Mol. See, inter alia, Mol (1998; 2002) and Mol and Berg (1994).

55. We are aware that these categories are no longer used. Please see note 8.

56. From interview notes with the staff at Castle Street Centre, Sandside, June 10, 1999, p. 38/6.

57. Ibid., p. 39/7.

58. Ibid., p. 38/6.

59. Ibid., p. 39/7.

60. Ibid., p. 39/7.

61. Ibid., p. 33/1

62. Ibid., p. 34/2

63. Ibid., p. 34/2.

64. Ibid., p. 35/3.

65. Ibid., p. 38/6.

66. For discussion of allegory see Kevin Hetherington and John Law (1998). On the distinction between figure and discourse see Jean-François Lyotard (1985). On absence/presence see John Law (2002a; 2002b). On motility see Kevin Hetherington and Rolland Munro (1997) and Kevin Hetherington (in press).

67. On the notion of conjoined alterity and absence/presence developed in an explicitly spatial context, see Law and Mol (in press).

68. Part of section 60 of the Leibniz (1973), "Monadology," p. 188.

References

Callon, Michel, and Rabeharisoa, Vololona. (1998). "Reconfiguring Trajectories: Agencies, Bodies and Political Articulations: The Case of Muscular Dystrophies." Paper presented to the workshop Theorizing Bodies, Paris, September 9–11.

Constant, Edward W. II. (1999). "Reliable Knowledge and Unreliable Stuff." *Technology and Culture* 40: 324–357.

de Laet, Marianne, and Annemarie Mol. (2000). "Zimbabwe Bush Pump: Mechanics of a Fluid Technology." *Social Studies of Science* 30: 225–263.

Haraway, Donna. (1992). "The Promises of Monsters: A Regenerative Politics for Inappropriate/d Others." In *Cultural Studies*, ed. Lawrence Grossberg, Cary Nelson, and Paul Treichler, 295–337. New York: Routledge.

Haraway, Donna J. (1997). *Witness@Second_Millenium.Female_Man©_Meets_ Oncomouse™: Feminism and Technoscience*. New York: Routledge.

Hetherington, Kevin. (in press). "Consumption and Disposal." *Theory Culture and Society*.

Hetherington, Kevin, and John Law. (1998). "Allegory and Interference: Representation in Sociology." Available at www.comp.lancs.ac.uk/sociology/reskhjl1.html.

Hetherington, Kevin, and Rolland Munro. (1997). "Introduction to Section IV." In *Ideas of Difference: Social Spaces and the Labour of Division, Sociological Review Monograph*, ed. Kevin Hetherington and Rolland Munro, 223–227. Oxford: Blackwell.

Law, John. (1994). *Organizing Modernity*. Oxford: Blackwell.

———. (2000). "On the Subject of the Object: Narrative, Technology and Interpellation." *Configurations* 8: 1–29.

———. (2002a). *Aircraft Stories: Decentering the Object in Technoscience*. Durham, NC: Duke University Press.

———. (2002b). "On Hidden Heterogeneities: Complexity, Formalism and Aircraft Design." In *Complexities: Social Studies of Knowledge Practices*, ed. John Law and Annemarie Mol, 116–141. Durham, NC: Duke University Press.

———. (under consideration). *The Method Assemblage*.

Law, John, and Annemarie Mol. (2001). "Situating Technoscience: An Inquiry into Spatialities." *Society and Space* 19: 609–621.

Law, John, and Vicky Singleton. (2000). "This is Not an Object." Available at www.comp. lancs.ac.uk/sociology/soc032jl.html.

Leibniz, Gottfried Wilhelm. (1973). "Monadology." In *Philosophical Writings*, 179–194. London: J.M. Dent.

Lyotard, Jean-François. (1985). *Discourse, Figure*. Paris: Editions Klincksieck.

Mol, Annemarie. (1998). "Missing Links, Making Links: The Performance of Some Artheroscleroses." In *Differences in Medicine: Unravelling Practices, Techniques and Bodies*, ed. Annemarie Mol and Marc Berg, 144–165. Durham, NC: Duke University Press.

———. (2002). *The Body Multiple: Ontology in Medical Practice*. Durham, NC: Duke University Press.

Mol, Annemarie, and Marc Berg. (1994). "Principles and Practices of Medicine: The Coexistence of Various Anaemias." *Culture, Medicine and Psychiatry* 18: 247–265.

Mol, Annemarie, and John Law. (1994). "Regions, Networks and Fluids: Anaemia and Social Topology." *Social Studies of Science* 24: 641–671.

Moreira, Tiago. (2000). "Difference and Ontological Fluidity: Cerebral Angiography and Neurosurgical Practice." *Social Studies of Science* 30: 421–446.

———. (2001). "Incisions: A Study of Surgical Trajectories." Unpublished Ph.D. dissertation, Lancaster University.

Moser, Ingunn, and John Law. (1999). "Good Passages, Bad Passages." In *Actor Network and After*, ed. John Law and John Hassard, 196–219. Oxford and Keele: Blackwell and the *Sociological Review*.

Sherlock, Sheila. (1989). *Diseases of the Liver and Biliary System.* 8th ed. Oxford: Blackwell.

Singleton, Vicky. (1996). "Feminism, Sociology of Scientific Knowledge and Postmodernism: Politics, Theory and Me." *Social Studies of Science* 26: 445–468.

———. (1998). "Stabilizing Instabilities: The Role of the Laboratory in the United Kingdom Cervical Screening Programme." In *Differences in Medicine: Unravelling Practices, Techniques and Bodies*, ed. Marc Berg and Annemarie Mol, 86–104. Durham, NC: Duke University Press.

Singleton, Vicky, and Mike Michael. (1993). "Actor-networks and Ambivalence: General Practitioners in the UK Cervical Screening Programme." *Social Studies of Science* 23: 227–264.

Strathern, Marilyn. (1991). *Partial Connections.* Maryland: Rowman and Littlefield.

Strauss, Anslem. (1993). *Continual Permutations of Action.* New York: Aldine de Gruyter.

About the Editors and Contributors

Frank Blackler is professor of organizational behavior at Lancaster University Management School. He is interested in the relevance of applied social science to the management of innovation and new approaches to organization and the paper included in this collection reports a study he led in a design engineering firm. In recent years he has been working on leader development within the UK National Health Service (NHS).

Isabelle Bouty is assistant professor in strategic management at the University of Paris X-Nanterre, Paris, France. She received her Ph.D. in strategy and management from the University of Paris X. Her current research interests focus on the competence- and knowledge-based view of the firm, social networks, and intellectual capital.

Norman Crump is a lecturer in the department of behavior in organizations, Lancaster University Management School. His research interests are focused on the development of cultural historical activity theory for the analysis of organizational change. The empirical sites of interest at the present time are the UK NHS, with particular emphasis on the changing role of medical staff as they attempt to respond to the changes demanded by both government and management. A further research interest is management education, with particular regard to undergraduate education and the often tense relationship between management education and the management of education.

Yrjö Engeström is professor of communication at the University of California, San Diego, and professor of education at the University of Helsinki, Finland. He is director of the Center for Activity Theory and Developmental Work Research at the University of Helsinki. Engeström applies cultural-historical activity theory in developmental studies of work. His research focuses on transformations in work organizations and formation of collaborative expertise through expansive learning. His recent books include *Cognition and Communication at Work* (1996, edited with D. Middleton) and *Perspectives on Activity Theory* (1999, edited with R. Miettinen and R. L. Punamäki). His current work deals with the transformation of the multiorganizational field of medical care in the Helsinki area, Finland.

Silvia Gherardi is professor of the sociology of organization at the Faculty of Sociology in the University of Trento, Italy. Since 1993 she has coordinated the Research Unit on Cognition, Organizational Learning, and Aesthetics at the Department of Sociology and Social Research. Her main areas of interest include the exploration of different "soft" aspects of knowing in organizations, with a peculiar emphasis on cognitive, emotional, symbolic, and linguistic aspects of organizational process. She has also extensively studied gendering practices in organizations and the promotion of the development of women's competences and participation in organizations. Prof. Gherardi served as a chairperson of the European Group for Organizational Studies (EGOS) in the years 1997–2000.

Carole Drucker-Godard is an assistant professor in strategic management at the University of Paris X-Nanterre, Paris, France. She received her Ph.D. in strategy and management from the University of Paris IX-Dauphine. She was awarded for the best dissertation in strategic management in 2000 (Fnege-AIMS). Her current research interests include managers' agenda-setting, CEO priority-management methods, decision-making process, and strategy implementation.

Marie-Léandre Gomez is assistant professor at ESSEC Business School, Cergy-Pontoise, France. She received her Ph.D. in strategy and management from the University of Paris-Nanterre, France. Her research interests include the dynamics of organizational knowledge, social learning, and epistemology.

John Law is professor of sociology and director of the Centre for Science Studies at Lancaster University. He works in the sociology of science, technology, and organizations, and in particular on large technical systems, aircraft projects, railways and rail disasters, and health technologies. His interest in fractional objectivities and subjectivities is explored in his recent book *Aircraft Stories* (2002), and in *Complexities: Social Studies of Knowledge Practices* (2002), which is co-edited with Annemarie Mol. His concern with theory and method is explored in his forthcoming book, *The Method Assemblage*.

Seonaidh McDonald, Ph.D. is a lecturer in strategy at Sheffield University Management School. She has two main fields of interest. The first centers on a range of closely related strategic issues such as the management of change, organizational learning, innovation, and knowledge management. She has an interest in studying the strategy-making processes themselves as well as their content and outcomes. Her other area of interest is waste management. Her research in this field is also concerned with change, but focuses on the household rather than the organization. This work aims to understand and to increase public participation in domestic waste-recycling schemes.

Davide Nicolini is contract researcher at the Department of Sociology and Social Research and founding member of the Research Unit on Cognition, Organizational Learning, and Aesthetics of the University of Trento (Italy). Prior to this he worked for five years as Senior Social Scientist at the Tavistock Institute. His background combines studies in sociology and individual and social psychology with interests in applied human sciences. His recent work focuses on practice-based approaches to knowledge, learning, power, and change in organizations. Other areas of interest include the study and facilitation of innovation process and organizational change, the advancement of action-research and reflection practice and its application to interorganizational relations, and cross-boundary and project-based learning.

Anne Puonti holds a masters in education and is finishing her dissertation on the collaboration between authorities in economic-crime investigation at the Center for Activity Theory and Developmental Work Research, University of Helsinki. She works as a development manager at the National Bureau of Investigation, Finland.

Laura Seppänen graduated from the University of Helsinki in horticulture. She has worked for many years in organic agriculture, in both advisory and research capacities. She is currently finishing her Ph.D. dissertation about changing work practices and learning in the organic vegetables farming sector. Her recent publications include "Creating Tools for Farmers' Learning: An Application of Developmental Work Research," which appeared in *Agricultural Systems*, and "Societal Integration in Organic Vegetable Farming: Exploring Learning Challenges," in *The Journal of Agricultural Education and Extension*.

Vicky Singleton is lecturer in women's studies and a member of the Centre for Science Studies at Lancaster University. She works in the sociology of science, technology, and health care. Her work on the complexities and ambivalences of health programs and health guidelines, including UK health initiatives on cervical screening and sudden infant death syndrome, are explored in a series of book chapters and in papers published in *Social Studies of Science.*

Antonio Strati is associate professor and lectures on the sociology of organizations at the Universities of Trento and Siena, Italy. He received his action research training in organization studies at the Tavistock Institute of Human Relations in London, UK. He is a founding member of the Standing Conference on Organizational Symbolism (SCOS-EGOS). His research interests focus on symbolism, aesthetics, tacit knowledge, cognitivism, and the significance of hypertext and "aesth-hypertext" in organization studies. His most recent publications include the book *Organization and Aesthetics* (1999), the textbook *Theory and Method in Organization Studies* (2000), and the editing (with P. Guillet de Montoux) of a special issue of *Human Relations* (no. 7, 2002) on Organizing Aesthetics.

Lucy Suchman is professor of anthropology of science and technology in the Department of Sociology at Lancaster University. She spent twenty years as a researcher at Xerox's Palo Alto Research Center before taking up her present position. Her research has centered on the sociomaterial practices that make up technical systems, explored through critical studies and through experimental, interdisciplinary and participatory interventions in new technology design.

Etienne Wenger, Ph.D., is a recognized thought leader in the field of communities of practice and their application to organizations. He was featured by *Training Magazine* in their "A New Breed of Visionary" series. A pioneer of the "community of practice" research, he was the co-author with Jean Lave of *Situated Learning* (1991), where the term was coined. More recently, he was the author of *Communities of Practice: Learning, Meaning, and Identity* (1998), a book that lays out a theory of learning based on the concept of communities of practice. He has recently published *Cultivating Communities of Practice: A Guide to Managing Knowledge* (2002). Co-authored with Bill Snyder and Richard McDermott, this new book is addressed to practitioners in organizations who want to base their knowledge strategy on communities of practice.

Dvora Yanow is professor and chair in the Department of Public Administration, California State University, Hayward. Her research focus is directed by an overall interest in the communication of meaning in organizational and public policy settings. She has published articles in major international journals on public policies as collective identity stories, the ways in which built space communicates meaning, and the meanings of "race/ethnicity" in social policy practices (in Israel and in the United States), as well as on organizational metaphors, myths, culture, and learning, and interpretive philosophies and methods. She is the author of *How Does a Policy Mean? Interpreting Policy and Organizational Actions* (1996), *Conducting Interpretive Policy Analysis* (2000), and *Constructing "Race" and "Ethnicity" in America: Category-Making in Public Policy and Administration* (2003, M.E. Sharpe).

Index

Abduction, 103–4
Accountability, 188–89, 190, 191
Activity networks
  activity objects, 128–29, 131, 132–33,
    136, 140–41, 142–43
  activity-theory approach, 127–29, 130*t*,
    142–46,147n.2
  analytical framework, 136*f*
  boundary innovations, 131, 132*f*
  collaboration, 128, 129, 131, 132, 134,
    135, 138, 140, 141–42
  community of practice, 128, 131–32
  conflict, 128, 133, 136, 138, 139, 141
  contextual innovations, 132
  disturbance-producing systems, 128
  domain innovations, 131, 132*f*
  expertise, 131, 132, 133–34, 137,
    138–39, 140, 141–43
  explicit knowledge, 127–28
  fragmentation, 129, 134, 142
  heterogeneity, 132, 133–34, 141,
    142–43
  HighTech (United Kingdom), 126–27,
    132–34
  horizontal relations, 131, 134
  introduction, 126–27
  organizing processes, 129, 131–32,
    137–40, 142, 148n.4
  overview, 16–17, 18, 126–127
  perspective making, 131, 132*f*, 134,
    136, 137*f*, 139*f*, 140*f*, 142, 143
  perspective shaping, 132, 134, 136,
    137*f*, 139*f*, 140*f*, 142, 143
  perspective taking, 131, 132*f*, 134, 136,
    139*f*, 140*f*, 142, 143
  research directions, 146, 148n.4

Activity networks *(continued)*
  research methodology, 135–36
  situated knowledge, 127
  social competence, 127–28
  Strategy Development Groups, 134–43
  tacit knowledge, 127–28
  theoretical contrast, 128, 129, 147n.3
  theoretical origins, 128, 147n.2
  vertical relations, 131
Activity theory. *See* Cultural-historical
    activity theory
Actor-network theory
  bridge-building, 187, 188, 189, 192–93,
    194–95, 199–200
  practice-based approach, 4, 12, 18–20,
    24–25, 29n.2
  safety knowledge circulation, 209–21
Aesthetic knowledge
  aesthetic defined, 55, 102
  aesthetic judgment, 54–55, 56, 58, 63,
    66, 67
  analytical philosophy, 54, 56, 57, 67
  art, 54, 55–56
  artifacts, 55, 65–66, 69
  bicycle riding, 66–67
  cognitive knowledge, 53, 54, 55, 56,
    67–68
  cognitive theory, 53, 56, 68, 71, 72
  community of practice, 70, 71
  conclusions, 69–72
  conflict, 58, 70
  continental philosophy, 54
  conversational analysis, 60–62
  cultural interpretive perspective, 39–40
  empirical research, 54, 57, 58, 65, 72
  epistemology, 67–68